Until I Return
The Selected Plays of Ismail Khalidi

Until I Return
The Selected Plays of Ismail Khalidi

Truth Serum Blues
Tennis in Nablus
Final Status
Foot
Sabra Falling
Dead Are My People

Edited and with an Introduction by
HALA BAKI *and* MICHAEL MALEK NAJJAR

methuen | drama
LONDON • NEW YORK • OXFORD • NEW DELHI • SYDNEY

METHUEN DRAMA
Bloomsbury Publishing Plc
50 Bedford Square, London, WC1B 3DP, UK
1385 Broadway, New York, NY 10018, USA
29 Earlsfort Terrace, Dublin 2, Ireland

BLOOMSBURY, METHUEN DRAMA and the Methuen Drama logo are trademarks of
Bloomsbury Publishing Plc

First published in Great Britain 2025

Copyright © Ismail Khalidi, 2025
Foreword © Naomi Wallace, 2025
Critical Essay, "Arab, Palestinian, American—The Theatre of Ismail Khalidi" © by Edward Blaise Ziter, 2025
Introduction, Playwright's Chronology and Interview © Hala Baki and Michael Malek Najjar, 2025

The authors have asserted their right under the Copyright, Designs and Patents Act, 1988,
to be identified as authors of this work.

For legal purposes the Acknowledgments on p. x constitute an extension of this copyright page.

Cover design by Matt Thame
Cover image by Santiago, from the play *Foot* by Ismail Khalidi

All rights reserved. No part of this publication may be reproduced or transmitted in any form or by any means, electronic or mechanical, including photocopying, recording, or any information storage or retrieval system, without prior permission in writing from the publishers.

Bloomsbury Publishing Plc does not have any control over, or responsibility for, any third-party websites referred to or in this book. All internet addresses given in this book were correct at the time of going to press. The author and publisher regret any inconvenience caused if addresses have changed or sites have ceased to exist, but can accept no responsibility for any such changes.

No rights in incidental music or songs contained in the work are hereby granted and performance rights for any performance/presentation whatsoever must be obtained from the respective copyright owners.

All rights whatsoever in this play are strictly reserved and application for performance etc. should be made before rehearsals to A3 Artists Agency of 350 Fifth Avenue, 38th floor, New York, NY 10118, USA. No performance may be given unless a licence has been obtained. No rights in incidental music or songs contained in the Work are hereby granted and performance rights for any performance/presentation whatsoever must be obtained from the respective copyright owners.

A catalogue record for this book is available from the British Library.

A catalog record for this book is available from the Library of Congress.

ISBN: HB: 978-1-3504-6547-3
PB: 978-1-3504-6546-6
ePDF: 978-1-3504-6549-7
eBook: 978-1-3504-6548-0

Series: Methuen Drama Play Collections

Typeset by RefineCatch Limited, Bungay, Suffolk
Printed and bound in Great Britain

To find out more about our authors and books visit www.bloomsbury.com
and sign up for our newsletters.

To my parents, Mona and Rashid, who always believed in the power of art.
And to my beloved kids Nur and Elias and the children of the camps.
May the future bring the light of liberation, love, and joy.

Contents

Foreword by Naomi Wallace, playwright viii
Acknowledgments x
Playwright's Chronology xiii

Introduction by Hala Baki and Michael Malek Najjar 1

The Plays
Truth Serum Blues 25
Tennis in Nablus 49
Final Status 101
Foot 149
Sabra Falling 161
Dead Are My People 213

Critical Essay: "Arab, Palestinian, American—The Theatre of Ismail Khalidi" by Edward Blaise Ziter 285
Interview: "The reason Palestine matters . . . is because it is about everything" 293

Bibliography 305
Contributor Biographies 311

Foreword

Almost twenty years ago I sat in the Pangea World Theater in Minneapolis listening to the voice of a young playwright that repeatedly jolted me. The play was imbued not only with a muscular lyricism but with a vision that was so combustible that it threatened to set the air alight.

The play I was watching was *Truth Serum Blues*. It is a post-September 11, 2001 era play written by the then twenty-two-year-old Palestinian American, and ahead of its time in terms of its intersectionality and its genuinely radical critique of the overlapping matrices of empire, Islamophobia, and white supremacy. *Truth Serum Blues* takes us to Guantanamo Bay inside the tortured body and mind of Kareem, a young Arab-American man lost in his own memories and deprived of his most basic rights. At that time, I had read and seen a good amount of new theater, but I hadn't come across anything quite like Ismail (Sim) Khalidi's work.

Since then, this playwright—both a diasporic and an American writer—has gone from strength to strength. This collection of plays is original, disruptive, and pulls no punches when it comes to staging the human intricacies, not to mention intimacies, of colonialism and war, be they in the Middle East or the USA. Here you have a body of work that refuses to trade in easy political rhetoric or clichés. Indeed Sim's work is filled with a palpable tenderness towards even the most brutal of his characters. In this collection what is compelling aesthetically (and of course runs parallel theoretically) is how the plays continually interrupt themselves, both their form and content. They refuse to be comfortable cultural places in which we can rest (assured); each seeks to dis-lodge us. Here a reader will find a daring political curiosity that never lapses into sentimentality or stereotype. Sim's re-membering and reimagining of what has been erased is always done with humor, and with rhythms that are at once of the Americas and the Arab world.

Another important aspect of these plays is how Sim produces the body on stage. In *Foot*, a meditation on soccer, love, and death under occupation, as recounted by a member of the Palestinian national team, the body, and its extension (in this case a soccer ball) tell a fragmented story. As the form of the play is dis-jointed, so is the body, and the story that the body tells. *Foot*'s unsettling nature, where there is no unified body or way of seeing given the radical disjunction in a world seen through a colonial lens, draws as much from Brecht as it does from James Baldwin.

Tennis in Nablus is set in British Mandatory Palestine in the year 1939, a turning point in the history of Palestine that is rarely explored on the US stage. The play boasts a rich and varied cast of characters, all forced to make decisions about the course of their struggle and their loyalties. With a historian's sense of the epic and a poet's ear for the tragic, Sim's play unfolds into naturalism, but it does so with a dark and irreverent humor that continually undermines the notion of naturalism on stage. Indeed, the "naturalism" found here is fractured with the presence of ghosts, as well as absurd and hilarious encounters.

That Sim's plays are not more widely produced is largely due to the milquetoast nature of mainstream American theater, especially when it comes to questions of Palestine and illegal occupations or properly interrogating Orientalist, anti-Arab, and

Islamophobic narratives. Hegemonic narratives are protected, leaving untouched the pernicious and poisonous assumptions that imbue one set of humanity with legitimacy and erases the history of others. Sim's work demands permission to narrate a hitherto suppressed experience.

In the twenty years since I first saw his work, I've had the pleasure of working closely with Sim. We've co-adapted two novels for the stage: Ghassan Kanafani's *Returning to Haifa* and the Iraqi writer Sinan Antoon's *The Corpse Washer*. At present, Ismail and I are collaborating on a new play that takes place in the ocean, and within the imagination of a refugee from Gaza. I will always be grateful for encountering Ismail's work, learning from it, being renewed by it.

As I write this foreword, Gaza is suffering an annihilating bombing campaign. With Israel's ongoing ethnic cleansing of Palestine—a joint operation with the US—unfolding in all its mind-numbing horror on our screens, it is heartening to know that there exists in our devastated, delicate, and beguiling world a playwright with Ismail's talent. His work is, I think you will agree, an act of defiance to—as opposed to a cultural distraction for—empire and colonialism.

Ismail's plays are the best of what "good theater" is meant to be: they are designed not to comfort but to confound. But this body of work is also a form of creative resistance to what diminishes and divides us, giving space and utterance to those voices that have been blocked from our stages for too long.

Naomi Wallace
Playwright

Acknowledgments

Ismail Khalidi:

Thank you to my parents Mona and Rashid and to my sisters Lamya and Dima for always having my back and telling stories around the table.

Many thanks to my extended family in Palestine, Beirut, and beyond. Deep gratitude to Naomi Wallace, one of the kindest and most radical writers around; to Bill and Bernardine for being my second parents in Chicago; to Meena, Dipankar, and the Pangea team; to Francisca and Carolina, and to a constellation of folks I love, cherish, and rely on, including but not limited to: Abe Paulos, Ameer Saleh, Ayinde Bennet, Khaled Mohammed, the Hirschmann Levys, Bridgette Bissonette, Bruce McLeod, Hadi Eldebek, Devin Atallah, and Constantino Marzuqa.

Last but not least, thank you to my luminous and wise little ones, Nur and Elias, who teach me daily and whom I adore beyond words.

Hala Baki:

Many thanks to Ismail Khalidi for sharing his work with us and the world. You are a true poet and worldmaker, and I hope that your voice continues to sing the stories of Palestine and its people for generations.

To my dear friend and mentor Malek, thank you for your passion and exemplary scholarship. I am so grateful for our collaborations.

I am also grateful for the support, patience, and enthusiasm of the team at Methuen Drama, especially Dom O'Hanlon and Sam Nicholls. It's been an absolute pleasure working with you again. Thank you for supporting Palestinian voices even as they face suppression everywhere.

To our contributors Naomi Wallace and Ted Ziter: Thank you for lending this anthology your words and wisdom. Thank you also to the various artists and institutions that helped bring it all together: Pangea World Theater, Meena Natarajan, Jeff Gaines, The Alliance Theatre, Kate Moore Heaney, Tess Mayer, Noor Theatre, Carolina Villar Castillo, and Arena Theatre, Chile.

Above all, thank you to my beloved family. *Habibi* Ben and Zayn *'omri*, I love you beyond words.

Michael Malek Najjar:

I am grateful to Ismail Khalidi for allowing us to publish these astonishing plays. Your work chronicles the history and lives of Palestinians who have endured almost a century of occupation, yet still remain defiant in the face of overwhelming odds. Your plays are a quintessential aspect of Arab American theater.

To my friend and collaborator Hala, thank you for another wonderful opportunity to work with you to bring these important plays to the American theater canon. You are truly amazing.

Special thanks to Dom O'Hanlon and the excellent staff at Methuen Drama, with whom I've had the pleasure of working on several books and anthologies. You always make the process of writing and editing these anthologies an absolute delight. I would also like to thank the amazing contributors to this book: Naomi Wallace, and Ted Ziter. Thanks also to Pangea World Theater, Meena Natarajan, The Alliance Theatre, Kate Moore Heaney, Noor Theatre, and Ismail Khalidi for permission to reprint the enclosed photographs.

Lastly, to my extraordinary wife Rana and my precious daughter Malak: I love you always and forever.

Playwright's Chronology

1982	Born to Rashid Khalidi and Mona Khalidi in Beirut, Lebanon.
1983	The Khalidis move to the United States.
2005	Receives BA from Macalester College, St. Paul, MN, with International Studies major and English and Theatre minors. *Truth Serum Blues*, directed by Dipankar Mukherjee, has world premiere at Pangea World Theater, Minneapolis, MN, September 29–October 8. Named "Best Solo Performance of 2005" by *Lavender Magazine*.
2008	Co-Recipient of Goldberg Playwriting Award, NYU Tisch School of the Arts, for *Tennis in Nablus*.
2009	Receives MFA in Dramatic Writing from Tisch School of the Arts, New York University. *Final Status* receives MFA Thesis Reading, The Public Theater, New York, NY, May 9. Recipient: *Tennis in Nablus,* The Quest for Peace Playwriting Award, Kennedy Center/American College Theatre Festival. Co-Recipient, *Tennis in Nablus*, The Mark Twain Award for Comic Playwriting, Kennedy Center/American College Theatre Festival. Recipient, *Tennis in Nablus*, Grand Prize, Kendeda National Graduate Playwriting Competition.
2010	*Tennis in Nablus*, directed by Peggy Shannon, receives its world premiere at The Alliance Theatre, Atlanta, GA, February 3–21. Finalist, *Tennis in Nablus*, L. Arnold Weissberger Award for Playwriting, Williamstown Theatre Festival.
2014	Honorable Mention, Middle East America Distinguished Playwright Award.
2015	Co-edits (with Naomi Wallace) and published *Inside/Outside: Six Plays from Palestine and the Diaspora,* Theatre Communications Group.
2016–17	Directs premiere and subsequent productions of Spanish translation of *Foot* (translated by Carolina Muñoz Proto) in Chile with Teatro Amal; wins Best Play of 2016 from the Instituto Chileno Arabe de Cultura.
2017	*Sabra Falling*, directed by Dipankar Mukherjee, receives its world premiere at Pangea World Theater, Minneapolis, MN, September 15–October 1.
2018	*Returning to Haifa*, directed by Caitlin McLeod, receives its world premiere at Finborough Theatre, London, UK, February 27–March 24. *Dead Are My People* workshop production, directed by Leah Gardner, produced at Noor Theatre and New York Theatre Workshop Next Door, November 4–11.
2019	*The Corpse Washer*, directed by Mark Brokaw, receives its world premiere at Humana Festival, Actors Theatre of Louisville.
2024	*Guernica, Gaza* (co-written with Naomi Wallace) receives its world premiere with Ashtar Theatre (Palestine) at the Uncaging Our World International Youth Theatre Festival (Mandal Theatre), Oxford, UK, July 20–7.

Introduction

Hala Baki and Michael Malek Najjar

"I know that the battle is inside me, and that, above all, it needs to be fought right here in America; it needs to be fought slowly and wisely, in, out, above, below, and around the system. I know it is not just about Palestine. Rather, Palestine is everything; it is about so much more than Arabs and Jews, and until we can make this an international struggle about human rights, human dignity, and freedom from racism and foreign military rule, then we are not doing enough. We cannot do it alone. Palestine is about everything."—Ismail Khalidi[1]

Committing oneself to writing about the Palestinian experience in any genre is a fraught enterprise; doing so for the American theater is tantamount to artistic immolation. The Palestinian–Israeli conflict is what one might call the "third rail" of American politics, ruining the careers of many who dare to speak in favor of the Palestinians and their cause for self-determination and statehood. For centuries the inhabitants of the land known as Syria Palaestina, or Palestine, be they Jewish, Druze, Bedouin, or other, have been subject to occupations—Roman, Ottoman, British, and Israeli. This history is either forgotten or erased by many who wish to believe that this area was a "land without people for a people without a land." Because Palestine was not a formal "nation state" by European standards, those who came from European nation states believed that it was a territory worth occupying and co-opting for their own purposes (be they political or religious) despite the wishes of the multi-religious, multi-ethnic populations who resided there. This sense of deep history is one that pervades Ismail Khalidi's plays. Khalidi, who is a descendant of a long line of Palestinian writers and intellectuals, and whose parents are known as the foremost scholars and chroniclers of Palestinian life, has taken the rich and scholarly tradition he inherited, transmuting this lineage into the form of theatrical playwriting. By doing so, Khalidi is one of several second-generation Arab Americans (of all the Americas) who has absorbed his people's history and has transfigured those stories into a theatrical form that is both potently artistic and politically committed.

Biography

Ismail Khalidi's paternal grandfather, Ismail Raghib Khalidi, was a Palestinian Muslim born in Jerusalem, Ottoman Syria, who worked as a senior diplomat for the United Nations Department of Political Affairs.[2] His grandfather's brother, Hussein, was the first elected mayor of Jerusalem and later the Prime Minister and Foreign Minister of

---

[1] Dan Berger, Boudin Chesa, Farrow Kenyon, and Dohrn Bernardine, *Letters from Young Activists: Today's Rebels Speak Out* (New York: Nation, 2006).
[2] "Ismail Khalidi, 52, U.N. Official, Dies." *The New York Times*, September 6, 1968. https://timesmachine.nytimes.com/timesmachine/1968/09/06/77313233.html?pageNumber=43.

Jordan. His paternal grandmother, Selwa Jaha, was born in Bishmezzine, Lebanon, and immigrated to Brooklyn where she met Ismail Raghib Khalidi. They planned to return to Palestine to have their son Rashid but could not due to the 1948 Nakba (النَّكْبَة). Rashid Khalidi, Ismail's father, was Columbia University's Edward Said Professor of Modern Arab Studies, and his mother, Mona Khalidi, is Columbia University's Assistant Dean of Student Affairs and Assistant Director of Graduate Studies of the School of International and Public Affairs. Rashid Khalidi received a BA from Yale University in 1970, and a PhD from Oxford University in 1974. He served as the advisor to the Palestinian delegation to the Madrid and Washington Arab–Israeli peace negotiations from October 1991 through June 1993. He has also published many of the most academically recognized books about the history of Palestine and the Palestinians including *The Origins of Arab Nationalism* (1991), *Palestinian Identity: The Construction of Modern National Consciousness* (1996), *The Iron Cage: The Story of the Palestinian Struggle for Statehood* (2006), and *The Hundred Years' War on Palestine: A History of Settler Colonialism and Resistance, 1917–2017* (2020).[3] During the 1970s and 1980s, Mona Khalidi worked at the Palestine News & Information Agency (WAFA), and served as president of the Arab American Action Network. Ismail's sister, Dima Khalidi, is an activist, attorney, and founding director of Palestine Legal, an organization protecting "people speaking out for Palestinian freedom from attacks on their civil and constitutional rights."[4] His sister Lamya is an archaeologist who specializes in the Middle East and the Horn of Africa.

Ismail Khalidi himself was born into this notable family in Beirut, Lebanon, in 1982, during one of the most violent eras of the Lebanese Civil War. In discussing his birth and the play *Sabra Falling*, Rashid Khalidi stated:

> He [Ismail] wasn't born when Sabra fell, and we were living in Beirut and my wife, Mona, was pregnant with him, so he was very much affected by the 1982 War, in his mother's womb. She had to flee the bombing at one stage, running five months pregnant with him, in June 1982. He was born in November of that year. It's a testament to the fact that you can, not having lived through something, you can write a play like that play . . .[5]

The Khalidi family first moved to New York City where Rashid Khalidi taught for Columbia University. He then joined the faculty of the University of Chicago in 1987 as a professor, director of the Center for Middle Eastern Studies, and the Center for International Studies.[6] In 2003 he re-joined the Columbia University faculty.

Given his Lebanese-Palestinian heritage, saturated in Palestinian history and politics, it is little wonder that Ismail Khalidi felt compelled to explore his Palestinian roots through art. In 2005, he graduated from Macalester College as an International Studies major and an English and Theater minor. During that time he served as the

---

[3] "Khalidi, Rashid." Columbia University. https://history.columbia.edu/person/khalidi-rashid/.
[4] "Dima Khalidi, Director." Palestine Legal. https://history.columbia.edu/person/khalidi-rashid/.
[5] NYUAD, "Narrating Palestine: A Conversation with Rashid Khalidi and Ismail Khalidi," YouTube, June 8, 2020, video, 1:01:26, https://youtu.be/BwQHgZC4B00?si–Xrzy2T-G9W6_NUU.
[6] "Khalidi, Rashid." The University of Chicago Photographic Archive. https://photoarchive.lib.uchicago.edu/db.xqy?one=apf1-10227.xml.

Education and Community Outreach Coordinator for Pangea World Theater in Minneapolis, and he wrote and performed in his play *Truth Serum Blues*, directed by Pangea's co-Artistic Director Dipankar Mukherjee. The production was awarded Best Solo Show of 2005 by Lavender Magazine. In 2009, he received his MFA from NYU Tisch School of the Arts in the Department of Dramatic Writing. During his time at NYU, he wrote his play *Tennis in Nablus*, which was the co-recipient for the Goldberg Playwriting Award and the Grand Prize for The Kendeda National Graduate Playwriting Competition. The Kennedy Center/American College Theater Festival awarded Khalidi the Quest for Peace Playwriting Award, and he was the co-recipient for The Mark Twain Award for Comic Playwriting. It was also the finalist for the L. Arnold Weissberger Award for Playwriting at the Williamstown Theatre Festival. The play was given a full production at The Alliance Theatre in Atlanta, GA in February 2010 and Stageworks Hudson in September 2011. Subsequent readings were given at Queens Theatre in the Park, the Goodman Theatre, New York Theatre Workshop, Emory University Center for Ethics, the American University of Beirut, Columbia University School of the Arts and the Center for Palestine Studies, and Silk Road Rising. The play garnered positive reviews in the press. In his review of the play, Wendell Brock of *The Atlanta Journal-Constitution* wrote, "For a play about a brutal 1939 rebellion in British-occupied Palestine, Ismail Khalidi's 'Tennis in Nablus' is a remarkably funny play . . . Khalidi defuses the solemnity of his story by masking it with comedic zest, and yet he never negates the horror of the final twist."[7] In his review of the play for the *Columbia Spectator*, David Froomkin wrote, "Westerners have themselves to thank for today's Palestinian mess, Khalidi suggests, implying that American imperialism is just as unwelcome today as British imperialism was 70 years ago . . . 'Tennis in Nablus' inspires laughter and tears—and the frequency of the former serves masterfully to ensure the efficacy of the latter."[8]

His next work, *Final Status*, received a reading at The Public Theater in New York on May 9, 2009. Meanwhile, *Sabra Falling* premiered at Pangea World Theater in September 2017, coinciding with the 35th anniversary of the massacres at Sabra and Shatila, again under the direction of Dipankar Mukherjee. Subsequent readings followed at the Shubbak Festival of Contemporary Culture in London, Noor Theatre in New York, and Golden Thread Productions in San Francisco. Khalidi's major plays up to this point in his career clearly demonstrated an ethos he was creating as a playwright of conscience focused upon the history of Palestine and the Palestinian people who were suffering under the injustices of occupation, displacement, and war.

During this time, Ismail Khalidi and renowned American playwright Naomi Wallace began a collaborative partnership. Their first play was a commissioned co-adaptation of the Ghassan Kanafani novel *Returning to Haifa*, which was slated to premiere at New York's Public Theater in 2014. However, according to Michael Billington of *The*

---

[7] Wendell Brock, "'Tennis in Nablus' Has Got Game: World Premiere Mixes Tragedy, Comedy, Political Tension." *Atlanta Journal-Constitution* [Atlanta, GA], February 6, 2010, D2. *Gale OneFile: News* (accessed February 15, 2024). https://link.gale.com/apps/doc/A218376024/STND?u=euge94201&sid=bookmark-STND&xid=5c840b69.

[8] David Froomkin, "Reading Takes Intimate Look at Middle East." *Columbia Spectator*, October 9, 2012, 6.

Guardian, "this play never reached the stage because of pressures from the board."⁹ Pressure by the governing boards that oversee theaters has led to many other cancellations of both Palestinian and Israeli dramas including Katharine Viner and Alan Rickman's adaptation of *My Name Is Rachel Corrie* at New York Theatre Workshop in 2006 and Motti Lerner's *The Admission* at Theater J in 2013, to name only a few. According to Wallace, "Even if you disagree with the voices, they still deserve to be heard ... The American theatregoing public doesn't even know about what it isn't allowed to see."¹⁰ This form of board-sanctioned censorship is an unfortunate consequence of donors having gained greater control of theater budgets and boards that are too risk-averse to confront those donors when so-called "political plays" are presented, especially those dealing with the Israel–Palestine conflict.

Khalidi and Wallace's collaboration continued, and in 2015 they co-edited an anthology of Palestinian and Palestinian-American plays titled *Inside/Outside: Six Plays from Palestine and the Diaspora*. In the Preface, Khalidi and Wallace explicitly highlight the challenges faced by Palestinian plays or plays about Palestine, writing:

> Plays written by Palestinians have an uphill battle in order to see the light of the stage. Palestinian dramatists do not so much write against the grain, though many do, but write against the odds. And the odds are stacked against them: their work is culturally delegitimized, derailed and delimited by the Israeli–Palestinian "conflict" wherein the Israeli perspective is always/already privileged ... This collection of compelling, feisty and imaginative plays fits into the long struggle of Palestinian and other oppressed and marginalized people who insist that they do not need permission to narrate their own stories, their own history, and their own visions of the future.¹¹

Khalidi and Wallace's anthology proved to be yet another stepping stone in their continued relationship. Soon after, they were commissioned by the Actors Theatre of Louisville for another co-adaptation, this time of Sinan Antoon's novel *The Corpse Washer*. The play was staged at The Humana Festival of New American Plays in 2019, directed by Mark Brokaw. In 2024, Wallace and Khalidi received a commission to write a play for Ashtar Theatre in Palestine, to be directed by Artistic Director Emile Saba. It is inspired by Picasso's "Guernica" and loosely based on Fernando Arrabal's play by the same name. At the time of this publication they were also commissioned by Interrobang Theatre in Chicago to co-write "an original play titled *Nostomania: An Oceanic Meditation at the Edge of the Continental Shelf*, a play about a young girl forced to leave her home by boat, and her imagined friendship with the Greenland shark."¹² Khalidi and

---

⁹ Michael Billington, "Returning to Haifa Review–Disturbing Drama is a Plea for Peace." March 5. Available online: https://www.theguardian.com/stage/2018/mar/05/returning-haifa-review-finborough-london-palestine-palestinian-israeli (accessed February 16, 2024).

¹⁰ Lyn Garner, "'Voices That Deserve to Be Heard': When Art Meets Activism." September 30. Available online: https://www.theguardian.com/stage/theatreblog/2016/sep/30/theatre-art-activism-freedom-flotilla (accessed February 16, 2024).

¹¹ N. Wallace and I. Khalidi (eds.), *Inside/Outside: Six Plays from Palestine and the Diaspora*. 1st ed. (New York: Theatre Communications Group, 2015), p. xi.

¹² N. Wallace, Email with authors. February 18, 2024.

Wallace's plays represent a powerful collaboration between two writers of disparate backgrounds who have found a fertile partnership at the nexus of theatre and Palestine. Their work together has added a new dimension to the corpus of plays addressing the Palestinian issue on US and UK stages. Khalidi has embraced collaborative writing projects and is currently working with co-authors Caitlin Nasema Cassidy, Noelle Ghoussaini, and Mohamed Yabdri on a drama titled *The Magic Bullet*, a play about Algeria, colonialism, and magic. Khalidi divides his time between New York and Chile where he lives with his two children, Nur and Elias.

Truth Serum Blues

Truth Serum Blues is a monodrama that dramatizes issues of governmental persecution, intergenerational trauma, and the indefinite detention of prisoners in US Black site prisons. Set sometime between 2002 and 2007, Khalidi's play employs multimedia, a chorus, and can be staged either as a one-person play or with multiple actors. In its original production, Khalidi played the role of the protagonist, Kareem. Kareem labels the prison in which he is incarcerated "Dubya's Gitmo," a reference to George W. Bush's establishment of the Guantanamo Bay Naval Base (GTMO/GITMO). He jokes about the difference between the Cuba of his imagination—replete with cigars, rum, and the Buena Vista Social Club—and the brutal totalitarian atmosphere he experiences there. Using his customary wit, Khalidi calls it, "more or less a mix of Attica and Alcatraz . . . with a militaristic Caribbean vibe—a collection of chicken and razor-sharp barbed wire" (*Truth* 28). The most resonant statement he makes, especially in lieu of subsequent administrations' promises to close down the prison, is "this place will always be around! Even if they shut the motherfucker down" (*Truth* 28). As of January 2024, the prison has cost US taxpayers over $400 million per year, has only released ten detainees, and most of the thirty people still detained there have been cleared for release. At its peak in 2003, the facility held 680 detainees.[13] However, Khalidi's ominous implication is, even without GITMO as a physical prison, the governmental persecution of Arabs and Muslims will continue indefinitely.

Kareem's incarceration is dramatized through a series of graphic torture scenes intercut with flashbacks to his past with his Palestinian cousin, Abu Ali. Echoing what might be Khalidi's own upbringing with a Palestinian academic, Kareem tells Abu Ali:

> My father used to give us lectures on Arab history, about Salah al-Din freeing Palestine from the invading Frankish barbarians . . . I listened as he talked between innings. Always between innings. See, Pops taught us about baseball and Holy Wars, but never taught us kids to be religious . . . just history, politics and baseball, stats and dates, the recitations and repetitions of invasions and uprisings: '36, '48, '67, '82, '87, '91, '96, 2000, 2002, 2003 . . . What's next? (*Truth* 29–30)

---

[13] C. Echols, "Why Won't Biden Close Gitmo?" Responsiblestatecraft.org. January 11, 2024. Available online: https://responsiblestatecraft.org/biden-close-guantanamo/. (accessed 22 February, 2024).

The audience discovers that Kareem is incarcerated specifically because of his relationship with his cousin, who is a doctor, whom the antagonist in the play, named only "Interrogator," insists is cooperating with Hamas. The recurrent traumas endured by the Palestinian people are recounted here in a long series of dates marking the loss and mourning of what used to be Palestine.

Khalidi then adds what he calls characters who are named "Intellectual Factors"—conservative pundits who appear and discuss the Israeli–Palestine conflict in terms of "the Arab mentality," "pathological anti-Semitism," and a "life and a culture of hatred" (*Truth* 33). These talking heads are dramatic representations of neo-conservative television and radio talk-show hosts, providing a larger polemical context to the political imbalance of the situation. Kareem's flashbacks with Abu Ali add moments of levity to the pervasive seriousness of the drama. As with many Arab Americans, having divided loyalties between one's land of birth and one's ancestral homeland causes feelings of displacement, disattachment, and guilt. Added to these psychological factors, the contemporary paranoia regarding perceptions of terrorism pervades all of the play's dialogues. Khalidi demonstrates that any feelings of resentment or anger Kareem harbors were the direct result of the prejudice and trauma he endured being an Arab in America.

After being beaten for no reason on an American street, Abu Ali returns to Gaza to help the wounded, only to find he became another target:

> Trying to live with some dignity is an act of terror as far as they're concerned. I'm a bloody insomniac, man, stitching up wounds, trying to cheat death by running to hospitals with headless infants, i.e., lil' Ahmad's brains and teeth rested in the back seat, bloodstains already crusted from the heat. My hospital and ambulances stay under siege, under lock and the only place I could reach was one of the Islamic Movement funded clinics . . . Six degrees of incrimination, you get it? (*Truth* 36)

For his part, Kareem describes the torture he endures in the detention camps, including extreme temperatures, sleep deprivation, verbal abuse, physical exertion, and broken bones. These physical abuses are also echoed by radio transmissions broadcasting Amnesty International reports of inhuman and degrading treatment of "aliens." By combining physical traumas with actual reports of abuses that have taken place in US Black sites, Khalidi merges fact and fiction in order to heighten the effect of the drama. Khalidi posits that the struggle people of color have endured in the United States from its founding is all part of the same hegemonic, racist ideology:

> Look what they did to the panthers, Huey an' Fred Hampton, the Chicano movement, man y'all, they are always ready . . . AIM . . . SNCC, MLK, Malcolm . . . FIRE! And the list goes on and on and it ain't just about Hoover or Nixon, or even the Bush boys . . . it's all of them, Democrats an' Republicans . . . 'cause this country, this country was founded on the backs of slaves, the bloody tracks of genocidal plagues of extermination, seeds that germinated into trade and expansion, open markets and mansions . . . Just divide and conquer in fashion, on runways, take off, drop off, and land, one-ton loads that explode from 30,000 feet, the same imperial magic show on repeat mode . . .
> (*Truth* 39)

The title *Truth Serum Blues* refers to the "truth inducing drugs—barbiturates," that The Interrogator injects into Kareem throughout the interrogation process. The primary antagonist, a character named Colonel Sangerson, justifies the use of torture by repeating old tropes about Islamic fundamentalism, Arab terrorism, and orientalism. "'Cause the real issue is what risks you all are willing to take to protect yer loved ones from these zealots! Is it worth getting one of these rag-heads a lil' tipsy to make him talk, to save lives in a fine hardworking American city? Well, to take a line right out ole Rummy the defense secretary's book of gems, I would say: 'heavens yes!' (*Truth* 41). Like many US Administration officials that justified torture, waterboarding, and other "enhanced interrogation techniques" after 9/11, Sangerson becomes just another soldier carrying out illegal orders in the so-called "War on Terror."

The tragedy that ends *Truth Serum Blues* is one that affects both Kareem and Abu Ali. After Abu Ali is killed when his medical clinic is obliterated by a missile strike, Kareem's guilt overwhelms him. In the play, cable news networks report that the clinic was a terrorist hideout, but Kareem refuses that indictment:

> ... there was no burden of proof, no room for me to question their version because the verdict had been passed, the punishment swift, just blood and broken glass ... No names, no faces, no ages, just the parroted statements of colonels and majors, analysts and haters justifying death of the other ... but this time it was the death of me, the death of my brother in struggle, in the hustle. And I cried for our mothers who would rather die a thousand deaths before burying a son or a daughter ... any mother any mother, anywhere, from Buchenwald to Bosnia and back ... and I cried ... 'cause any way you cut it I was guilty. ... I am guilty ... I was guilty any way you cut it! Because I am part of it, complicit in this terroristic existence ... no matter what I know or believe, or believe I know, it is my tax dollars that helped send that missile, that Apache—made and paid for here—to the apartheid regime that occupies your breath and finally took it too ... And that's terror, man ... sheer fucking terror!
>
> (*Truth* 45–6)

Kareem realizes that, as a US citizen, he is still a complicit actor in a situation that is directly afflicting his family and his people by virtue of the fact that his tax dollars are directly funding the weapons that are systematically destroying Palestinians in Palestine. The play's bleak ending is a mirror for the Palestinians living in the diaspora helplessly witnessing their homeland being annexed, bombed, occupied, and diminished decade after bloody decade.

Tennis in Nablus

Khalidi's *Tennis in Nablus* is a thought-provoking play set in the tumultuous time of British Mandate Palestine, specifically in the city of Nablus during the 1936 Arab Revolt. This pivotal period of Palestinian history saw a nationalist uprising by the Arab population against British colonial rule. During the Revolt, Palestinians resisted colonial policies that favored European Jewish immigration, land acquisition, and economic development at the expense of the native population. They aspired, like many nations in the interwar era, to achieve national independence from colonial rule and fought for this goal through both peaceful and armed resistance.[14] Nablus, a major urban center of northern Palestine, quickly became a focal point for Arab political and military organizing. In response, British colonial forces and Zionist militias retaliated with extreme repression and violence, including a campaign of public hangings of Arab revolutionaries meant in part to deter resistance. The campaign "left 14 to 17 percent of the adult male Arab population killed, wounded, imprisoned, or exiled."[15] Overwhelmed by the imbalance of power, the Arab Revolt ultimately failed to achieve its goals of Palestinian national independence and of halting European Jewish immigration. Its consequences, however, would reverberate well beyond its end in 1939.

Tennis in Nablus delves into the lives and worldviews of various characters from this period, including British officers, Palestinian nationalists, and Zionist settlers. It illustrates how these diverse individuals—and their fates—intertwine within the complex matrices of colonialism, nationalism, and identity. The play reveals the deep-rooted tensions and power dynamics prevalent during the period, not only between Palestinians and non-Palestinians but more significantly among Palestinians themselves.

The Al-Qudsi family serves as a microcosm for Palestinian society in this period and includes Yusef, the once-exiled rebel leader; Anbara, his intellectual revolutionary wife; and Tariq, their assimilationist entrepreneurial nephew. The play opens with Yusef and Anbara reuniting in their home after two years of separation due to Yusef's exile. He reveals to her that after his release, he immediately returned to his insurgency, stealing guns, ammunition, and an officer's uniform from the British, because "the revolution can't wait" (*Tennis* 54). Meanwhile, Anbara reveals that during Yusef's absence she maintained her practice of writing political propaganda pieces under various pseudonyms, the latest of which was "Mohammad Ali Baybars," a nod to the medieval Mamluk sultan renowned for defending the Islamic world against Crusaders (*Tennis* 56). The couple immediately reads as the embodiment of the dichotomy of Palestinian rebellion during the Arab Revolt. One party rebels through militant violence and the other through intellectual warfare. Their methods differ but they are united in their desire for national independence and view the power dynamics in the region with relative clarity.

On the other hand, their nephew Tariq lacks their critical attitude and instead favors collaboration with both the British and the Zionists. He is a businessman whose drive for self-preservation leads him to assimilate into the political and economic status quo, even going so far as selling his own family's land to Zionist settlers. This rift among the Al-Qudsi family comes to a head when Yusef invites Tariq to his home in order to convince him to join the cause of the rebellion. He claims that a man of Tariq's standing, with intimate knowledge of the British, could strengthen the revolution, but Tariq refuses to enable or participate in violent resistance.

We learn through their exchange during this visit that not only do the two men differ in their political outlooks but they also have a history of injury between them:

---

[14] Eugene Rogan, *The Arabs: A History* (New York: Basic Books, 2017), 201–7.
[15] Rashid I. Khalidi, *The Hundred Years' War on Palestine: A History of Settler Colonialism and Resistance, 1917–2017* (New York: Picador, 2020), 44.

Tariq Let's not confuse my business with who I am as a person.

Yusef Fine.

Tariq Though, such a notion surely didn't cross your mind as you sent my investments into flames in '36, dear uncle!

Anbara *gives* **Yusef** *a look.*

Yusef Yes. Well . . . I wanted to . . . apologize for that incident. It was unfortunate.

Tariq It was a betrayal, Yusef. It was utterly foolish and unjust. / It was—

Yusef —It was a rebellion, Tariq! There was a rebellion going on! Your people. You remember who your people are?! And that business of yours was breaking the boycott.

Tariq I was making a living for myself, not to mention my workers; our fellow countrymen!

Anbara Quiet! Both of you. A patrol could hear you from a mile away. Don't give them an excuse to come in.

Yusef (*in a near whisper*) Your "business as usual" helped the British to undercut the revolt! Is all this lost on you?

Tariq I'll tell you what I lost. I lost years of hard work! I lost contracts, employees, investments, thousands and thousands of pounds.

Yusef And I lost friends. I lost two years of freedom. (*Tennis* 61–2)

This exchange clearly underscores the price of intra-Palestinian divisions at a time when unity was most crucial. It sheds light on the complexity of building a resistance movement that draws on the strengths and competing interests of various sectors of society. It highlights the challenges to Palestinian unity when members of the same family, and by extension the nation, have to find a way forward past self-inflicted injuries and broken trust. Khalidi invites the audience to embrace this complexity by humanizing Palestinians and their cause while also disrupting the often reductive representation of Palestinian resistance so prominent in Western (particularly US American) discourses.

Despite Yusef and Tariq's divergent views, both men ultimately end up in the same position: arrested and chained together on a tennis court. The British officers, who Khalidi paints as racist buffoons, punish the men for their alleged treason by forcing them to be ball boys for their tennis games. This demonstrates their sheer disdain for and dehumanization of Palestinians. Khalidi further reinforces this colonial power dynamic by citing derogatory language used by British characters to refer to Palestinians, such as "Arab beast" and "damned Semite scum" (*Tennis* 68). Therefore, while Palestinians are seen struggling for their homeland, their rights, and their futures, the British are shown subjugating Palestinians through sick games and derogatory language.

Yet Khalidi does not reduce the British colonial entity to a pair of caricatured officers but complicates the equation by adding two colonial soldiers into the mix, one Irish and one Indian. Michael O'Donegal is a young, Irish "criminal" forced to serve in the

British army to avoid jail, and Rajib is a conscript from Britain's Indian colony. While the two men guard Yusef and Tariq in jail, they bond with the prisoners over their shared experiences of colonization and their contempt for the British, making their oppressors the butt of many jokes. Khalidi utilizes the relationship between these Irish, Indian, and Palestinian characters to draw astute historical parallels across diverse contexts and groups. All three nations experienced direct colonial subjugation, economic and cultural exploitation, and imposed partition at the hands of the British that left a legacy of ongoing conflict in their homelands. By including these characters and intertwining their stories, Khalidi reminds audiences of British colonialism's vast reach and builds bridges of solidarity based on shared struggles for liberation. In fact, Michael and Rajib act as go-betweens connecting Yusef and Anbara, and they eventually agree to help Yusef escape from jail.

Their covert resistance helps reignite Anbara's own efforts just as she was contemplating her next move. Following Yusef and Tariq's arrest, she crafts a fierce and poetic article denouncing Arab leaders who are "far too comfortable under the tutelage of their Western masters to be of any use" and, alongside them, the British for "play[ing] the Arab and the Jew like so many chess pieces." She implores readers to rise up and not recede into silence lest they "find [themselves] strangers in [their] own land" (*Tennis* 76). This powerful critique makes her (or, rather, "Baybars") a target of British, Zionist, and British-aligned Palestinian factions interested in silencing her. The British want to arrest her, the Palestinian Mufti wants to kill her, and the Jewish Agency wants to pay her off to be quiet. Anbara decides to take the money and is seen struggling to decide what to do with it—run, buy back land, buy rifles, etc.—when Michael and Rajib arrive with a message from Yusef. In that opportune moment, she decides to give them half the money to help free Yusef and sends a message to Yusef recommitting herself to her writing under a new pseudonym (*Tennis* 92).

Anbara's renewed resistance seems snuffed out by news of Yusef's sudden hanging, as we learn that she was not even able to bring herself to attend his funeral. But in the final scene of the play, we see that the flame of resistance has passed onto Tariq. He visits Anbara in her home after a rally following Yusef's funeral and describes how the experience transformed him:

> **Tariq** I walked up to the front of the crowd. I was pushed. Carried even. I got up on the fountain and I . . . spoke. I felt . . . intoxicated. I was holding something, a flag maybe, or a rock, a gun, I don't . . . even remember. It was as if . . .
>
> **Anbara** As if Yusef was speaking.
>
> **Tariq** And they cheered me, Anbara. They roared, and we marched. Moving like a sea.
>
> **Anbara** And then the shots.
>
> **Tariq** Yes.
>
> **Anbara** Always the shots.
>
> **Tariq** We scattered in every direction. Blood and shoes on the ground. I ran. Like a boy escaping a beating, not seeing or hearing a thing. Just the explosions echoing in my head. (*Tennis* 99)

The traumatic events Tariq experienced, not least the brutal hanging of his uncle, shook him into a political awakening. He realized what Yusef had tried to make him see from the beginning, that "the days of looking the other way are over" (*Tennis* 63). With his new understanding of the rebellion, he informs Anbara that he is exiling himself to Beirut and has come to say goodbye. He hands her a ring of three old iron keys and says, "The keys for what's left. What I haven't sold or seen burn. Take them. Until I return" (*Tennis* 100).

Of course, for most audiences or readers of this play, the foreshadowing in Tariq's statement leaves one with an eerie awareness of impending doom. The decade following the Arab Revolt, culminating in the Nakba (النَّكْبَة, the Catastrophe), saw the complete destruction and permanent displacement of over 750,000 Palestinians. The defeat of the Great Revolt paved the way for this unfolding disaster by leaving a legacy of continued foreign interference and inter-Arab rivalry. As the historian Rashid Khalidi puts it, "These problems were compounded by intractable Palestinian internal differences that endured after the defeat of the revolt, and by the absence of modern Palestinian state institutions."[16] *Tennis in Nablus* serves as a poignant reminder of this history and complicates its tragic consequences as they relate to ongoing debates over Palestinian nationalism, identity, and liberation.

Final Status

Between 1987 and 1993, Palestinians rose up against Israeli occupation in a popular uprising that became known as the First Intifada (الانتفاضة الأولى, Arabic for "shaking off"). It began in the Jabaliya refugee camp in Gaza in response to the killing of four Palestinian workers by an Israeli truck driver and quickly spread across the occupied territories of Gaza and the West Bank. This Palestinian resistance, marked mostly by peaceful strikes, boycotts, and other means of civil disobedience but including violent attacks such as stone throwing and bombings, was met with disproportionate counter-violence by the Israeli military.[17] As the popular uprising dragged on and Israeli violence escalated, its profound impact on global public opinion generated international pressure for ending the conflict through peaceful resolution.

Meanwhile, as grassroots activists took lead in the Occupied Palestinian Territories, the Palestinian Liberation Organization (PLO) struggled to maintain its position as the sole legitimate representative of the Palestinian cause. The PLO leadership, with Yasser Arafat at its head, had been exiled to Beirut in 1967 and then again to Tunis after their defeat in the 1982 Israeli invasion of Lebanon. According to historian Rashid Khalidi, they were "taken by surprise by the outbreak of a grassroots-led uprising and lost no time trying to co-opt and profit from it."[18] PLO leaders-in-exile felt threatened by the potential rise of alternative Palestinian leadership, particularly as they did not have a full understanding or direct experience of the conditions of occupation on the ground. As a result, Arafat's PLO politically inserted itself into the Intifada from abroad. They

---

[16] Khalidi, *Hundred Years' War*, 58.
[17] Charles D. Smith, *Palestine and the Arab–Israeli Conflict, Fourth Edition: A History with Documents*, 4th ed. (Boston: Palgrave Macmillan, 2001), 412–21.
[18] Khalidi, *Hundred Years' War*, 175.

jostled for control of the uprising with the newly created Islamic Resistance Movement (حركة المقاومة الإسلامية) in Gaza, known by its Arabic acronym Hamas. Both parties sought to claim the leadership of the Intifada, one within a secular national frame and another with Islamist aspirations.

This context brought about major consequences for the future of Palestine when eager PLO leaders pursued peace negotiations with Israel on terms disadvantageous to the Palestinian cause. They issued a Palestinian Declaration of Independence in November of 1988 which effectively abandoned the organization's claim to all of historic Palestine, accepted a two-state solution, and agreed to a peace conference on the basis of UN Security Council resolutions 242 and 338.[19] In doing so, they failed to secure parameters of peacemaking that included critical issues such as borders, Jerusalem, and the right of return for Palestinian refugees. The PLO even failed to secure itself a seat at the table as it was not allowed to directly participate in peace negotiations, agreeing instead to a joint Jordanian–Palestinian delegation that included politically unaffiliated Palestinian individuals.[20] In Rashid Khalidi's words, "instead of using the intifada's success to hold out for a forum framed in terms of [. . .] liberatory ends, the PLO allowed itself to be drawn into a process explicitly designed by Israel, with the acquiescence of the United States, to prolong its occupation and colonization, not to end them."[21] Thus the talks that began in 1990 and ultimately ended with the 1993 Oslo Accords served only to perpetuate the status quo of Palestinian dispossession, prolonging the occupation of Palestinian territories and paving the way for de facto annexation of the West Bank and Gaza by Israel.

These negotiations and their complex power dynamics inspire Ismail Khalidi's *Final Status*. The play dramatizes the behind the scenes tensions and maneuverings of Palestinian and Israeli negotiators in Madrid and Washington—which, as mentioned before, his father Rashid was directly involved in. Khalidi's intimate knowledge of the talks and his translation of them to the stage reveals the nuances of peace making, power imbalances, and the pitfalls of disunity among Palestinian leaders. In the process, it illuminates the shortcomings of the Oslo agreement and the roots of its eventual dire consequences, both predictable and not.

From the outset, in the Prologue, Khalidi establishes the clear imbalance of power between Palestinian and Israeli negotiation teams. The scene opens with Edriss, a man in his mid-sixties, standing at a podium and addressing the press at the 1991 Madrid Peace Conference during the first round of peace negotiations: "I should start by thanking you all for finally recognizing the Palestinian people at an international summit. But I won't . . . One shouldn't ever have to thank another for his inalienable rights" (*Final* 103). Lighting shifts from the podium to Motti, a man in his fifties, addressing an unseen group of colleagues with Edriss' picture projected behind him. The audience quickly realizes that he is briefing the Israeli team on their opposition: "Dr. Edriss Abul Hajj. From Gaza. Well-respected. And no one's bitch . . . not *yet*" (*Final* 103, emphasis original). This split stage scene provides the necessary exposition

---

[19] Rogan, *The Arabs*, 434–6.
[20] Rogan, *The Arabs*, 465–6.
[21] Khalidi, *Hundred Years' War*, 180–1.

by introducing central characters, laying out their backstories in the form of an intelligence briefing and foreshadowing the conflicts of the play through key information. It also establishes the power imbalance at play by painting the Palestinian team as "untested" yet confident and committed while it depicts the Israeli team as well-prepared and following orders to "keep the negotiations on [their] terms" (*Final* 104).

Act One jumps to two years after the Prologue, twelve rounds of negotiations later at a hotel in Washington, DC. The first scene makes it clear that Arafat's PLO has been meddling with the negotiations from abroad, making Edriss' job frustrating and unproductive. His colleague, Faisal, reveals that Arafat is sending his right-hand man Mazen from Tunis, presumably to monitor the negotiations but in truth to exert influence despite his exclusion from the process.

> **Faisal**   The old man [Arafat] hasn't listened to a word we've said for the past year.
>
> **Edriss** (*calmly*)   He's vulnerable, Faisal. He's isolated in Tunis. He walks like a rooster but he feels like a mouse.
>
> **Faisal**   And the Israelis can smell it. That's what worries me.
>
> **Edriss**   We can handle the Israelis. I assume the old man's smart enough to realize that.
>
> **Faisal**   You know he's suspicious of Hala. Because of her support in the West Bank. Same goes for you in Gaza. The Intifada / showed—
>
> **Edriss**   —Showed him he's not as relevant as he thought? I know. I read your article in the *New York Review of / Books*.
>
> **Faisal**   *London Review of Books*.
>
> **Edriss**   Look, they can fax and phone all they want, but in the end we're still the ones at the table. (*Final* 106)

This exchange reveals the limitations of the negotiating team and the nuances of the process of negotiation amid irreconcilable, intra-Palestinian tensions. It sets up the three negotiators—Edriss, Faisal, and Hala—and Mazen as stand-ins for the various interests representing Palestinian aspirations in the West Bank, Gaza, and diaspora.

In the course of this scene, the young Palestinian American lawyer Ibrahim enters the fray of the negotiations and finds himself swept up in the unspoken game of tug of war between competing visions. He serves as the new legal advisor for the team, replacing an incompetent lawyer hand-picked by the PLO who could barely speak English, the language of the negotiations. The impressionable young Ibrahim quickly becomes a target for Mazen, who is eager to have eyes and ears at the negotiations. Mazen plants the idea in his head that Edriss and the rest are pursuing their own agendas, adding, "Which is why I need someone here who I can trust totally. Someone who's committed to the struggle of Palestinians everywhere, not just the ones on the inside. The old man [Arafat] and I need someone sharp, from the outside. Like you" (*Final* 114). Again, Khalidi highlights the internal divisions among Palestinians as well as the insecurity of PLO leadership that led them to undermine the negotiation process in pursuit of self-interest.

In addition to internal struggles, Ibrahim gets drawn into mind games being played between Israeli and Palestinian negotiators. Khalidi sets up parallel adversaries in the characters of Edriss and Motti, the older negotiators, and Ibrahim and Uri, the younger counsels of the Palestinian and Israeli team respectively. In their standout scenes, Edriss and Motti face off in a battle of wits that is subtle in its subtext and heavy with the weight of years of experience as well as secrets. In contrast, the scenes between Ibrahim and Uri reveal their youthful competitiveness as they spar more directly and sarcastically with one another, each trying to intimidate the other.

These dynamics ultimately play into the major turning point of the play, a confluence of internal and external sabotage for Edriss and his team. Towards the end of Act One, Uri hints at secret talks happening in Oslo and reveals that he and Motti were instructed to stall things at the Washington negotiations. Soon after, the Israeli negotiators, along with Mazen and Ibrahim—now fully co-opted by the PLO—disappear. Edriss and his team learn that a deal has been made. The PLO agreed to the same terms that the Palestinian negotiators had been resisting and that the Israelis and Americans had been trying to force for over a year. Heavy with disappointment, Edriss returns to Gaza, but not before pleading with Mazen to loosen his grip on the young Ibrahim and tell him "I'll smack him across his pretty face the next time I see him" (*Final* 130).

He does in fact get this chance in Act Two, fifteen years later, when Ibrahim and Mazen suddenly show up at Edriss' door in Gaza as bombs and sirens can be heard in the background. Ibrahim initially claims that he has come to take Edriss to safety since an Israeli invasion was imminent. However, after Mazen enters the scene, we learn that the two have an ulterior motive: to enlist Edriss to negotiate a truce between Israel and Hamas. Not only does this visit demonstrate the further unraveling of Palestinian leadership, now split into warring factions in Gaza (Hamas) and the West Bank (PLO/Fatah), but it further shows the extent of PLO–Israeli coordination at the expense of everyday Palestinians.

The play highlights the deterioration of Palestinian life in the wake of the Oslo Accords, directly tying it to the repercussions of the deal and failures of PLO leadership. Edriss alerts Ibrahim to the consequences of Israel's complete siege on Gaza, among them: lack of electricity, lack of water, and destruction of infrastructure. He accuses Mazen of sounding "just like the fucking Americans" and suggests that he—and by extension the PLO—is their puppet, easily manipulated to fulfill American and Israeli goals. Finally, when Edriss realizes that he cannot get through to the other men, he decides to play a game with them called "Final Status Oslo Edition" (136–141).

In this farcical climax of the play, the various Palestinian positions that competed in the first act come to full blows. Edriss assigns roles to each of the characters in the scene: Edriss plays Mazen; Mazen plays the Israelis; Moose (a buffoon guard) plays Arafat; and Ibrahim plays the ghost of his father, the poet and martyr. Ibrahim, ironically, is played by an inanimate lamp. Together they recreate the Oslo negotiations within the frame of the game.

Mazen (as the Israelis) offers Edriss (playing Mazen) the deal: "mutual recognition, immediate withdrawal of IDF troops out of most of Gaza, save for some settlers, and we'll throw in Jericho ... Plus, we are letting the PLO into Palestine." Edriss then makes him "pinkie promise" to "talk about all the important stuff later"—meaning the status of Jerusalem, right of return for refugees, and the dismantling of settlements

(*Final* 143). The characters continue, in absurdity and confusion, to unpack the deal and in the process confirm the naivety and pettiness of the PLO negotiators which saddled Palestinians with disadvantageous terms.

Eventually, by the end of the game, Ibrahim comes to self-awareness as the reenactment turns into a metatheatrical character study of the young lawyer:

Moose   What does Ibrahim think?

They all look at the lamp. Silence.

Mazen   That's a yes.

Ibrahim   Maybe it's a no. Maybe he's too scared to say no.

Edriss   The son of Salim Abu Eid, scared? I don't believe it.

Mazen   He's more practical than his father was, he's a politician, not a poet.

Ibrahim   Maybe he's in over his head. Not scared but intimidated. And young.

Edriss   And deferential in the presence of leaders who he grew up hearing about,

Ibrahim   Old men who knew his father,

Edriss   Who use his name, tell him he can become a real Palestinian hero, like his dad.

Ibrahim   Maybe. (*Final* 145)

Ibrahim realizes that he has been taken advantage of by both the Israelis and the PLO leaders, all of whom were pursuing their own interests while he believed he was serving a cause. He also realizes that the Palestinian team had the entire game rigged against them, setting up a "damned if you do, damned if you don't" dilemma (*Final* 146).

As dawn breaks and the visitors prepare to leave, Ibrahim tries once again to convey his concern for Edriss and convince him to escape to the West Bank. Edriss, of course, refuses. When Ibrahim declares that he will stay behind with him, Edriss rejects his offer, adding "stop following us old men around, waiting for your orders. Clean up the mess we've made. You and the *shabab* [young men]. And the women. Too many men onstage for fuck's sake" (*Final* 147). In this closing statement, Khalidi seems to speak to Ibrahim's entire generation, encouraging them to acknowledge the failures of their predecessors and forge their own new path for the Palestinian cause. The playwright further emphasizes the need for women's inclusion, valuing their contributions and echoing their implicit endorsement through the portrayal of Hala—the only female character in the play. In this way, *Final Status* begs audiences to consider the blind spots of well-meaning leaders and how their blind spots, coupled with pride, could lead the collective into disastrous pitfalls.

Foot

While not explicitly, Ismail Khalidi's monodrama *Foot* connects to *Final Status* "by a tendril," according to the playwright (Interview 294). Set in 2007, two Intifadas later and roughly where *Final Status* leaves off, the play presents a young footballer in his twenties, unnamed, confined to a walled refugee camp in Gaza and to his imagination. From the beginning of the play, we see the man's poetic curiosity riff on clichés about feet and list the endless obstacles of occupation in the most beautiful alliterations. We learn that he studied journalism and poetry before his university was shut down, and he displays his prowess in the seamless weaving of tales and metaphors.

He imbues every anecdote about his life with poetic might. For instance, he describes his olive farming "fans" as the "old ones, the traders of our rotting but resilient agricultural heritage; mourners over the corpses of our fallen sustenance" (*Foot* 153). He muses about Palestinian dispossession and erasure through the metaphor of football in the Holy Land. He compares it to the popular dish falafel: "It is appropriated, cleansed and exiled. It's easy. Just sweep away the rubble, annex it, rename it, re-package it and you have a mythology on which to plant your feet; the mythology of a sandwich, a bean dip, a record, a war, a game . . . and finally a state to promote on the international stage" (*Foot* 153–4).

The young man does not reserve his poetry to just bemoaning Palestinian loss and suffering. He also paints football as a rallying call to the Palestinian cause for people to answer from across the diaspora. He describes the descendants of refugees from all over the world, "answer[ing] a call to play for an idea . . . For a team full of phantoms suddenly back from the dead" (*Foot* 154). For him, Palestine may not have statehood but its nationhood emanates out of the ghosts of its children and grandchildren, no matter what corner of the world they come from or what language they speak. They come together to form an entity; thus the team becomes the nation.

But just as the nation is tested and threatened by oppression, so is the team. We learn that this scrappy beacon of Palestinian agency, what the young man calls proof of existence, faces tremendous obstacles and losses at the hands of Israeli occupation. Less harmful obstacles, like checkpoints and curfews, affected the team's ability to practice or travel to competitions. Other, more deadly, effects of occupation make the players question how they could go on. One example he shares is of the killing of the team's midfielder, a man named Tareq, by an Israeli sniper. The young man grapples with the devastation of such a senseless loss, citing other incidents in which the team pushed themselves to go on, "because you have no choice . . . Because your feet tell you to and you listen" (*Foot* 157). Khalidi highlights the power of perseverance under suffering and the resilience of Palestinian life despite its invisibility and dehumanization in the eyes of the world.

The young man mourns that invisibility as he mourns Tareq, even as he dreams of a future at the World Cup. "Millions of people will see that match, I thought . . . but they won't see Tareq," he says, "He'll be invisible" (*Foot* 158). These themes of invisibility and spectrality weave throughout the play and serve as subtle foreshadowing for the surprise turning point that follows. The playwright suddenly blindsides the audience when the young man says, "All those thoughts, to know the future then, suddenly brought the past back in shots" (*Foot* 158). He goes on to narrate vignettes of memories, the simple pleasures of love, joy, and excitement cut short by a bullet to the neck. It turns out that the young footballer is the ghost of Tareq, recounting his own journey toward death.

As this reality sinks in for the audience, the young footballer concludes his memory of death:

And my feet, melting into blackness, into the words of one of our poets; words written in the five languages of my team:
"On the day you kill me
You'll find in my pocket
Travel tickets
To peace,
To the fields and the rain,
To people's conscience.
Don't waste the tickets."

(Foot 159)

This poem by the Palestinian poet Samih al-Qasem invites the killer themself to take up their victim's intentions for peace, freedom, and humanity despite their own deadly one. In the final moments of the play, Khalidi makes a parallel invitation. As Tareq prepares to take a penalty kick, the sound of a large cheering crowd rises. He suddenly stops, turns his back to the ball, and before exiting, says "Don't waste the tickets" directly to the audience. Khalidi's choice to end on this line invites audiences, as witnesses to this dead man's testimony, to take up the intentions he had for joy and life which were unfairly cut short. He implicates the audience as bystanders to his fate, placing responsibility on them to act towards preventing history from continuing to repeat itself. In this way, *Foot* follows a similar implicit call to action which can be found at the end of many of Khalidi's thought-provoking plays.

Sabra Falling

Sabra Falling takes place during one of the most catastrophic periods of Palestinian history during the Lebanese Civil War. The attack on the Sabra and Shatila refugee camps, and the subsequent massacres that occurred there at the hands of Phalangist Lebanese militias under the cover of the Israeli Defense Forces, were among the most horrific losses that Palestinians have endured prior to the cataclysmic war in Gaza after October 7, 2023. "While accurate figures on the number of people killed are difficult to ascertain, estimates have put the death toll at between 2,000–3,500 civilians."[22] The prominent British journalist Robert Fisk wrote of the massacres in his book *Pity the Nation: The Abduction of Lebanon*:

> There had been fighting inside the camp. The road near the Sabra mosque was slippery with cartridge cases and ammunition clips and some of the equipment was of the Soviet type used by the Palestinians. The few men here who still possessed weapons had tried to defend their families. Their stories would never be known.[23]

---

[22] AJ Staff, "Sabra and Shatila Massacre: What Happened in Lebanon in 1982?", *Al Jazeera*, September 16, 2022. (accessed July 30, 2024).

[23] R. Fisk, *Pity the Nation: The Abduction of Lebanon* (New York: Thunder's Mountain Press/Nation Books, 2002), 365.

Khalidi's *Sabra Falling* is a play that refuses to let the stories of these fighters and innocent civilians remain unknown.

Following the story of the Akawi family living in the Sabra refugee camp in West Beirut August and September of 1982, the play opens with a massive crash of an Israeli pilot who lands in his ejection seat directly into the middle of the family's living room. The matriarch, Leena, stops her son Hani, who is a PLO fighter, from executing the man. Sofyan, the patriarch of the family, a theater director, gradually believes that The Pilot is his lost son Eyad. The specter of their lost child hangs over the play as the family contemplates what they should do with their unwelcome guest. Sofyan reminds his son Hani that his people have been caught up in wars before from the British to the Zionists, to the Israelis. All along the betrayal of their fellow Arabs stings them, as Sofyan recounts:

> Hear that? That's the tick tock of a clock and we're running out of time. Who will come to our aid? The Syrians? Their air force was wiped out. Those shits in Saudi Arabia? Ha! Bunch of hypocritical swine with oil pumping in their veins and cash the only cause they care about? Will they ride to our rescue? The Soviets? The French? The Americans?! . . . That's why I'm telling you we can win only when we show them they can never win. By laughing at their tanks and jets. By creating beauty where they have left us none.
>
> (*Sabra* 173)

With the departure of the PLO fighters, Hani decides to depart Beirut despite Dalia's protestations. The fighters, like so many in the Palestinian diaspora, would find themselves scattered around the world as they continued their struggle for a Palestinian homeland.

Sofyan's slide show of pre-1948 Palestine is both a reminiscence of what was, and a reminder of what now is. Where Sofyan sees his ancestral village, The Pilot knows new houses, parking lots, and supermarkets. The notion of disappearance also permeates the play. Dalia shouts at the awaiting soldiers:

> I can see you laughing behind your tanks, assholes! Hey you! Don't you want to go home? You drive us from our land and you're not even there! It wasn't enough to chase us out and build your parks over our villages? To erase the names and make them your own?! . . . So what more do you want from us?! You've hunted us into the sea, blown us into the sky and driven us under the earth. Now there's nowhere for us to go!
>
> (*Sabra* 206)

This speech, born of decades of displacement, war, and exile, expresses the horror Palestinians endured, and continue to endure, in their ongoing desire for liberation. The play ends with the arrival of the Phalangist militias and the sounds of shooting and screams outside. The inevitable massacre has arrived and the family now stand with their backs to the door awaiting their terrible fate. The previously nameless and faceless victims of the Sabra and Shatila massacres now have names and faces that audiences must contend with. As the cacophony of violence crescendos, the last stage direction reads, "*Light cuts to black . . . All is silent. All is still*" (*Sabra* 208). That horrific stillness is recounted by Robert Fisk, who was at the Sabra and Shatila camps directly after the massacres:

They were everywhere, in the road, in laneways, in backyards and broken rooms, beneath crumpled masonry across the top of garbage tips. The murderers – the Christian militiamen whom Israel had let into the camps to 'flush out the terrorists' – had only just left. In some cases, the blood was still wet on the ground. When we had seen a hundred bodies, we stopped counting. Down every alleyway, there were corpses – women, young men, babies and grandparents – lying together in lazy and terrible profusion where they had been knifed or machine-gunned to death. Each corridor through the rubble produced more bodies.[24]

At Sabra and Shatila today there is nothing but a small rectangular marble marker that commemorates the massacre. Unfortunately, these horrific events which were perpetrated September 16–18, 1982, have faded in historical memory. Khalidi's play is a drama that seeks to memorialize the lives lived, and lost, in the camps. Although *Sabra Falling* is set decades in the past, it remains a testament to Palestinian lives lost in every conflict from the 1920 "*ām al-nakbah*" to the present day. Palestinian American poet Hala Alyan writes, "In the face of incomprehensible destruction, what does the diasporic witness have to offer? What do we build in a rift the size of countries? Our poetry? Our hoarse voices at a protest, seared by what we've been spared? A last name pronounced in two languages. The promise of a long, unruly memory."[25] Khalidi, like Alyan, is a diasporic witness whose "long, unruly memory" will not allow the dead of Sabra and Shatila to die in vain.

Dead Are My People

In 2018, Khalidi wrote the book for *Dead Are My People* through a collaboration with composer Hadi Eldebek, with lyrics by Ismail Khalidi, Hadi Eldebek, and Patrick Lazour. The "play with music" was produced by Noor Theatre and presented at New York Theatre Workshop in November 2018 under the direction of Leah C. Gardiner. The play was based on the real-life story of the lynching of the Syrian-Lebanese immigrant N'oula (Nola) and the police killing of his wife Hasna (Fannie) Romey in Lake City, Florida in May of 1929.[26] Khalidi's play is not a factual retelling of the Romey murders, but rather utilizes this pivotal moment in Arab American history as an inspiration for a similar story with haunting repercussions.

Khalidi's interweaving of anti-Arab, anti-Black, and anti-immigrant narratives which define so much of US history, provided the milieu for Khalidi's dramaturgy. In her review for *Arab America*, Sarah Moawad wrote:

---

[24] Fisk, *Pity the Nation*, 359–60.
[25] H. Alyan, "'I am not there and I am not here': a Palestinian American Poet on Bearing Witness to Atrocity." *The Guardian*, January 28, 2024. Available online: https://www.theguardian.com/world/2024/jan/28/gaza-palestine-grief-essay-poetry (accessed 29 January, 2024).
[26] "The Romey Lynchings" (no date) *Khayrallah Center for Lebanese Diaspora Studies, NC State University*. Available at: https://lebanesestudies.ncsu.edu/explore/publications/projects/romey-lynchings/ (accessed July 30, 2024).

Khalidi is remarkably talented at weaving the historical with the contemporary to demonstrate how little progress has been made in the last hundred years. His work does not shy away from the fiercely and unapologetically political, and, by drawing upon historical memory, reminds us that oppression does not happen in a vacuum – that the roots of colonialism, racism, imperialism, and white supremacy are all intertwined.[27]

The script, based partly on Sarah M. A. Gualtieri's book *Between Arab and White: Race and Ethnicity in the Early Syrian American Diaspora*, further demonstrated Khalidi's ability to meld Middle Eastern history with contemporary dramaturgy. Gualtieri's chapter "The Lynching of Nola Romey: Syrian Racial Inbetweeness in the Jim Crow South" was the chronicle of the May 17, 1929 lynching. Gualtieri writes:

> Once the event receded from the headlines, the lynching began to fade into the silence of the past. It was never systematically researched, and it received no attention in the substantial literature on the subject of lynching. Scholarship on Arab Americans rarely mentions it, despite the claim by community leader Salloum Mokarzel in 1929 that the lynching was "one of the saddest tragedies in the history of the Syrians in America."[28]

Gualtieri places the lynching within the larger, more horrific, history of extralegal violence against Blacks in the American South.

Lynching, which punished and terrorized newly enfranchised African Americans in the Jim Crow South, also affected others who were outside of the "white" category of the American racial imaginary. The Romeys, both Christians from what is now Lebanon, fled Ottoman persecution in their native homeland in 1906, immigrating to the United States with the desire to leave political persecution behind them. What they found instead was a cruel and punishing racial hierarchy that placed them outside of the white supremecist order. Following his Syrian cousin to Lake City, Florida, N'oula Romey could not imagine that, by the time he arrived there, he would already have been targeted by the KKK who, in Valdosta, Georgia, flogged him. He and his wife then moved to Lake City, Florida where, for a short time, they were allowed to operate a grocery store. After a series of events that led to the police killing Hasna Romey in her store, N'oula Romey was beaten, arrested, and later shot to death by a mob on the outskirts of town. Their four children were orphaned and raised by the local Syrian community. According to Gualtieri, "the lyching of Nola Romey and the murder of his wife *were* about race and the work that race did in a town where they were foreigners and outsiders."[29] This event remains unmemorialized and to this day there is no historical marker commemorating the site of the lynching. Khalidi's deep understanding

---

[27] S. Moawad, "Ismail Khalidi's 'Dead Are My People' Examines White Supremacy & Immigration in America." *Arab America*. October 8. Available online: https://www.arabamerica.com/ismail-khalidis-dead-people-examines-white-supremacy-immigration-america-now/ (accessed February 16, 2024).

[28] S. Gualtieri, *Between Arab and White: Race and Ethnicity in the Early Syrian American Diaspora* (Berkeley, CA: University of California Press, 2009). 114.

of this history, exemplified by his dramaturgy and the extensive works cited found at the end of his play, forms the foundation for his drama.

Khalidi titled the play *Dead Are My People* after the poem by the same name in the renowned Lebanese poet Kahlil Gibran's collection *Secrets of the Heart*. It is fitting that Khalidi would echo Gibran, who wrote the poem in exile, while lamenting his people's fate at the hands of famine and occupation. In particular, Khalidi finds solidarity between the struggles of Black Americans and Palestinians, seeing both communities oppressed by power structures that thrive on white supremacy, extrajudicial acts, and domination through military might. N'oula Romey was lynched the same year that the 1929 Buraq Uprising (ثورة البراق) took place in Palestine in which 116 Palestinians were killed. For Khalidi, the past is present, and his plays are replete with historical resonances that echo and mirror the past at every turn.

By dramatizing Weevil and Nicola as two sides of a particularly American coin, Khalidi is positing that African Americans and Arab Americans share a similar type of persecution in the US and, because of this fact, they are partners in the same struggle. Utilizing a chorus much like the one seen in his *Truth Serum Blues*, the "Chorus of Hoods" that represent the KKK are a menacing force that symbolize the hegemonic white power structure that ultimately serves to crush both communities. While both Arabs and Blacks came to the Americas by boat, Weevil reminds Nicola there was a difference:

> **Nicola**   I never want come to America like others. Why I need a street made of gold? But I have nowhere to run. So I hide in little boat, then in very big boat over the big sea. To America.
>
> **Weevil** (*half to himself*)   Funny, ain't it? How much depends on the kind a boat you arrive in. And where you was sittin' on it. (*Dead* 249)

The confluence of African American and Arab American histories in the play highlights the shared histories of "the other" in American life. Whereas Weevil works diligently to help Blacks escape to the north and to assure that their extrajudicial murders are documented, immigrants like Ellis and Helene do their best to assimilate, to stay within societal bounds, and to ensure they are deemed "white." Arabs and Arab Americans, who often have the privilege of "passing" as white eventually realize that, no matter how much they believe they are accepted by their society, they will always be otherized no matter the racial categories the government gives them.

Nicola, who was forced to flee his native land due to his anti-Ottoman activities, finds himself in another society where he faces oppression. His dream to find a new homeland filled with freedom and economic prosperity becomes a nightmare of racism and fear. Perkins, Aldridge, and "The Hooded Ones" are an ever-present reminder that white supremacy is supreme, and that those who are allowed to live and work in these communities do so at the behest of those in power. Lines (or "delineators" as Weevil calls them) are drawn throughout the play, demarcating the boundaries of the conditional citizenship the Arab and Black characters inhabit. "Form your lines, brothers and strike

---

[29] Ibid., 120.

the bell. Protect what's white, come high waters or hell!" the Chorus sings (*Dead* 226). Perkins draws a line denoting where Ellis can place his groceries on the sidewalk, and Weevil and Nicola are not allowed to cross certain lines in the cemetery, leading Weevil to say: "Let's just say it can be hard to know exactly where one stands all the time. What with all the lines drawn by certain men. In the sand, in the air, the seas and rivers, even in the blood" (*Dead* 248). It is no coincidence, then, that the lines drawn by the British and the French that created the map of the modern Middle East are also mocked and called into question.

At play's end, the sacrifice made by Tanios for Weevil is repaid by Weevil for Nicola. Nicola's vandalism of Aldridge's statue, and Weevil's willingness to take responsibility for it, reinforces and dramatizes the shared history of oppression and political activism Khalidi envisions between Arabs and Blacks in the United States. As recompense, Nicola absconds with the documents, taking them north for W. E. B. Du Bois, thereby completing the mission for justice begun by Weevil and Tanios. As Weevil helps Nicola secure a gravestone for his lynched uncle Tanios, Nicola helps Weevil smuggle the documents to New York. Unlike the Romeys, and the countless Black victims of lynching in the US South, for whom justice was never served, the characters in *Dead Are My People* find a way to work together to right a historical wrong. Weevil and Nicola's improbable escapes provide a satisfying conclusion for a story whose historical antecedent ended only in tragedy.

Conclusion

In the introduction for his edited volume about Palestine for *Mizna*, Ismail Khalidi wrote:

> So we create and write and speak so we may recover our histories and rewrite our future, and "so we may know the end of this travel." And we cultivate steadfastness from the knowledge that it is those who oppose human dignity and freedom who are truly bound in chains.[30]

As his body of work attests, he is, in an Adornoian sense, a committed artist. His poetry, plays, performances, articles, and critical writings comprise a body of work that speaks for Palestine and the Palestinian people artistically in the same manner that Rashid Khalidi's academic works did so academically. For Khalidi, Palestine really *is* everything: an inspiration, a cause, a people, a revolutionary struggle, a life-long calling. While his contemporaries are content creating lighthearted works that entertain for profit, Khalidi is a stalwart voice of his people in the diaspora speaking out against the endless injustices faced by Palestinians. Because Khalidi's plays are a direct challenge to the hegemonic ideals of our so-called democracies, they are rarely produced, frequently censored, and relatively unknown by the American theater establishment. One must ask why, unlike his contemporaries, Khalidi's works do not receive productions at major American theater companies? What is it about the

---

[30] I. Khalidi, 'Foreword.' *Mizna*, 19.2 (2019): 5–8.

Introduction 23

American theater that seems to have unlimited opportunities for some playwrights, but not for others? Khalidi's plays deserve the same attention and space as other plays about the Israeli–Palestinian conflict, yet they are relegated to singular productions by theater companies that focus solely on the region itself. This myopia, if not outright censorship, but the wider American theater establishment, is nothing short of a travesty. This anthology is one attempt to remedy this injustice.

Truth Serum Blues

Characters

Kareem*, *Arab-American, twenties.*

Abu Ali, *Palestinian, Kareem's cousin, thirties.*

The Interrogator, *an unseen force. A voice.*

Intellectual Factors #1–3, *pundits on screen.*

The Official, *a government man.*

The Colonel, *a military man.*

The Scientists, *a man of science.*

Setting

Time: Time is fluid, but sometime after 2003.

Place: A Guantanamo Bay cell. The Midwest. The Mideast. Nowhere.

The Set: Minimal. There is fencing or chicken wire (or the suggestion of it,) cutting the stage and separating it from the audience. Wires and bald light bulbs hang here and there. There is a stool where interrogations take place, and a syringe hanging from the ceiling above it. A mop, a suitcase and other basic props and clothing items mentioned in the play can be placed around the stage at the director's discretion. There should be a space, perhaps downstage, where Kareem feels he is in his cafe back home. But mostly the feeling of confinement and disorientation prevails. Somewhere there is a bare wall on which images are projected.

Truth Serum Blues originally commissioned and produced by Pangea World Theater in 2005 and created as a multimedia piece in collaboration with filmmaker Bassam Jarbawi. It was directed by Dipankar Mukherjee.

"The 'Arab malaise' is inextricably bound up with the gaze of the western other – a gaze that prevents everything, even escape. Suspicious and condescending by turns, the other's gaze constantly confronts you with your apparently insurmountable condition . . . You could conceivably overcome, or even simply ignore, the western gaze. But how can you avoid returning it, and measuring yourself against its reflection?"
—Samir Kassir

They killed me once
Then wore my face many times

—Samih Al-Qasim

---

* All characters should be played by same actor as Kareem, except perhaps for the character of Abu Ali, who only appears on screen, and the voice of the interrogator.

Prologue

Kareem *is barely visible, sitting upstage, talking on a pay phone, wearing a coat and wool hat. He does not face the audience.*

Kareem   Can I please speak to a human being!? . . . Yes. Thank you . . . Right, and the first name is Kareem. No, it's K-A-R-E-E-M. Yeah, you got it . . . 55 West 79th St. Across from the diner. I Just thought I should contact you all, be on the safe side. Well, thank you, sir. Yes, yes, sir, no problem.

He hangs up the phone as the sound of sirens and doors slamming rises. The lights fade to black.

Scene One

Kareem *is curled on the ground against a wall. He wears shorts and an undershirt now. All is in partial darkness.*

The barking of dogs is heard and an alarm buzzes. The sound of doors slamming open and shut.

Light hits the stage, as if a door is opening on a dark room, or the sun rising in the morning.

He splashes his face with water from the bucket near his bed. As he speaks, a stream of images of Havana appear on the screen, gradually speeding up as salsa music can be heard faintly, growing louder.

Kareem   It's funny, but I always wanted to visit Cuba . . . Maybe even for medical school . . . Best in the world, they say. Mamma always said I'd be a good doctor. Then again, moms always say that about their kids. At least Arab moms.

I always imagined arriving in Havana – under American radars of course – stepping out into the street and hailing a cab . . . "taxi"!

He hails a cab, sees it and gets in.

. . . A sky-blue 1957 Chevy. A beauty with beads hanging from the mirror and a statuette of Yemayá on the dashboard. Behind the wheel sits a cigar chompin' Cubana who, as it happens, also holds a PhD in comparative Latin American literature . . . ooh, leeme algo lindo, mamacita . . . mid-morning I run into Ibrahim Ferrer and Compay Segundo with the rest of the Buena Vista cats shooting the shit in the shade between gigs. Then, a straight white rum on the beach, the sound of Silvio Rodriguez singin' something poetic from an old radio perched on a windowsill somewhere behind me. After lunch, I attend a six-and-a-half-hour Fidel speech, meet him in his office afterwards to rap about politics over a fat-ass Cohiba . . .

He breathes the reverie in then freezes at the sound of gates closing and dogs barking; he is jolted and frantically runs for cover, speaking faster now.

... but Cuba is nothing like that. More of a totalitarian atmosphere, so don't believe the happy-go-lucky shit you hear! This ain't the Cuba Libre they talk about. No. This right here ... this is Dubya's Gitmo! Guantanamo Bay!

Muffled news reports and the grating sounds and sirens of a high-security prison.

Yes. Yes, yes, you've heard about it, I know ... read about it too ... Seen pundits debate how it is run, agreed wholeheartedly with some op-ed in *The New York Times* about the legality of it all ... you might've even written a letter to your congressman ... exercised your God-given constitutional, democratically elected, and upheld rights to speak out ... You even demonstrated! Held witty signs to the camera, shouted into the heavens, to the tops of skyscrapers about the Geneva Conventions, habeas corpus, and human rights ... Or perhaps not. Well, this is it ... More or less a mix of Attica and Alcatraz ... with a militaristic Caribbean vibe—a collection of chicken and razor-sharp barbed wire—high fences with an oh-so-unsavory clash of orange and military green confined on either side of the divide.

He is looking for something and he starts rummaging through an old leather suitcase on the floor, almost as if getting ready for work.

Some more sentimental than me might say there's more than human rights flushed down the toilets here ... But of course, as Americans ...

He's found it. He pulls out a folded orange jumpsuit and a skull cap.

... As Americans ...

He tosses it, still folded onto the ground, and grabs a cigarette butt from a hiding place.

... you can make your own decisions, draw your own conclusions. But let me tell you one thing, before I am swallowed whole: this place, this place will always be around. Even if they shut the motherfucker down.

He lights the cigarette butt.

... There's been approximately 784 men and boys of forty nationalities encaged here since ... since *you know*. And, well, I ain't gonna lie, most of these guys ... are nothin' ... but simple peasants or preachers caught at the wrong place at the wrong time, some of 'em just kids, and a good number were sold at random to American forces by warlords out for a buck or revenge, or both. Anyway, you've probably heard all about it on NPR so I'll ...

He mimes zipping his mouth shut. After a moment he shouts to all directions offstage.

No, no, no, no! This is NOT the fucking Buena Vista Social Club! This ain't no Silvio Rodriguez sing-along! No, sir, Allah knows it ain't even close ...

Speaking again, more calmly, back towards the audience.

... it's more like the ... uhh ... Bin Laden psychological club, coz in Gitmo, everyone wants to know about Uncle O-Sama.

He grabs a roll of toilet paper and squats on the bucket, now covered with a white toilet seat.

I for one don't know much about the man, except what you know, and they know of course, which is that he is the son of a Yemeni-born millionaire, controversial member of one of the richest families in Saudi Arabia who went on to take part, financially and personally in the CIA-backed Jihad against the Soviet Union in the eighties—blah blah yes yes we know, we know . . . leader of the once celebrated mujahideen – trained, armed, and funded by the US' astounding intelligence!

He wipes his bum and looks at the results.

One could say Bin Laden is simply the rotten fruit of America's poisonous seeds planted in the Mideast and Central Asia—who now finds himself in opposition to his estranged partners. Just one pigment on the jumbled canvas that is the new world disorder . . . And when he's gone there'll be another Grendel, another dragon, another commie or Chinaman, another monstrous A-rab to unify the West for yet another crusade in the name of capital or Christ . . . .

He gets up, adjusts his pants, and "flushes" the toilet.

Perhaps it is worth mentioning that I have yet to talk to anyone here who has ever met *him*, all of us just seen pictures of him on CNN and Al Jazeera. Some cats insist they've seen his tracks and others have found his droppings, but nothing more than the shit myths are made of.

Here he kneels down and runs his fingers over the ground as if tracking an animal.

. . . Except one man . . . Hajj Malik, Sector C. While herding his flock of sheep in the hills of Eastern Afghanistan, swears he saw Bin Laden's silhouette:

He becomes old Afghani man, Hajj Malik:

"Clear as a clip from the TV. Tall and slender, rising above the horizon, speaking on large cell phone" . . . (*As* **Kareem**.) he said (*Back to Hajj Malik*) "this long tall Bin Laden, he scare the sheep away" . . . of course, they—the interrogators— misunderstood him, thought he said that Bin Laden scared the jeep away, which led to some questions about

He is shouting now as if he is the interrogator:

"Who exactly was inside that jeep you smelly fuck" . . . Well, Hajj Malik, taken aback, could only reply that: "No one entered the sheep, sir, man, it is *haram* to fornicate with sheep in Islam" . . . (*Beat.*) . . . Lost in translation I guess. Happens all the time here.

Kareem *"irons" and "inspects" his jumpsuit, now spread on the floor, while talking . . .*

My father used to give us lectures on Arab history, about Salah al-Din liberating Palestine from the invading Frankish barbarians . . . I listened as he talked between innings. See, Pops taught us about baseball and Holy Wars, but never taught us kids to be religious . . . just history, politics, and baseball, stats and dates, the recitations and repetitions of invasions and uprisings, '36, '48, '67, '82, '87, '91, '96, 2000, 2002, 2003 . . . What's next? Who's next? Surely more payloads and target lists are being prepared. My internal air-raid sirens seem to wail night and day over the drumbeat of impending doom and the drone of a pulsating breed of grief.

You know what they say? They say we're in a slump, the Arabs are in a slump. Prompting questions like: "What went wrong? Why so hostile, so underdeveloped? Why do they hate us?" On paper the slump theory holds some water . . . I mean crusade after crusade, colony after company, with a lot of bad decisions and backstabbing thrown in over the centuries has left us with . . . slumped shoulders to say the least . . . but I don't speak for the Arab mind . . .

He starts to put on the orange jumpsuit.

. . . Nope, can't speak for the Arab mind any more than the African or Asian mind or the white European mind . . . Whatever the fuck that means.

But, I think I know what you're thinking.

He is now fully dressed, buttoning up the final buttons of the orange suit.

You're thinking: My, he speaks so very well. His English is really so good for one of . . . them!

So how did I end up here? I, whose mechanics with a bat or a ball far outshine my mechanics for submission to a higher power or ignition of soaring towers.

Well, I don't know! Maybe it's my name. Or my beard?! Or perhaps in the end the answer can only be that sometimes terrorism is just . . . (*Pause.*) a state . . . (*Pause.*) of mind . . . a state of guilt that we can't escape . . .

Sound of muezzin's call to prayer can be heard.

And like clockwork, it is time to take my orange ass to the high priest for confession . . .

The prison soundscape/alarm comes in abruptly cutting through and replacing the call to prayer. **Kareem** *forcefully slumps into a praying/kneeling position and comes up blindfolded and cuffed.*

Scene Two

Kareem *walks blindfolded, feet and hands bound, and sits on a stool, a syringe on a string dangling above his head, and above it is a light bulb attached to the ceiling. Light focused on* **Kareem**. *Directly in front of him sits the bucket of water/toilet.*

Interrogator (*off/audio*)   You in a talking mood today, boy?

Kareem *lifts his chin and hisses/sucks his teeth in Arab disapproval.*

Interrogator   I take that as a yes . . .

Kareem (*to the audience*)   Another typically Arab custom, which may aggravate cops or officials, or anybody for that matter, is that Arabs say "no" by moving their head up and down—so the chin is upright—rather than the Western habit of moving their head left and right. In this context, "yes" actually means "no."

Interrogator   Give us names and maybe we can get you out of here, closer to home.

Kareem   Home?

Interrogator   Yes.

Kareem   I don't know where that is anymore, sir?

Interrogator   Well, you do hold a US passport do you not?

Kareem   But I like Cuba, sir, it's sunny here.

Interrogator   Do you know why you're here?

Kareem   No . . . yes . . . because I know about terrorists . . . because . . .

Interrogator   That's what we think. That's what your friends in sector C are telling us. In fact you told us that when you were apprehended—

Kareem   —Me?

Interrogator   You practically / invited us in . . . you—

Kareem (*interrupting*)   —Greeted you with flowers and cheers . . . as liberators right?!

He is shouting joyfully, but stops abruptly after receiving a violent blow to his head, then grabs a syringe and administers a shot to his own neck, slowly and painfully yet deliberately.

Interrogator   Ok, here we go one more time, big boy, tell us everything one more time for the record.

So, you're a Pakistani extremist living in the US, funneling money to terrorist groups abroad, including those linked to Al-Qaeda?

Kareem   Palestinian . . . sir

Interrogator   Pakistanian?

Kareem   Sure.

Interrogator   But you drive a taxi. Look, we know that you drive the taxi illegally.

Kareem   Like I said, the taxi's to pay for school . . . but don't tell my mom, she has no idea, she'd kill me, man, she thinks I'm doctor material . . . wha . . . wha . . . What's going on?

Interrogator   So you're Palestinian?

Kareem   Correct.

Interrogator   And how'd you become Pakistani? To join Al-Qaeda?

Kareem   What?!

He shakes his head to try to combat the grogginess brought on by the drugging.

Interrogator   And the one in Khamuss? Your cousin.

Kareem   Who?

Interrogator   He goes by Abu Ali.

Kareem   Oh, you mean Waleed . . . pfff . . . No, no, no . . . Waleed is clean, bruh.

Interrogator   He's not in Khamuss then? What about Al-Qaeda?

Kareem   No way, sir, he's not into that kinda shit . . . sir?

Interrogator   Tell us why you and your cousin are sending Khamuss money?

Kareem   I'm not

He is struck repeatedly by the invisible interrogator, his head reacting to the blows . . . The interrogator's voice gets angrier.

Interrogator   You're sending your cousin money and you said he's in Khamass! They're on the terror list, which means that's material support, son. You understand the gravity of your predicament? Where is your cousin? Is he trying to get into the US? The Israelis insist he's missing. Is he headed here?

Kareem   Sir, excuse me but which terror list would you be referring to sir? Perhaps we have different lists, kinda like how there's the metric system and then there's the other one that no one else uses . . . the uhh . . . the inch system, sir. But the rest of the world uses the metric system you know? Mrs. Nettles, third grade teacher, she used to tell us "the metric system is only for reds and homosexuals"—

He is slapped.

Interrogator   TALK!

Kareem   I said he's NOT innovled!

Interrogator   Are you? You in Khamuss?

Kareem   No.Yes, well no, I just send money to my cousin.

Interrogator   Where?

Kareem (*groggily*)   In Pakalakustan . . . . Palistan . . . . Palestine, sir, Palestine! Sir, I don't know what they teach you at West Point or the School of the Americas, but Palestinians, like other displaced and colonized and occupied follks, well we sometimes just need a lil' scratch you know, money, a bit a bread, want life, the basics. You know, Waleed has a Green Card . . . I mean "Abu Ali" . . . he came to school here. He's a doctor . . .

Interrogator   You an anti-Semite? You hate the Jews, don't you?

Kareem No, sir. And with all due respect, I am a Semite, sir. I am pretty much pro-Semitic I think. (*Beat.*) Maybe you're the anti-Semite, sir?

Interrogator Here, let me find it, we have you on the record, umm, you said . . . Look at me! You said . . .

Abu Ali *appears on screen—he is there yet elsewhere, Gaza perhaps, but nowhere.*

Abu Ali (*to* **Kareem**) He's gotta be kidding. Look, man, don't answer, that's a stupid fucking trick question. Typically American. Tell him your opposition to an illegal military occupation doesn't mean you don't like Jews. Tell him that there are Jews around the world opposed to this bloody apartheid hell they've trapped us in . . . tell 'im! Hey, wake up, K! Tell him a great scholar once said that, and I quote, "We need to think about two histories not separated ideologically, but together, contrapuntally. Neither Palestinian nor Israeli history at this point is a thing in itself, without the other. In so doing we will come up against the basic irreconcilability between the Zionist claim and Palestinian dispossession. The injustice done to the Palestinians is essential to these two histories, as is also the effect of Western anti-Semitism and the Holocaust." Tell 'im!

Abu Ali *flickers then fades away.* **Kareem** *is looking drugged and confused.*

Kareem I already did, man. Waleed? What does contrapuntally mean? . . Does it derive from Condaleeza?

A conservative pundit/intellectual appears on screen. He is **Kareem** *but different. He wears a blazer, hair gelled and an orange tie.*

Intellectual Factor #1 It's the leadership of the Palestinians that control their people and deprive them of a richer life in modern world. The two peoples now differ in psychological terms. The Palestinians have become a community of hatred and the Israelis have not! And for many in the Muslim and Arab world, Israel has become a central element of a collective obsessional delusion! Thus denunciation of Israel appears to be a component of a mass delusional system. In fact, the Arab mentality is made of "a sense of being a victim," "pathological anti-Semitism," and "a tendency to live in a world of illusions." Not surprisingly then, the Palestinian refugee camps are ideal environments for nurturing a paranoid view of life and a culture of hatred.

Kareem Who is that asshole? That's total bullshit, man. Who let that moron on TV?!

Interrogator Concentrate! And listen to me good. We have you on record saying incendiary stuff. You wanna tell us what yer planning? You wanna hit us too, huh? Use your American passport and your American accent and get us from the inside? Spit it out, you dirty fucking snake, answer me!

Kareem *is struck again.*

Interrogator You talk an' we can talk deal, let you play ball in the yard maybe. You'd like that wouldn't you?

On the screen a more progressive-looking pundit, also **Kareem**, *comes on the screen, a wall full of books behind him. He wears a tweed blazer, etc.*

Intellectual Factor #2 This is preposterous, gentlemen. By systematically attributing all manifestations of Arab and Muslim political behavior to religion, authentic political grievances are easily, and conveniently, avoided! The Palestinians, for example . . .

Intellectual Factor #2 is muted and visibly frustrated by it before flickering into oblivion.

Interrogator Tell me about your connection to Khamass and Yasser Arafat. What about Saddam?

Kareem Sir, have you been asking about hummus this whole time? Cause if so then I confess, I'm heavily involved with it. I support it being spread across the US and over bread and even crackers and, if absolutely necessary, on carrots in a white-party setting. We were indoctrinated at a young age, sir, I had no choice.

He laughs; he is visibly tipsy and drowsy. He is struck again. The screen flashes with images of older Arab women, grandmas, etc.

Kareem Sir, please! Help, I need to talk to my mamma. Can I call my mom? I still haven't gotten my one phone call, it's the law! One call. She's probably worried sick . . . Or a carrier pigeon? A raven? I'm sure they could find their way to the south side and my mamma's place—

Kareem *is slapped again.*

Interrogator Watch the lip, smart ass! Let him swim, boys, nice an' long. Keep questioning him and keep the tapes rolling.

Kareem *falls to the ground, to his knees, as if forced, and his head is dunked in the water of the bucket/toilet in front of him. He rises for air, gasping then dunks it again then raises his head and screams . . .*

Kareem (*shouting*) *Allahu Akbar*!

He once again submerges his head/is dunked violently as the lights cut to black.

Scene Three

Lights fade up on **Kareem** *standing, drying his face with a towel calmly, as if he has just washed his face in a bathroom. He grabs an apron, puts it on, and starts doing tasks in the diner back home: sweeping, putting out ashtrays and forks and knives, perhaps cooking something,. He is in a diner. He rings a bell and then shouts off to someone unseen.*

Kareem Number two! Getting cold, getting cold . . . (*To a customer.*) Hey, how you doin', Paulie? See that game last night? Worst call I've ever seen, swear to God. Take a seat, got that coffee comin' right up, cream and three sugars.

Abu Ali *appears behind* **Kareem***'s back. He doesn't notice him until he speaks.*

Abu Ali Inta irhabi? Wa ana Hamsawi? Pfff. [You, a terrorist? And me in Hamas?]

Kareem I know, Walid? Shitty umpire. What ya gonna do?

Abu Ali What was it? Slide hard, talk shit /

Kareem throw high and tight, and never forget to curse the umps,

Abu Ali and Kareem because there is no such a thing as an honest broker.

The two men laugh.

Kareem How you doing, cuz?

Abu Ali Been a while. You remember abu Lu'ai? Martyred . . . Two slugs to the head, in his underwear in the middle of the night—the army raided the building. Came to the window to see what was going down and "bam bam," just like that. And the fat grocer man, he still wakes me up before Fajr.

Kareem *is silent for a beat, almost frozen in thought.*

Abu Ali Your mother's worried sick, little cuz, on one of her sleepless binges . . . keeps calling what's her name, Ammou Salim's wife who does human rights law . . . I keep telling her you're fine . . you'll be ok . . . we all have run-ins with the law, right. I was arrested three times for throwing stones at the army jeeps before I was fifteen . . . And remember when they arrested me and Nazir in Chicago for not using our turn signal . . . Black man and an A-rab, in a fly ride. Forget about it, man, we should've known. Then again, we would've gotten pulled over driving your bucket, too.

Kareem Damned if you do, damned if you don't. Anyway, don't worry about me, fam. You holdin' up ok?

Abu Ali Curfew here, haven't left the house in a week, can't get to work at the hospital half the time. Oh and before I forget, the next time they talk to you, tell 'em—the tarboush man was sellin' Kharoob—plastic cups, capitalist gadgets, dreams of golden-paved streets and battery-powered made-in-China fans. Everbody hustling at the checkpoints . . . Shorties running around, rocks for roadblocks, gunshot rhythms and ambulance melodies, tar revolutions sizzling and that tear gas gets the eyes and nose to confess to any crime.

Kareem They said you were Hamas, man . . . You didn't go funda-mental on a brotha, did you?

Abu Ali So what if I did. But listen, man, *Iftah ar radio* [turn on the radio].

Kareem *walks over and switches on a radio.*

Radio (*audio*) News flash: In Khan Younis peaceful demonstration turns deadly—four shot, as missiles hit a building said to be used by weapons smugglers.

Abu Ali   There's your answer.

Kareem *is silent.*

Abu Ali   Trying to live with some dignity is an act of terror as far as they're concerned. I'm a bloody insomniac, man, stitching up wounds, trying to cheat death by running to hospitals with headless infants, i.e., lil' Ahmad's brains and teeth rested in the back seat, bloodstains already crusted from the heat. My hospital and ambulances stay under siege, under lock and the only place I could reach was one of the Islamic Movement funded clinics . . . Six degrees of incrimination, you get it? . . . And what up with that twitch? *Leish bitrajrej*, man?

Kareem   What twitch?

Abu Ali *fades/flickers out of screen replaced by blinking hints of torture pictures, e.g., Abu Ghraib, West Bank crackdowns, police brutality. The radio now blasts snippets of news stitched together between static.* **Kareem** *rocks uneasily as he listens, increasingly disoriented.*

Radio (*audio*)   None of the more than 500 detainees still held at Guantanamo—believed to include at least three who were minors at the time of being taken into custody—has had the lawfulness of his detention judicially reviewed // Shot and killed in Harlem by officers // Amnesty International claims that all those currently held are arbitrarily and unlawfully detained // subject to various forms of torture and interrogation techniques banned under international law // the Department of Justice has concluded that under article 16 of the Convention on Torture there is still no legal obligation prohibiting cruel, inhuman, or degrading treatment with respect to aliens overseas // The lessons learned at these facilities have advanced the operational art of intelligence // strategic interrogations doctrine // providing valuable insights into the mindset of the terrorist and the continuing threat posed to the United States // Idir's hands were secured behind his back before the guards are said to have slammed his head repeatedly into a steel beam and then the floor // continued to pound his body then stuffed Mr. Naseer's face into the toilet, repeatedly pressing the flush button // the military denied the charges as outlandish, while the President called them lies and refused to comment // sprayed chemical irritant into his eyes // sleep deprivation // the detainees were subject to interrogation techniques such as extreme temperature manipulation, forced sitting for hours // sleep deprivation . . .

Kareem *has by now has walked backwards and stumbled from the diner back into the cell, half-blinded, shivering, hands tied.*

Kareem   They leave you in the room, in your underpants with the air-conditioning on max for three, four hours. Alarms going off, music on full blast every time you nod off! Then you got a bag over yer face an they make you sit then stand, sit, stand, get up, down, *stand up*! Sit down! Up! Stand the fuck down you fuckin' goat fucker! And when you finally fall asleep they pour cold water on you and you scream, fall upward as far as the chain gives, but it hurts with a shattered jaw from all the boots to the face and so you just cry, I cry, Waleed; listening to the troops celebratin' the fourth of July, fireworks lighting up a sky . . . that I can't even see.

He slumps into the floor deflated then slowly rises, unties his hands and, someone else, puts a blazer on over his orange jumpsuit. Once up, he struts. He is a spokesman talking to a crowd that is small and elite. He talks to the audience as if his colleagues and press.

The Official   Is America a nation at war? You bet. And at the direction of the President, we will defeat adversaries at the time place, *and in the manner* of our choosing. I repeat, in the manner of our choosing. So even though our strength as a nation will continue to be challenged by those who employ a strategy of the weak—using international forums, judicial processes, and terrorism—we will prevail. There is terror in our midst, hiding, lying in wait, ready to strike our democracies from New York all the way to London and Tel Aviv. This enemy hates our way of life and this enemy doesn't rest. He has no mercy. Nor shall we!

The Official *takes off the jacket, hangs it on a chair, and returns casually to the cell where he immediately slumps down onto the floor, exhausted, almost crying. He is* **Kareem** *again.*

Kareem   You get it, Waleed?

Abu Ali *has appeared on screen and there is a silence, as if all is understood, although* **Kareem** *has his back turned to the screen. Slowly* **Abu Ali** *begins to talk, the screen flickering as* **Abu Ali***'s speech gets faster, more intense.*

From this point **Kareem** *physically inhabits the role of* **Abu Ali** *and his attackers in the story as* **Abu Ali** *speaks.*

Abu Ali   You know I twitched for a while after that night at the bar when I got beat down on the street. The year after September 11th . . . I could never tell you, hard to talk about, getting my ass kicked like that . . . It happened fast . . . slow motion in retrospect but fast at the time . . . In commercialized war zones they pick fights and break you like Kit-Kat, for being not quite right, not quite white, out for the night with a Black girl and it was a wrap. Broke me down with fists and feet, broke me the fuck up in the jazz alley, Billy on the electric organ inside / while cats sit back, talk smack, and watch me get beat down by five of 'em, five frat boys ready to scrap, my head to the pavement / while wolves chewed over some race shit, some flag shit that didn't involve any part of me / maybe a little / right eye . . .

Kareem, *against the fence, his back to the audience, is punched in his eye.*

Abu Ali   My back, scrapes / aches / but basically . . .

Kareem *is hit in the stomach, slumps to ground.*

Abu Ali   The scream was from me, is me, with Waleed, Ali, Ibrahim, and Mohammad in my name // Went from not enough of a cracker to other to WTC attacker / like fire crackers on the fourth and five good ole Northern boys drunk on brew unleashed their hate on my terrorist air strikes from every direction, fists and spit flying fast and hard towards their target . . .

Kareem *now beating fence as if he is the attacker.*

Abu Ali   heard me speaking that rag-head tongue, and if it was Dixie or I was a shade or two darker maybe they would have hanged my ass too, turned me to strange fruit or left me headless, working through insecurities and bigotry and me, not protected by political correctness /

Kareem (*as attacker*)   You goddamn camelfucker rag-head motherfucker! You want some more . . . I'll fuck your mother, you terrorist motherfucker!

Kareem, *as the attacker, kicks and spits on the ground where Abu Ali's body is/was/should be.*

Abu Ali   But I was alright, bigger than any label. They beat my ass down for no good reason except that I was hard to pin down . . . But after that I was out. Back home to the *balad*. From one stolen land to another on the other side of the earth.

Kareem *falls with a blow and while collapsed takes a last kick to the ribs as if he is Abu Ali, or perhaps himself, on the ground after the beating.*

Kareem   Guilty . . . by birth.

He appears on screen as a third intellectual factor, a social-scientist, statistician, census bureau type. He speaks matter-of-factly.

Intellectual Factor #3   With between four and five million Arabs and Arab Americans nationwide, Arabs make up one of the faster-growing groups in the US. Arabs may have white skin and blue eyes, olive or dark skin and brown eyes. Hair textures differ, ranging from straight to kinky. The United States has at different times classified Arab immigrants as African, Asian, white, European, or as belonging to a separate group.

Kareem *is now back in torture mode, head against ground or in toilet. He shouts as he comes up for air.*

Kareem   You goddamn camelfucker rag-head motherfucker, you want some more . . . I'll fuck your mother, you terrorist motherfucker! Cry, bitch, cry!

Intellectual Factor #3   Most Arab Americans, however, identify more closely with nationality than with ethnic groups, and in many cases Arab Americans have dual loyalties . . . dual loyalties . . . dual . . .

Kareem, *curled up near the toilet, starts singing Al Green's "Tired of Being Alone" . . . lights down on interrogation part of stage up on diner with radio now playing Al Green . . .*

Kareem *walks into diner mode . . . dancing and talking to Abu Ali, who is now on screen listening but flickering on and off, in and out . . .*

Kareem   You remember that summer, after junior year, driving to work . . . no tapes, no CDs just one soul station and the sound of Manny and Munir's beat box in the back seat . . . Woo, the K-town crew!

A beat starts playing.

Kareem   As soon as we rolled up to those mansions with our ladders and paint buckets, those suburbanites would start sweating man; you remember how scared they got when we walked up? I mean, can you blame 'em: two rabs, two Black males, three CHicanos and a borricua packed into that stale beat up van rented from Hector's dad's uncle's girlfriend's cousin. We had plans, man, thought we were invincible . . . (*Music stops abrubtly.*) And maybe we were, for a moment, but they got us. Divide and conquer. One by one . . . they got us.

Lights shift, prison-scape sounds come up, dogs, fences, alarms. **Kareem** *runs frantically into the cell, shedding his apron as a spotlight comes up on him, raving, shouting, tugging on the wire fencing, shaking it and gesticulating as if delivering a sermon to the other unseen inmates to start a riot.*

Isma'u ya jama'a: Look what they did to the panthers, Huey an' Fred Hampton, the Chicano movement, man y'all, they are always ready . . . AIM . . . SNCC, MLK, Malcolm . . . FIRE! And the list goes on and on and it ain't just about Hoover or Nixon, or even the Bush boys . . . it's all of them, Democrats an' Republicans . . . 'cause this country, this country was founded on the backs of slaves, the bloody tracks of genocidal plagues of extermination, seeds that germinated into trade and expansion, open markets and mansions . . . Just divide and conquer in fashion, on runways, take off, drop off, and land, one-ton loads that explode from 30,000 feet, the same imperial magic show on repeat mode . . .

They can kill us fast or they can kill us slow. And the rest of us, the rest of us can be bought and sold . . . That simple. One by one they get us out of the picture so we can't interfere with grand plans hatched way back when from the yoke of British rule, fried on pans greased with cotton and sugar, tobacco then skewered with greed and gold, cocaine and soil and finally with that slick crude oil . . . Now, let that shit simmer. Add corporate sponsors, use freedom as the moniker . . . divide and conquer.

He is more calm now, down from wall, his hands and feet bound, he walks slowly in circles.

But now that whole American pie is kinda tasteless, just the lost epicenter of an empire of bases, 750 of 'em at least, bought, stolen, or leased . . . militarism speaks from the pulpit of freedom! Screamin' orders: Divide and conquer! Divine sponsors and the chalk lines of manifest destitution criss-cross eyes into blindness.

And one by one they got us . . . in the prison system with the other millions . . . broke as hell gas station fillin' . . . or sent to Iraq to do some killin—

Like our guy Munir, twenty-two years old, leg blowed out by a roadside bomb in Mosul, brains blown out by own hand went postal upon return as vet to his native land, Detroit, Michigan . . . one more victim of American terror, man . . . And you turn on the TV. Turn on the TV.! And there ain't a word about that reality! About 200,000, 300,000, half a million dead in Iraq, or even the lives of those suicided soldiers, 4,000 of 'em, died killing for something other than freedom and democracy . . . and there lies the hypocrisy, 'cause in the end we gotta apologize. And for what?

For being Muslim? For being Arab? Black? Poor! For being against the war?! It's us who gotta apologize and reform?!

Beat.

And here we are . . . here I am, Waleed . . .

He has walked to the torture platform by now, almost stumbled there, and drops onto the stool.

. . . in exile, missing, secretly awaiting trial incommunicado on Caribbean isle with the descendants of Torqamada hissing . . . in my ears . . .

He injects truth serum and slumps into a chair.

. . . It's been a while since I've seen myself smile . . . seems like years . . .

He slumps onto ground and slowly transitions in dim lighting into military figure putting on a green army coat and hat. In the coat is a book and a belt. He mimes roughing **Kareem**.

Scene Four

Colonel Sangerson   Get 'im out a here boys, put 'im in the freezer an' bring in another one.

He shouts this offstage and then handles, twirls, checks the syringe, making himself comfortable in the stool.

So what is, in layman's terms, referred to as "truth serum" could be any one of several truth-inducing drugs—barbiturates actually. Administering such chemicals in the context of tor . . interro . . . questioning yields results.

In effect, it's like injecting someone with four or five stiff alcoholic beverages at once so that all of a sudden they're drunk, and BOOM, the senses are diminished an' yer much less inhibited . . . Puts the subject into a state between sleep and wakefulness, a semiconscious limbo so ta speak, where the truth flies out freely. Scientist say that along with the truth can come loads of bullshi . . . *misinformation*, but as long as we get inside their heads, that's all that matters . . . Learned that from the Frogs in Algeria, then in Nam, south of the border with the Contras and our Israeli partners too. They know how to extract intel. Hell, I wanna know what these Hajjis shit looks like in the morning. I wanna know what kinda panties their mammas wore under their burqas!

Look here, this truth stuff is a lot nicer'n what I'd do to these boys without it . . . so to all of you faggoty human rights Genevagina Convention people, I say, sure, this stuff is "invasive," but it ain't wrong! And frankly speakin', in this new dangerous world we inhibit, actions and results are the name of the game, so I ask you if you think it is worth it. 'Cause the real issue is what risks you all are willing to take to protect yer loved ones from these zealots! Is it worth getting one of these rag-heads a lil' tipsy to make him talk, to save lives in a fine hardworking American city? Well, to take a line right out ole Rummy the defense secretary's book of gems, I would say: "heavens yes!"

Now, at my officer school, where I instruct and rear young men into fine military officers, this book (*he produces a book*), *The Way Arabs Think*, is the basis of my cultural instruction . . . it says, among other fascinating things, that . . . "Arabs only understand FORCE . . . and the biggest weakness of the Arabs is shame and humiliation . . . especially sexual variations since they, Arabs, are a severely repressed an' backwards society" . . . page 85, good stuff!

And let me clarify that unlike the pinkos breathing down my neck, when it comes to Arabs I do not have some sort of incurable romanticism for 'em . . . ridin' their camels in the dessert, drinkin tea, eatin lamb, impregnatin women . . . I mean hell, even when there's a war to fight they barely even show up to tha field of battle! But that's why I got into this business; helping people: introducin' some sense inta 'em, communicatin' with 'em!

Folks, they ask me, they say, "Colonel, Colonel. Is liberatin' hearts an' minds a full-time job?" And I reply, "Oh heavens yes" . . .

He uses the belt to whip the ground near the bucket where his victim lies. He, the interrogator, then falls to the ground, shedding his coat and hat on the way down, and becomes **Kareem** *again, curled on the floor protecting his head as lights dim.*

Screen shifts to a baseball game. The phone is heard ringing. **Kareem** *runs out of interrogation mode into the café to answer it. As he does so, he is also watching the game, talking loudly, shouting . . .* **Kareem** *answers, his attention clearly on the game . . .*

Kareem   Allo?

Abu Ali (*altering his voice and accent*)   Hello is this Kareem Khallef? This is agent Frank Stillwater of the Federal Bureau of Infestation . . . we'd like to talk to you 'bout certain acquaintances and activities of yours . . .

Kareem (*distracted*)   Yeah, this is . . . Did you say the Fed. Bureau of Infestation?

Abu Ali   That's right, the Federal Bureau of Intimidation . . .

Kareem   Shut up, Waleed, what do you want? Watching the game here.

Fixed on the game again.

Yes! Yes! Yes! No, No! Ahhh, shit! Extra innings, Tigers-Sox . . . *shoo fi*?

Abu Ali   I got the papers straightened out. I'm gonna try to come to the States with Leena and the kids, get 'em the hell out of here. The schools here are closed, army's everywhere you look, the situation is shit, man. Might as well get out while we can, put this Green Card to use before the tanks move in again . . .

Kareem   That's great, cuz. I heard. *Ehla wasahla*. And you know we're gonna throw a parade for you all when you arrive. Wait, hold up. . . . Fuck! Throw the ball to the base! The base!

Abu Ali   Also, K, gotta ask you something important—

He is cut off by **Kareem** *who hasn't heard him.*

Kareem   Habibi, listen, gotta go . . . I'll call you tomorrow from the house, you can talk to my mom too, she's worried about you . . . (*Back to the game.*) Really? Unbelievable! How much do they pay you, asshole? Yo, Walter!

Abu Ali   Don't call me Walter, *ya arse*.

Kareem   They pay this chump the GDP of several countries and *wallah*, and he can't even catch a fly ball!

Abu Ali   Hopelessly American. I'm worried about you. It's taking up too much space in your brain! That's why you're not gonna pass the MCATs!

Kareem   First of all, don't hate just because you can't understand the intellectually stimulating intricacies of of Beisbol! Secondly, you try studying for the MCATs while driving a taxi cab at night and flipping burgers by day.

Abu Ali   Try working at a bodega, driving a truck on weekends and having a baby.

Kareem   Touché.

Abu Ali   Listen, I need you to do me a favor.

Kareem   Waleed? Waleed? The line is bad. Can't hear you.

Abu Ali   Kareem?

Kareem   I can't. . . . Hello? I gotta get off now anyway, but I'll grab a phone card and call you as soon as I'm off work . . . Can you hear me? *Yallah*, bye, take care, yeah, and love to the kids.

He hangs up and continues to watch the game's finale, then starts yelling in celebration, and runs/transitions back into cell . . .

Kareem (*drugged, shouting to all and to interrogator*)   Safe! He's safe, I'm safe, under the tag, I'm safe! Sir, I'm safe aren't I . . . You know, sir, Cuba has given my career a new breath of life. In fact, I'm the captain of the Camp Delta team, the Gitmo Gippers . . . I also play all nine positions . . . (*As announcer.*) Batting ninth, number eleven, playing everywhere . . . Ka rhyme Kahaloofee!

You see, sir, we were always the weird names on the roster. Pops used to coach too—he called pitches from the dugout . . . in Arabic. No need for signs. Suspicious. . . . Right?

Interrogator (*audio*)   Abu Ali . . . Where is he?

Kareem   He went underground, into the shadows . . . He's planning to come back into the States . . . But you won't find him! Only I can, 'cause I know him like the back of my hand. He talks to me. We talk, on the phone, or meet in the diner ... like always ... In fact, I just talked to him, sir, and he told me things. He passed on information about his mission.

He is "pulled" up from the interrogation chair and walked to right in front of the toilet ...

Waleed's my guy from way back! He radicalized me.

He is brought forcefully to his knees and his head is dunked. As this happens, **Abu Ali** *appears again.*

Abu Ali   Mornin' to ya, K-Rhyme, *Sabah al Kheir*!

Kareem (*head out of toilet, gasping*)   *Sabah al nour habibi* ... coffee straight black, my brotha, *no cierto*?

His head is dunked again. Lights cut.

Abu Ali   Sugar, two spoons.

The lights flicker back to reveal **Kareem** *again in diner, drying his face with a towel.*

Kareem   *Mazbout!* Sugar, I knew that! Where's my head, man? (*Beat.*) Yo, I drove that night shift again. Took a mamma to the airport to pick up another cheap flag-draped coffin comin' back from Babylon. And Mamma still doesn't know I'm driving the taxi either! I have to park it over at Ricardo's crib so she won't see it ... She'd flip out! "Oof a taxi, *eish hada*?! *Shu*, my son is driving a taxi! What if they rob you? Ooooof! ..."

Abu Ali   How about poker and a couple drinks on Thursday?

Kareem   Dude, keep your voice down about that when Hajj Radi is on premises! Save us both the lectures, please ... (*Now imitating Hadj Radi, an older man*). "Beer and cards! Fear Allah, son, and put on the Qu'ran. This silly willy hibby hobby is heavy on the ear. They have Sheikh Abdl-Basit on CD these days—"

They laugh together. **Kareem** *then turns around, looking off stage, as if at Hadj Radi across the diner. He raises his hand in salute, speaking very loudly and deliberately to the old man.*

Kareem   *esSalam-ou alaykoum ya Hadj. Hamdullilah, Hamdulilah, Y3ateek el a3afieh.*

He turns back towards Abu Ali (*Waleed*).

Kareem   Luckily for us he is one deaf ole man ... Cute but deaf. Poker sounds like a plan. Let me grab your food ...

He starts to cross but stops as the interrogator's voice breaks in.

Interrogator   SPEAK!

Kareem *is frozen in place then collapses in terror into a kneeling position. He is cowering, twitching. Worlds are overlapping. He stumbles and crawls back into cell area and stands on the stool, connecting electric wires to his fingers, around his neck, all with his back to the audience.*

Kareem They keep asking me how I got into the country. You ask and ask and I say: I grew up in the US, but they keep pressing . . . the button (*electric shock*) . . . So I insist. Ever since she set foot on Ellis Island I been here too (*another shock*) . . . tell 'em she came to this country in 1920, me too (*shock*) . . . yeah, just before they changed the immigration laws to keep the undesireable hordes of Asiatics out. She came here with her mom and her brother—the rest of the family was gonna follow but laws change so plans change and lives change . . . They posted up in Brooklyn and her brother joined the US Navy. Then she met *Jidou*, my grandfather . . . Here from Palestine to study. He didn't know that between his arrival in this country with one bag and his planned time of return, the Palestine he knew would disappear forever . . . They met in New York City . . . "New Yaowk Cityyy!"

He calls out "New York City" as if announcing a train leaving or arriving. **Kareem** *then becomes his grandfather.*

"Your grandma, wow . . . she was a beautiful girl from the mountains of Lubnan, very American but those eyes, *ya salam*, those eyes! You know she was Christian, didn't convert but I didn't care, too beautiful to care, so we married and had your father . . . and then your uncle . . . and then your other uncle . . . *Ya salam* those eyes . . ."

(*Back to* **Kareem**) My jidou had lost Palestine but his suitcase turned to furniture and his memories into sons and he wasn't a religious man but he prayed that one day he could take them all back:

Kareem *is now his grandfather again and he cradles the suitcase as if a young son and talks to it as such.*

"I'll take you to Jerusalem, to Bab el silsilee, Bab el A'moud, Haram-eh-shareef, to the Galilee, to the walls of Akka, ya bayee, rising out of the sea . . ."

(*Back to* **Kareem**) And he hoped, kept hoping until those six nights in '67 when the rest of Palestine was lost and it became even more unthinkable that anything could return to way it was, the way it was supposed to be, but it wasn't meant to be.

He slumps down to the ground.

And in the end it killed him. And once again the fam dispersed, globally . . .

A driving tabla/drum beat arises from every direction as he rattles off the names of cities.

Beirut, Amman, London, Santiago, Marseille, Cairo, Chicago, Cincinatti, Detroit, Damascus, Tunis . . . Inspired and kept alive by bad-ass mammas migrating with families on their backs through fire, from war to war, haven to haven, followed by phantoms, black hawks, and ravens . . . always holding it together somehow . . . and we can only stand and watch in awe, the way our grandfathers and then our fathers did . . . gangsta-ass Arab women: You can't beat 'em . . . you gotta just follow orders and believe in miracles.

He falls into an unstable sleep, tossing and turning to video clips of Apache helicopter strikes and flashes of Abu Ali's face in black and white interspersed with

TV commentators talking in fast-forward but muted . . . He tosses and turns, the lights flicker.

Scene Five

Kareem *shoots upright in bed as the clip of the helicopter firing a missile plays over and over again, almost as if skipping.*

Kareem I remember, Waleed . . . Your mom called that day . . . Now I remember. And I knew it was your mom, I knew it from the way my mom ran to the phone, the silence that swept through the house room by room. You know how it is. The way a mother has that sense, knows when family is calling. Calling with bad news . . .

She been watching the news upstairs, Apache attacks near Jenin, and when I heard Mamma scream . . . I knew that the missiles from that chopper had slammed into your clinic . . . taken you along with the all the patients, the patience you had sworn to protect . . . CNN said it was an attack against a terrorist threat. But there was no burden of proof, no room for me to question their version because the verdict had been passed, the punishment swift, just blood and broken glass . . . No names, no faces, no ages, just the parroted statements of colonels and majors, analysts and haters justifying death of the other . . . but this time it was the death of me, the death of my brother in struggle, in the hustle. And I cried for our mothers who would rather die a thousand deaths before burying a son or a daughter . . . any mother, any mother, anywhere, from Buchenwald to Bosnia and back . . . and I cried . . . 'cause any way you cut it I was guilty . . .

He has walked slowly toward the opening in the fence and upon starting to speak again, he walks through it, into the diner, and speaks to the emptiness where Waleed is/should be.

I left the house, just walked straight out, couldn't see Mamma's face.

I just walked out onto the street like nothing had happened . . . that's how people acted . . . walked past the guys watching the game at the bar, people on dates, the recruiting office closing up for the day and it was just another evening, another day coming to an end in the USA and even the game made me sick. Baseball, Waleed, my lifeline to this country, made me want to throw up, throw a stone through a fucking window . . . wanted . . . to get Hector's piece and end it (*he holds his finger to his head, like a gun*), strap dynamite to my chest, walk downtown, and scream at the top of my lungs: "Waaaaaake uuuuuuuuuup, motherfuckers, wake up!"

After a moment he picks up the mop and begins to mop furiously.

'Cause as I saw it I had two choices: stay, pay my taxes, live my life, this life, go to the game, hold it in, forget about it . . . or just leave. Disappear.

. . . 'Cause . . . I am guilty . . . I was guilty any way you cut it! Because I am part of it, complicit in this terroristic existence . . . no matter what I know or believe, or believe

I know, it is my tax dollars that helped send that missile, that Apache—made and paid for here—to the apartheid regime that occupies your breath and finally took it too . . . And that's terror, man . . . sheer fucking terror!

He starts retreating back behind the fence, still speaking to Waleed and us.

. . . And I am guilty 'cause I sent you money every other month, I too would have died to protect you, aided and abetted you if given the chance . . . And *they say* you are a terrorist! And what they say goes! So any way you cut it, I was funding, loving, supporting terror . . .

Ismail Khalidi performs in his play *Truth Serum Blues*, directed by Dipankar Mukherjee, produced by Pangea World Theater, 2005. Photo by Marc Norberg. Photo courtesy of Ismail Khalidi.

Kareem *is now back to pay phone from opening scene, again in a winter hat.*

So yeah, I did it. I went to a pay phone and called the only people who might understand, make it all go away. (*On the phone now.*) Kareem is the first name, K-A-R-E-E-M, yeah . . . (*Beat.*) That's right . . .

He drops the phone and looks back towards Waleed.

I figure I did my part in the war on terror . . . Maybe saved others from what I was scared I might do, from what they told me I must be! Sirens approaching.

As the sound of sirens gets closer, he slips back to the café and sits down, hastily picks up a pen and scrap of paper, writing furiously.

Wrote a note to mamma . . . wrote, "Dear Mamma . . . I'm sorry . . . Gone away, to settle some things, maybe go to Cuba too. Will call, at least once. Don't worry about me, I'll be back to get you. You are pure light, in this world of demons and charlatans, Ma. Do not lose faith . . . Eternally yours, your son, Kareem."

He rises, leaves the note on the table, and walks slowly towards center stage then stops.

"P. S. I'm sorry I never told you about the taxi . . . I promise I didn't shame the family name. I was one of the drivers you would have liked: the kind that talk, but not too much, kept the cab clean and the music low . . . Never lied about where I was from when people asked, never pasted American flags to the windows, even to protect my ass. I'm leaving, but I'll be back when all this passes."

He turns his back to us. Suddenly light hits the stage as if a door has been forcefully opened—a crash, more police sirens, dogs, and shouting is heard.

Kareem's *hands go up behind his head. With his back to the audience, he falls to his knees, hands still on his head . . .*

Lights cut out to black.

Fin.

Tennis in Nablus
A tragipoliticomedy in two acts

A Brief Historical Note

Palestine was under British rule from 1917 to 1947. During this time Jewish immigration to Palestine increased dramatically as a result of the growth of the Zionist movement, the Balfour Declaration of 1917 (which promised a Jewish homeland in Palestine), as well as growing anti-Semitism in Europe.

This period coincided with the rise of Arab nationalism across the Middle East as well as the rise of a Palestinian national consciousness.

The years 1936–9 saw a revolt among the indigenous Arabs of Palestine against British rule and growing Jewish immigration from 1933 onwards. Promises of Arab independence were not kept by the British who were also promising Palestine to Zionist leaders.

By 1939 the British had succeeded in brutally smashing the Arab rebellion using tactics similar to those employed to suppress uprisings in other parts of the empire such as India and Ireland. Although the Zionist militias in Palestine had been incorporated into the British army in order to defeat the Palestinian rebels, the Zionists would break with the British after the onset of World War II in response to the London-issued 1939 White Paper which challenged Zionist nationalist aims by putting quotas on Jewish immigration from Europe.

The Palestinian independence movement never recovered from the defeat of the revolt in 1939, and less than a decade later, in 1947–8, nearly three-quarters of a million Palestinians were violently driven from their homes by Jewish militias as the state of Israel was born in the vacuum created by the British withdrawal.

Time   1939

Place   Nablus, Palestine. A tennis court, a balcony, a house, and a jail cell.

Characters

Anbara – *mid-thirties, a Palestinian writer and the wife of Yusef al-Qudsi. She is modern but not necessarily Western. She is never melodramatic or sentimental.*

Yusef – *mid-forties, a notorious Palestinian rebel.*

Tariq – *mid-thirties, a successful, Westernized Palestinian businessman and the nephew of Yusef.*

Michael O'Donegal – *an Irish "criminal" in the British army in Palestine.*

Rajib – *an Indian conscript in the British army. He wears a turban but other than that is in British army attire.*

General Falbour – *mid-sixties.*

Lieutenant Douglas Duff – *thirties, a British officer, not without ambition.*

Samuel Hirsch – *forty, British-educated German Jew and a respected member of the growing Jewish community in Palestine.*

Hajj(a) Waleed(a)** – *seventies, works for and lives with Anbara and Yusef. S/he is more an uncle/aunt than a servant.*

Soldiers* – *British soldiers.*

Reggie* – *a British businessman, young and energetic, only recently arrived in Palestine.*

Emiliano Zapata* – *a ghost*

The Set (suggested)
The set should be minimal and versatile.

On the backstage wall we might see the façade or suggestion of British headquarters, perhaps with arched windows. Connected to it is a raised balcony or raised platform of sorts, which overlooks the stage.

The suggestion of the tennis court should run horizontally right to left on the stage, with the (removable) net cutting vertically across center stage.

The stage (or part of it) also serves as the interior of a Palestinian home, simple, minimalistic, perhaps sharing the back wall of the British HQ. Likewise the stage (or part of it) serves as the office of Tariq in Act One, Scene Two, and then the prison-cell area.

---

* Reggie and Zapata can be double/triple cast by the actor playing Samuel Hirsch.
** Hajja Waleeda can also be played as an older man (in which case he would be called Hajj Waleed) with appropriate changes to gender in the dialogue.

Prologue

A summer night. Nablus, Palestine, 1939. The creaking of wheels on a donkey-drawn cart can be heard, then the cocking of a rifle.

Soldier (*offstage*)   Halt! Step down from the carriage with your hands in the air.

Out of the darkness **Waleeda**, *an older woman in simple embroidered robes, enters with her hands raised. From the opposite direction a British soldier.*

Soldier   What's in the carriage, old crone?

Waleeda   *Bidenjan*, your . . . highness.

Soldier   What?

Waleeda   Eggplants, sir. Aubergines. I want to take them to the early morning markets up north.

Soldier   Eggplants?

Waleeda   No relation to eggs, sir. Cousin to the potato and tomato. Who would have known such a dark elegant purple orb was related to the fat lumpy white potato? The world is a mysterious place, sir, and God has a way of making a kind of poetry with his creations, no?

Soldier   Let's see what's in the / cart.

Waleeda (*enthusiastically*)   The word aubergine, for example, your highness, derives from the Spanish "Berenjena" which comes from the Arabic "Bidenjan," which in turn is from the Persian "Badin-gan," all derived originally from the Sanskrit, "Vatin Gameh."

Soldier   Bloody fascinatin'.

Waleeda   Yes, I think so.

Soldier   Why are you driving up in the dead of night? There's a curfew, you know.

Waleeda   Because eggplants are in the nightshade family, sir. It is their custom to move at night. Wilt under the sun. When they travel in darkness they arrive at the market pregnant with the night; full of the whispers of their friend the moon . . . And this way I sell twice as many as the farmers who transport their produce in the morning heat! Shall I tell you about the harvesting of the eggplant sir? It really is / interesting.

Soldier   Just piss off! Be on your way, and stay off the main roads!

Waleeda *bows and exits into the shadows.*

Act One

Scene One

Later that night in an old Nablus house: There is a table with a typewriter on it. On the back wall hangs an Ottoman sword.

A man enters quietly. He wears a British officer's uniform. He removes oranges from his various pockets. One after another.

Anbara *enters from behind him. She silently grabs the sword off the wall and places the blade on his neck as he is about to sit down. He raises his hands.*

Yusef (*in a posh British accent*)   Have you escaped from your harem to seduce a British officer such as myself, young lady? Or am I being knighted?

Anbara   It doesn't suit you.

He looks down at the uniform.

And you were about to sit in my chair. /

Yusef   This chair belongs to His Majesty King George! I—

Anbara   Yusef.

She touches his face.

Yusef (*disarmed, in his normal voice*)   Anbara. You look—

Anbara   Shut up.

Yusef   Two years . . . It's been / two—

Anbara *pushes him into the chair.*

Anbara   Two years. Yes. I know.

Yusef   . . . I've gotten older.

Anbara   But you've been giving the Brits hell since they released you.

Yusef   Seven days, / non-stop.

Anbara   At least that's what everyone in Nablus is talking about.

Yusef   Really? What are they saying?

Anbara   Tell me: after two years apart, it took you seven days to make your way to your wife?

Yusef   Blame the British, my dear.

Anbara   I do.

Yusef   If it weren't for them I'd be playing the oud for you every night.

Anbara   I'd like that. /

Yusef Like I used to. But that life is gone, Anbara. So as soon as I was released I went to work. The revolution can't / wait—

Anbara Don't lecture me like some young recruit from the hills.

Yusef I came as soon as I could.

Anbara I waited as long as I could.

Yusef I had to see if I still had it in me . . . Wait, what does that / mean?

Anbara Never mind. So? Do you still have it? In you?

Yusef Naturally.

Anbara I've missed you.

Yusef Naturally.

Anbara Still so modest. (*Beat.*) So you've come home? To me?

Yusef In the flesh.

Anbara And who said you could? Come here, I mean.

Yusef You are my wife. This is my house.

Anbara And what if I have a guest over and this isn't a good time? Did you think about that?

Yusef What do you mean?

Anbara A younger man perhaps? Or a woman. To keep me company. Fleeing out the bedroom window at this very moment.

Yusef *tries to peek into the other room but* **Anbara** *closes the door with her foot before he can.*

Yusef Somehow I imagined this homecoming differently.

Anbara That my clothes would fall to the ground the moment I saw you?

Yusef For instance.

She lights a cigarette, takes a drag, and then hands it to him.

Anbara It's dangerous, Yusef, the British will be after you.

Yusef Hence the disguise.

Anbara You look ridiculous.

Yusef But you're dying to hear how I got it.

She ignores him

Yusef The English, as you know, my love, are formidable opponents: They're ruthless, callous, and greedy . . . *But*!

Anbara Tea? Or a drink?

He nods to the bottle and continues.

Yusef But . . . they have a weakness which allows a quick-witted opponent in need of a disguise to get their uniforms off their backs quicker than a Turkish prostitute.

Anbara And you have experience with such women?

Yusef It's a figure of speech. Please. Ask me how I did it.

Anbara No thanks. /

Yusef Simple. *Costume parties*. They'll drop *everything* at the mere mention of a themed ball.

Anbara I have noticed that.

Yusef The idea came to me when I arrived to Haifa last week with the other prisoners set for release. We docked before dawn and on shore I could see the officers' corps in costume, returning from a night out. Once free, I made my way down the coast and then inland, village to village, town to town.

Anbara Like the old days.

Beat.

Yusef Except half of my men from before are dead or in prison.

Anbara I've been to my share of trials and funerals while you were gone, Yusef.

Yusef You hate funerals.

Anbara Almost as much as I hate trials. And stories that drag on.

She refills his cup and he throws it back.

Yusef Right! So yesterday, finally, I arrive in Nablus.

Anbara Not to see me, apparently.

Yusef Not yet, no. Patience, dear. I went to the residence of the General in charge of our noble district. Falbour. But he wasn't in. Off playing cricket. Or tennis. With Lord so-and-so.

Anbara But you went in anyway / . . .

Yusef Disguised as a servant of the house I entered through the kitchen and up the back stairs, where I convinced a one Lieutenant Douglas Duff that he was late for the India-themed ball at the High Commissioner's house in Jerusalem. The man was dressed and out the door in fifteen minutes!

Anbara Leaving his uniform for the taking.

Yusef Precisely. And with it I was able to *borrow* from the Nablus armory fifty brand-new 1939 edition Enfield rifles; enough ammo for a month's campaign, and a supply of dynamite to derail British trains. (*A bow.*) Thank you, thank you very much.

Anbara Impressive. (*Beat.*) And where is all of it now? Not here I hope.

Yusef No! Hajja Waleeda's taken it up to the fighters in Jenin . . . Hidden under her eggplants.

Anbara You shouldn't make the old woman run your errands! She won't last if they catch him.

Yusef Waleeda's been with my family for years. She was fighting the Turks before you finished grade school!

Anbara Exactly.

Yusef And if all fails she can bore anyone to death with the details of the eggplant or the olive harvest.

Anbara How they must regret the day they set the famous rebel Yusef al-Qudsi free.

Yusef Imagine! They wanted to send me to London for the negotiations.

Anbara You refused. I heard.

Yusef They thought I'd scurry off to England to beg them for terms with the others!

Anbara Don't underestimate them, Yusef.

Yusef I know the Brits; I know precisely what they're after. They want to conquer everything south of their dreary little isle in order to kidnap the sun to brighten the place up.

He starts to shed the uniform, as if it burns his skin.

It's hot. (*Beat.*) You know, I still get nervous every time I see you. A rugged rebel made speechless by a beautiful peasant girl.

Anbara Your fantasies are so predictable, Yusef.

Yusef *kisses* **Anbara** *for the first time. A beat.*

Anbara Drifting in at the strangest times.

Yusef (*pointing to the typewriter*) And you, writing away at the strangest hours.

Anbara Well, how would you have become a revolutionary if it weren't for my ideas?

Yusef When's your deadline?

Anbara Noon. Arabic and English editions. To go to print before the British release their report on the London meetings. Mohammad Ali Baybars. At your service.

They shake hands.

Yusef A pleasure, Mr. Baybars. I hear you're quite a thinker. You also have a lovely smile and divine—

Anbara   Go. I'll follow. When I'm done.

Yusef   Exile is lonely.

Anbara   I know. My husband was imprisoned on an island at the end of the earth for six hundred and thirteen days . . . What's with the oranges?

She nods to the oranges on the table.

Yusef   Stole them. From that grove on the road from Jaffa to Tel al Rish.

Anbara   Your family's land?

Yusef   Not anymore. New ownership: It's a Jewish farm now.

Anbara   Tariq.

Yusef   He's been busy while I was gone.

Anbara   There's a killing to be made on real estate these days. Your nephew isn't one to miss out.

Yusef   When Waleeda returns I'll have her fetch Tariq for a friendly talk.

Anbara   He didn't get the message last time.

Yusef   I'm his uncle, he'll listen . . . Finish that article . . . before the old lady returns from Jenin.

He exits. **Anbara** *begins to type. She stops, gets up, and follows him. Lights fade.*

Scene Two

A Western-style office. **Tariq** *sits at the desk. He wears a European suit, reads the paper. It is early morning. The call to prayer is heard. He turns on the radio.*

Radio (*voiceover*) And from Palestine, British commanders hail the success of anti-terrorist measures against the "Arab Revolt," which has raged since 1936. High Commissioner MacMichael announced that "the violent unrest of the Arab population is in its last throes." His assessment was confirmed by commanders of Jewish units fighting alongside British troops. On the European front, escalating tensions between Germany and Britain—

A knock. **Tariq** *turns the volume down.*

Tariq   Come in.

Reggie, *a young British functionary, enters.*

Reggie   Mornin', Rik! Here early.

Tariq   Couldn't sleep. You?

Reggie   Haven't slept since I got here. All that chanting from the mosque at five in the bloody mornin'.

Tariq You'll get used to it.

Reggie When'd you get back from Alexandria, mate?

Tariq Last night. Late.

Reggie Business as usual, then?

Tariq Everything in order, yes.

Reggie Well, it's good to have you back, Rik.

Tariq Any news?

Reggie Just talk of war back home and how to get the Arabs on our side if we fight the Huns.

Tariq Let's hope for the best.

Reggie (*lowering his voice*) Though it's no secret that war is good for business, ey. Right, almost forgot. That Hirsch fellow came by to finalize the deal on that land in . . Beyt . . . Beyt something or other. Said you'd know the place.

Tariq I know it. Just have to convince the owners to sell.

Reggie Alright then, cheers.

He exits then pops his head back in.

By the way, party at the governor's place Friday. You gonna come along?

Tariq I might drop by.

Reggie I'm goin' as a Bedouin chieftain of the Hijaz. I make Lawrence of Arabia look like an amateur, yeah.

Tariq Weren't you a Bedouin chieftain last time, Reggie?

Reggie No! I was a Turkish sultan. Get it straight, man. Not all Orientals are the same.

Tariq No they're not.

Reggie I *am* using a bit from that costume actually . . . but I can lend you the rest if you like.

Tariq I might just put on the old Venetian mask again. Keep it . . . simple.

Reggie Suit yourself.

He exits then pops his head in once again.

Tariq Yes, Reggie?

Reggie Sorry, got someone out here waiting to see you.

Tariq Hirsch?

Reggie An Arab. Granny-type lady.

Tariq   Send her in.

Reggie *exits.* **Tariq** *picks up an Arabic newspaper then picks up the English paper then switches again. As the door opens he has one in each hand. As* **Waleeda** *enters,* **Tariq** *pretends to read both at the same time.*

Waleeda   Good morning, Tariq *effendi*.

Tariq   And to you, Hajja Waleeda.

Waleeda   I never knew you were such a two-faced man, young Tariq.

Tariq   What is that supposed to mean?

Waleeda   Well, you are reading two newspapers at the same time. Very impressive.

Tariq   How can I help you, auntie?

Waleeda   You're invited to your uncle's house.

Tariq   Yusef?

He springs up, making sure no one is outside.

He's in Nablus? Since when?!

Waleeda   He wants to see you immediately. He's cooked you breakfast.

Tariq   Send him my regards. I'm busy.

Waleeda   He insists. It must be now. It's important.

Tariq   It's barely eight o'clock! I haven't read my papers or . . . or had my tea.

Waleeda   He's your uncle, Tariq.

Tariq   Uncle?! He had my store in Jaffa looted and burned, then made my workers strike.

Waleeda   So, what should I tell him then . . . "Rik"?

Tariq   What did you call me?

Waleeda   It's what the English one out there called you, no? I thought maybe you changed your name to "Rik."

Tariq   It's a nickname. At the office. I didn't / even—

Waleeda   Shall we go?

Tariq, *deep in thought, doesn't answer for a beat.*

Tariq   I'll be there around nine. I have an urgent matter to attend to. Is that all?

Waleeda   Since you ask, I wonder if we could talk about the land in Beyt Naqquba? That land has been in my family for hundreds of years / and—

Tariq   I assure you I have everyone's best interests in mind, including your cousins, when I conduct my business. Now if you don't mind . . . .

Waleeda *exits.* **Tariq** *picks up the phone.*

Tariq   Get me Lieutenant Duff, please.

Scene Three

Later that morning at the house. **Yusef** *prepares food.* **Waleeda** *reads.*

Waleeda   Who wrote it?

Yusef   Mohammed Ali Baybars. A friend. He sent over a draft.

Waleeda   Reminds me of the writing of that other boy who used to write for the weekly journal, before they shut it down. What was his name?

Anbara   Mustafa el Badawi . . . I believe. No?

Yusef   Similar styles, yes, but I think this Baybars is even smarter.

Waleeda   He's a damn genius if you ask me.

Tariq   And pretty.

Waleeda   Did you say / pretty—?

Yusef   Pretty *likely* the most important thinker between Cairo and Baghdad.

A knock at the door . . . **Yusef** *draws his pistol and melts into the shadows.* **Anbara** *lets* **Tariq** *in.* **Yusef** *emerges from behind him.*

Yusef   You look *richer*, nephew.

Tariq   Still armed, I see. And utterly unreformed after all these years.

Yusef   Unrepentant, too. Now give your uncle a hug.

He grabs **Tariq** *and hugs him.*

Yusef   I made *ful*. Still the best beans this side of the Sinai.

They sit. **Yusef** *puts his pistol near his plate.*

Tariq (*calmly*)   Are you threatening me, uncle?

Yusef   Are you threatened by me, nephew?

Tariq   No need to mock me as if I were a little boy, you're only ten years older than me.

Yusef   Eleven, actually.

Tariq   Could you please put that *thing* somewhere else?!

Yusef *slides the gun a couple of inches away.*

Tariq   Further?

Yusef *slides it another couple inches away.*

Tariq   Like in another room perhaps!

Yusef   Well, maybe you'd like to hold it? Is that it? Here, take it!

Anbara *snatches the gun and tucks it into her robe.*

Anbara   Now, would you children like some food?

Tariq   Thank God your wife is more civilized than you, uncle.

Yusef   I'll take that as a compliment. Unless you're referring to British "civilization."

Tariq   And what if I was?

Anbara   Here we / go.

Yusef   Then I'd consider it an insult, since they were painting their bodies and drawing on caves when we were building fountains and universities and inventing / mathematics!

Anbara / Tariq (*in unison*)   Mathematics!

Tariq   Oh, such an example of refinement you are, sitting with a revolver on your plate!

Yusef   I am a hunted man! Look how they got Zapata in Mexico, / and—

Tariq   Oh no! /

Yusef   Don't "oh no" me. He was betrayed in his own territory. / Ambushed!

Tariq   Still comparing yourself to dead "revolutionary" heroes?!

Yusef   I'm protecting myself. I don't know who I can trust after all, have to watch my back.

Tariq   Spare me, Yusef! You're a petty thug.

Yusef   And you are a petty little capitalist. But believe it or not, I've missed you, Tariq . . . Or is it "Rik" now?

Tariq   It's Tariq! Let's not confuse my business with who I am as a person.

Yusef   Fine.

Tariq   Though, such a notion surely didn't cross your mind as you sent my investments into flames in '36, dear uncle!

Anbara *gives* **Yusef** *a look.*

Yusef   Yes. Well . . . I wanted to . . . apologize. For that incident. It was . . . unfortunate.

Tariq   It was a betrayal, Yusef. It was utterly foolish and unjust. / It was –

Yusef It was a rebellion, Tariq! There was a rebellion going on! Your people. You remember who your people are?! And that business of yours was breaking the boycott.

Tariq I was making a living for myself, not to mention my workers; our fellow countrymen!

Anbara Quiet! Both of you. A patrol could hear you from a mile away. Don't give them an excuse to come in.

Yusef (*in a near whisper*) Your "business as usual" helped the British to undercut the revolt! Is all this lost on you?

Tariq I'll tell you what I lost. I lost years of hard work! I lost contracts, employees, investments, thousands and thousands of pounds.

Yusef And I lost friends. I lost two years of freedom.

A beat.

Now shut up and eat your food!

Tariq *gets up from the table.*

Tariq You must excuse me, Anbara, but I won't take his abuse.

Anbara You're a free man.

She goes to open the door.

Yusef No. I'm sorry. Sit . . . Sit. Please. It's important.

Tariq Make it quick.

Yusef I need your help. As a fellow Palestinian. *We* need you, Tariq. Your people need you.

Tariq The answer's no.

Yusef Listen, the Brits think they've won, *but* if we can counterattack, make one last / push—

Tariq And what do I have to do with this *push* of yours?

Yusef We need a man of your standing, Tariq, with your *capital*, your knowledge of the Brit. If you were to support the revolt we could hold our ground. But this is our last chance.

Tariq (*laughing*) You're practically the only one still fighting.

Yusef If you joined me others would follow. You're my last hope, Tariq.

Tariq Our leaders went to the London conference. Give it up.

Yusef The Brits kill thousands, imprison thousands more and now they want to negotiate. They'll use us and throw us aside. Help us!

Tariq What would I need to do to help save your little revolution? Carry a gun around, mugging people, like you?

Anbara You could start by not selling off our lands to the Europeans.

Tariq You mean to Jews?

Anbara No, I said Europeans. They are Europeans to me. I have no interest which way they talk to God.

Yusef We've always had Jews among us, but they were Arabs, like us, Tariq. These Zionists are Europeans, they're colonizers, by their own admission, fighting side by side with the British Empire.

Tariq I happen to call many of them friends and associates and find they are equitable and / kind—

Anbara They're not just buying summer homes, Tariq. They're building a country on top of ours while the English hold us down.

Tariq That's a matter of opinion.

Yusef Perhaps you think those are toy guns they're carrying around?! The days of looking the other way are over. They want it *all* for themselves.

Tariq I must take my leave. I suggest you make yourself scarce. You are a hunted man after all.

Yusef Tariq, wait!

Anbara Just let him go.

The door is kicked open and a British **Soldier** *enters, his rifle pointed at* **Yusef**.

Lt. Douglas Duff *enters behind him with a pistol drawn. He wears a full maharaja costume.*

Lt. Duff Breakfast's over! Hands where we can see them.

(*To* **Yusef**.) Well, well. Hello again. I've been looking for you.

Yusef Good morning your maharaja-ship.

Lt. Duff (*to the* **Soldier**) Have this man cuffed and arrested.

The **Soldier** *hesitates.*

Soldier I think we arrest him and then cuff him, sir. Technically.

Lt. Duff *Technically*, I don't care which order you do it in. He's a rebel and a thief! Cuff him!

The **Soldier** *cuffs* **Yusef**. **Duff** *gets in his face.*

Lt. Duff I don't need my uniform to arrest you and have you exiled again to some God awful island or, better yet, executed. Now, if I hear one word out of you I'll have you all lashed and gagged . . . Or gagged and then lashed. Soldier, search the house

Tariq Sir. Lt. Duff, please. There is nothing here I assure you, upon the King's throne. You've got who you came for, now leave these people alone.

Lt. Duff And you are?

Tariq I don't believe we've had the pleasure, sir. My name's Tariq al-Qudsi. Here's my card.

He hands **Duff** *his business card.*

I'm in the import–export and real estate business.

Lt. Duff I've heard of you. Surprised to find you in the company of such a lawless bandit as this.

Tariq Family, sir. One can't choose them.

Lt. Duff I'll take your word on that. (*To* **Yusef**.) My uniform. I'd like it back.

Yusef It seems I misplaced it last night, your excellency.

Lt. Duff Take him away!

Anbara *draws the pistol, cocks it, and holds it to the back of* **Duff**'s *head.*

Anbara You'll be taking no one out of my house.

Lt. Duff (*to the* **Soldier**, *unable to see her*) Is that thing . . . real?

Soldier Looks pretty real to me, sir.

Lt. Duff I thought they were supposed to be timid and docile in the Orient?

Anbara I'm very outgoing, sir, and this gun is definitely real. Shall I test it out?

Lt. Duff That's quite alright, lady. (*To the* **Soldier**.) Shoot her.

Yusef Wait!

Lt. Duff I said *shoot* the bitch! Ready!. . .

The **Soldier** *prepares to fire.*

Yusef Anbara, put it down!

Anbara I won't let them take you.

Lt. Duff Aim!

Yusef I'll be fine. I'll be free in no time.

Lt. Duff (*to* **Yusef**) You'll hang!

Yusef Go to Baybars. What he writes makes a difference.

Lt. Duff Silence!

Yusef If he can't free me, at least he won't let me die in / vain.

Lt. Duff Shut up, everyone shut up or I'll have you all shot!

Yusef   Put the gun down, Anbara.

A beat. **Anbara** *lowers the weapon.*

Lt. Duff   Now arrest her and confiscate that weapon.

The **Soldier** *grabs* **Anbara** *and the gun.*

Yusef   I'll give you names. Let her go and I'll give you names.

Anbara   Yusef, shut up! Take me in.

Duff *once again gets in* **Yusef**'s *face.*

Lt. Duff   I want the financiers behind the revolt. Can you give me that?

Yusef   Yes.

Lt. Duff   Very well. Release her. Move out.

The **Soldier** *and* **Duff** *leave with* **Yusef** *in tow.*

Tariq   He was irresponsible to come here, to put you in danger, Anbara. The one place they'd know to look! I'll go at once to straighten this out. You'll see that my name and my way can achieve more than mere thuggery. Negotiations, compromise, deal-making! A calm discussion between adults.

Lt. Duff *re-enters, seen by* **Anbara** *but unbeknownst to* **Tariq**.

Tariq   You must assure me, however, that when I get Yusef out, you will make him see things my way. It's only with restraint and cooperation that we can advance our cause. I call it "rational nationalism." The revolution is about evolution. You'll see, I'll take care of this. The Brits will pay for their arrogance and see us once and for all as equals.

Lt. Duff   Bravo. Very inspiring. You were done, no? Or is there more?

Tariq   No, sir. Yes. Thank you. I was. Done.

Lt. Duff   I must inform you, then, that you're under arrest by the Mandatory Authorities of His Majesty, King George of England.

Tariq   For / what?!

Lt. Duff   For your clandestine role in assisting financially and materially the treasonous rebellion against the British Mandate in Palestine, Mr Qudsi.

Tariq   There's been a terrible mistake, sir –

Lt. Duff   Evidence doesn't lie. (*Beat.*) And if it does, oh well.

Tariq   This is an outrage, Lieutenant! Please, I demand to speak with the General.

Lt. Duff   Yes, perhaps you could give him your card.

Duff *slips the card* **Tariq** *gave him into* **Tariq**'s *front pocket and exits, leading* **Tariq** *out.*

Waleeda   God works in mysterious ways, Anbara. It's in his hands now.

Scene Four

The courtyard in the British compound. **Rajib** *and* **Michael O'Donegal** *play cards and drink tea.*

Michael Two kings. What do you have?

Rajib Two threes!

Michael Shit! Your hand. Again.

Rajib I have never been this lucky at cards, Michael, I swear.

Michael How do I keep drawing fuckin' face cards? It's a bad omen. Damn useless royalty!

Rajib Agreed. A worthless lot the kings and queens. (*Beat.*) You owe me a pound, O'Donegal.

Michael Don't have it, Rajib. But I'll pay you back. Friday. Sunday latest.

Rajib Don't go gambling away money you don't have. At least not until after you've paid me.

Michael At this rate I'll never escape back to Ireland.

Rajib It was your idea to change the rules; "Bolshevik poker" was your idea, Michael.

Michael Oh we were both equally fond of that inbred bastard on the Thames. I didn't hear you complainin' when we made the change.

Rajib And I'm not complaining / now.

Michael I couldn't even *buy* a king before our glorious little revolution!

Rajib Also true.

Michael (*pacing*) Right! So one would then surmise that I'd keep drawing low cards and be winning under the new rules. But now that I don't bloody want 'em, I'm drowning in fuckin' high cards!

Rajib Technically the high cards are low cards and the low cards are high / but—

Michael And who are you, the Commissar of the People's Republic of Poker?!

Rajib Just a poor comrade like yourself, trying to get out of this powder keg before it blows. I don't want to die in Palestine either. I'd prefer Kolkata or Karachi any day.

Michael It's all shit.

Lt. Duff (*from offstage*) Guards!

They continue as if they heard nothing.

Michael Another cup of tea?

Rajib   Why not. Another hand perhaps?

Lt. Duff (*still offstage, louder*)   Privates Rajib and O'Donegal!

Rajib (*calmly*)   Sugar?

Michael   Two spoons. Whiskey?

He takes out whiskey, offers to **Rajib**.

Rajib   Too early for me.

Soldier *enters, winded.*

Soldier   Duff's back. Screamin' his head off for you two.

Michael   I didn't hear a thing. Did you, Rajib?

Rajib   I heard a dog barking / but . . .

Michael (*to the guard*)   Did his head *really* come off?

Soldier   No, O'Donegal. His head's still there.

Michael   Well, one can always hope.

Soldier   Your orders are to report. Immediately. Says he's got a job for the two of you.

Rajib   Maybe it's not too early. If you don't mind.

Michael *serves and they both gulp down the drink, grab their rifles and exit.*

Scene Five

The prison-holding area. **Tariq** *and* **Yusef** *cuffed.* **Duff**, *still in maharaja-wear, sits at the desk writing.* **Rajib** *and* **Michael** *enter.*

Lt. Duff   Thank you for coming, soldiers. Remind me to commend you to the General.

Michael   Really, sir?

Rajib   That's very kind of you, sir

Lt. Duff   No, it's not! I was being . . . never mind. At ease.

Rajib *stares at* **Lt. Duff**'s *outfit.*

Lt. Duff (*to* **Rajib**)   Yes?

Michael *subdues a laugh.*

Lt. Duff   Is there something you want to say, Private O'Donegal? No? Good. Now button your uniform!

Michael *rests the rifle against* **Yusef** *and buttons his shirt.*

Lt. Duff I'd prefer you didn't hand the prisoner your rifle, Private.

Michael Oh, you're right, sir, sorry. It woulda been a disaster; he might have shot you, sir.

He takes the rifle back.

Lt. Duff One more insubordination from you, Private, and I'll punish you. Understood?

Tariq Sir, I'd like to speak with the General, at once.

Lt. Duff You'll get your chance to chat to General Falbour soon enough.

Tariq Thank you.

Lt. Duff As it happens, he's the presiding judge of the military court you'll be standing in front of. (*To* **Michael**.) Private, these two men are from a very well-respected clan of Palestine. And Arabs are quite fond of their honor, so make sure they are treated accordingly.

Yusef You know, Lieutenant, our ancestors fought alongside Salah-a-din when he defeated your Richard the Kitten Heart and his crusader / hordes.

Lt. Duff King Richard the Lion Heart. Lion Heart!

Rajib Any orders for me, sir?

Lt. Duff Yes, actually. You can hop over to the tennis court and have it leveled and ready to go by eleven o'clock. Dismissed.

Rajib *salutes and exits.*

Lt. Duff Now that you look more like a soldier, O'Donegal, I'll ask you to escort these two men to cell five. Not four. Not three. Five. And do remember they are dangerous and will gladly slit your throat.

He leaves.

Yusef (*to* **Michael**) What's your name, young man?

Michael Well, it's not Paddy or Mick, I'll tell you that.

Yusef I enjoy being called "Arab beast," or just "Wog." I also like "damned Semite scum." It has a wider scope of targets for the British gentleman.

Michael Is that so, dirty Mohammatan.

Yusef Irish bastard /

Michael Bloody Bedouin goat-shagger. /

Yusef Filthy potato-eating pope-lover! /

Michael Two-timin' camel-ridin' / terrorist!

Yusef Tinker Mick taig monkey son of a Paddy whore!

Beat.

Michael Touché.

Yusef Yusef al-Qudsi. And this one here is my traitorous nephew Tariq. Say hello, Tariq.

He doesn't.

Michael (*to* **Yusef**) Michael O'Donegal. Cigarette?

He shares a cigarette with **Yusef** *who is still cuffed.*

Yusef Any relation to Sean O'Donegal?

Michael Me dad's second cousin, yeah. You know him?

Yusef We know of him. Fought the partition, gave the Brits a hiding in 1918. An inspiration.

Michael Well, he'd give me a hiding if he saw me in this uniform. But it was either rot in a Belfast prison for five years or this.

Yusef The choices we're left with. I was conscripted into the Ottoman army in '15; got a British bullet in my ass at Gallipoli for the trouble. Whiskey's the only thing that numbs the pain.

Michael I've got somethin' for what ails you, then.

He un-cuffs **Yusef***, gives him the flask. He drinks.*

Michael Not a pious Moslem?

Yusef More of a pious rebel, Michael.

Michael Amen. To the Empire!

Lt. Duff (*offstage*) O'Donegal!

Michael Well, duty calls

He puts cuffs back on **Yusef** *and exits. Another soldier enters to stand guard.*

Tariq This is absurd.

Yusef Yes: An army of pink, pig-eaters thousands of miles from their island telling us how to live. It's the height of absurdity.

Tariq I'm just going to sit here. In silence. I clearly can't have a conversation with you!

Yusef Fine. But you should know that communication with other human beings during imprisonment is key to maintaining one's sanity. Learned that in the Seychelles. Ended up talking to a banana tree after a week in solitary.

Tariq You gave Duff my name.

Yusef You know the worst part?! . . . I had to eat them afterwards.

Tariq What? /

Yusef The bananas. I killed then ate my only friends; my confessors, my comrades. We were fed mostly bananas. Imagine. Like monkeys.

Tariq You framed your own nephew.

Yusef I figured I'd return the favor.

Tariq Are you suggesting I turned you in? You're insane.

Yusef And *you* are guilty. Banana sandwiches . . . Banana kebab . . .

Tariq Guilty? / Of what?

Yusef Stuffed bananas! Surprisingly good.

Tariq What am I guilty of?

Yusef Doing monkey business, Tariq!

Tariq You've always been jealous. Because I built a fortune and a reputation.

Yusef But despite your "reputation," to them, you are just a dirty Arab *monkey*. Guilty!

Tariq I am well-respected by colleagues from Nablus to / London!

Yusef And yet here you are, in jail.

Tariq You've sullied my name.

Yusef Being in prison is the one thing that can save your name from being "sullied." If only you were lucky enough to *actually* be guilty of fighting for your country.

Tariq So you admit it? I'm innocent.

Yusef If by innocent you mean naive, then yes.

Tariq Naive? I'm the only one preparing himself realistically for the future of Palestine.

Yusef You're right. Because there won't be a Palestine to do business in before long! We'll be the foreigners soon enough and your business partners will be the citizens. But perhaps you'd trade it all for a flat in London? What a sight: A collaborating ape walking the streets of the imperial capital in a nice European suit.

Tariq I am no collaborator. And I am not going anywhere.

Yusef Banana with a little yogurt. That was my favorite.

Tariq And you wonder why I would turn you in?!

He starts writing with a small pencil and a piece of paper.

Yusef What is that? What are you writing?

Tariq   A request. For the prompt assistance of a respected man, a friend, who will vouch for my character and get me out of here. But not you, I'm afraid.

He returns to lead **Tariq** *and* **Yusef** *to "prison cell."*

Yusef   That's true, your friends would have me rot in here while you run free.

Tariq   Maybe because you are the perfect example of why we need to be ruled. At least until we learn how to behave and rule ourselves.

Yusef   You're right. It's better if you don't speak to me.

Both are led into their cell.

Scene Six

Later that morning on the balcony of the British compound: standing over a map is **General Falbour** *with an elephant-tail fly swatter in hand. He flicks away the occasional fly as he moves pieces around on the map.*

Lt. Duff *enters. He wears a white tennis outfit. He holds a stack of files.*

General   Douglas! Damn you, man!

Lt. Duff   What is it, sir?

General   You've once again withheld crucial information from me, Lieutenant Duff. Failing to remind me about the costume party this afternoon. Do you deny the charges?

Lt. Duff   No, sir! I mean yes. No! Sir, I . . . think there's been a / misunderstanding.

General   I'll have to go and see if I can dig up my Zulu chieftain outfit from last year.

He exits.

Lt. Duff (*calling off*)   Sir? I don't think that's necessary, sir.

General (*from offstage*)   I could have sworn that party was this Friday. And now you'll show me up with that smart little sailor's outfit you've put together.

Lt. Duff (*offstage*)   But, um, it's *Wednesday*, sir. Remember. (*Pause.*) . . . And I'm not a sailor, actually.

General (*offstage*)   Well, what are you supposed to be then?

Lt. Duff   A *tennis* player. Sir.

General (*offstage*)   Oh. Yes. Well done. You're missing the racket, though.

Lt. Duff   That's because it's . . . on the tennis court. We play tennis, Wednesdays, sir, after the briefing. Just got dressed a little early. So there's actually no costume ball, sir.

*The **General** re-enters behind **Duff**. He wears a Zulu headdress and holds a spear. His face is covered in crude blackface/war paint.*

General   No party?

*He exits before **Duff** can see him and returns, without the costume, his face still painted.*

General   Tennis it is. Shall we carry on with the meeting then, / Lieutenant?

Lt. Duff   Sir . . .

General   Before it's too hot to play.

Lt. Duff   Your face, sir. You seem to have put on your Zulu . . . war paint.

General   Yes. (*Beat.*) Of course. It's a . . . *prototype*, we're testing it out. A sort of anti-wog camouflage, Lieutenant. To blend in with the natives. I want to get your top-secret feedback before we deploy in the field. Maybe a shade lighter, but you get the idea.

Beat.

Lt. Duff   Great thinking, sir.

General   Turns out I couldn't find that Zulu costume after all.

Lt. Duff   It was stellar. The Spanish Consul was quite convinced, you know.

General   Yes, yes. He was wasn't he.

He wipes off the face paint.

Lt. Duff   And when you did your war dance in the fountain in the High Commissioner's garden . . . Now *that* was pure genius, sir!

General   It was, wasn't it.

Lt. Duff *studies the map.*

Lt. Duff   I see you're strategizing, sir. Studying the battlefield of the Levant? What's on your mind, General. Why have you moved this regiment here for instance?

General   Ah, funny. Funny. As you can see, this is in fact a miniature recreation of the Battle of Waterloo. Arrived yesterday from London. Even that mad little midget Napoleon was a more honorable foe than these Arab hostiles.

Lt. Duff   Right. Yes. I was joking of course. Now, shall we get on with the briefing, sir?

General   Yes. One moment.

*He exits. **Lt. Duff** looks at his watch then calls out from the balcony.*

Lt. Duff   Rajid! O'Donegal! Report to the courtyard!

Michael *and* **Rajib** *enter.*

Lt. Duff   I believe I told you two to have this raked and smoothed over by 11 a.m., did I not?

Michael   Not me, sir. Sorry.

Duff *points at* **Rajib.**

Lt. Duff   Well, then, I told you.

Rajib   I don't recall you telling me anything, sir?

Lt. Duff   Are you certain?

Rajib   Yes, now I remember . . . a very dashing maharaja told me something about tennis courts, sir, but I have not seen him since.

Michael (*under his breath*)   I've seen him. He was wiping the General's arse for him just this morning.

Lt. Duff   I warned you, O'Donegal.

He calls offstage.

Soldier!

Soldier *runs onstage.*

Lt. Duff Administer five lashes to Private O'Donegal for being a smug Fenian bastard. (*To* **Soldier**.) On my count . . .

Michael *removes his shirt. The* **Soldier** *stands over* **Michael**. *With every count,* **Michael** *is struck on his back with a leather strap.*

Lt. Duff One . . . . two . . . . three . . . four . . . and five!

This isn't Dublin or Belfast or Sligo or wherever your mother spawned you. You will follow orders and act civilized even if it is against your nature. And that goes for you too, Vikrum! I'll deal with you later.

The **General** *re-enters in his tennis outfit.*

General   Proceed.

Lt. Duff   Gladly, sir. As you know, the European front looks increasingly warlike. But here in Palestine our tough response to the "Arab Revolt" has paid off. We are within reach of crushing the terrorists.

General   Good, Lieutenant. And what of the "prison situation"?

Lt. Duff   We are down to seven thousand Arabs in custody. Also, the decision to bring the Black and Tans and other anti-terror experts from the Irish and Indian campaigns has been highly effective: confiscation of weapons is up as is the suppression of agitating publications.

General   Good, good.

Lt. Duff. Similarly, the pattern of executing convicted rebels in military courts has clearly sent a message to the average Arab. Just as you predicted, / sir.

General Damn, it's hot.

Lt. Duff And last but not least, sir, I am happy and proud and honored to announce to you here that just this morning we've apprehended a most foul and dangerous renegade. His name is Yusef al-Qudsi.

He hands a file to the **General**.

Lt. Duff As you can see, he was behind the strikes in Jaffa, Haifa, and Nablus in '36. And he fought us to a standstill in Tulkaram in '37. He was captured, exiled, and recently released.

Which turned out to be a bad idea as he, unsurprisingly, returned immediately to his treasonous ways. But he's in our custody again. I personally oversaw the operation, sir.

The **General** *has tracked a fly on* **Duff**'s *shoulder and swats it.*

General Well done!

Lt. Duff Thank you, sir.

General You're welcome. Now, what do you say we bring the Arab you caught out to the court today?

Lt. Duff I believe in swift justice as much as the next man, sir, but we do need time to prepare for the trial.

General I mean the tennis courts, Lieutenant. For our match.

Lt. Duff Oh, yes. Though I doubt he's up to our level of play sir—

General Not to play, Lieutenant. To fetch our balls.

Lt. Duff Ball boy, sir?

General (*casually confiding*) In Rhodesia and Tanganika, Douglas, we'd march the Pygmy prisoners to our cricket matches where we'd have each one stand in as the wicket. Then our batsman would miss on purpose so the bowler could knock one right on the Blackies' jewels. I thought Africa was hell. Until I came to Palestine. There was water there at least, and not an Arab or a damned Jew in sight.

He leans confidentially towards **Duff**.

General And the problem with the Jews, Lieutenant, is I don't quite know whether to fear them or have contempt for their groveling and jockeying. They're not as simple as the Arab.

Lt. Duff Nor quite as short as the Pygmies, sir.

They enjoy the joke as **Samuel Hirsch** *enters the courtyard.*

Hirsch Hello, gentlemen . . . May I?

General Of course, Mr. Hirsch, join us. We were just finishing up.

Rajib *enters with a tray of tea after* **Hirsch**.

Lt. Duff Two sugars in mine. None for the General.

Rajib Yes, sir, sugar, sir. Two.

Lt. Duff (*to* **Rajib**) And next time do inform us beforehand if a guest arrives. Dismissed.

Rajib *exits.*

General How can we help you, Mr. Hirsch?

Hirsch I've come by to follow up on our last meeting, sir. I've also brought our counter-proposals in regard to the Jewish immigration and land-purchase quotas, as Lieutenant Duff requested.

Lt. Duff *takes the document*

Lt. Duff By the way, thank your comrades in the special night squads for their assistance in suppressing the Arab rebellion. Quite a job they've done.

Hirsch That isn't my doing, sir. Not my field of expertise. But I'll be sure to pass on your thanks if I get the chance.

Lt. Duff (*to the* **General**) The Jewish units have proven quite competent and fierce fighters actually, sir. It's been quite a pleasant surprise.

Hirsch What is that supposed to mean, / Lieutenant?

General Oh, don't take it badly, Mr. Hirsch, it's a compliment. Anything else we can do for you?

Hirsch There is one other matter, which is the worsening situation in Europe this summer, sir. Our community is deeply worried, and I hoped you could pass on our growing concern to / your superiors.

General Yes, we're all very concerned, Mr. Hirsch.

Hirsch You can call me Samuel, sir, or Sam if you'd like.

General And I assure you, Samuel, that in England we are vigilantly watching Mr. Hitler.

Hirsch Thank you, sir / but—

General And we are *deeply* committed to the plight of the Jews, in Europe and everywhere, as I believe we have proven time and again here in Palestine.

Hirsch That's reassuring, thank you, sir. I simply wanted to convey that it is of the utmost importance that something is done at the highest levels to stop the coming / storm.

Lt. Duff *sips from his tea and spits it out all over himself and* **Hirsch**.

Lt. Duff   Good God!

General   What is it, Douglas, what's got into you?

Lt. Duff   My tea's full of fucking salt, the incompetent / bastard!

General   These servants, from God knows where! You can't trust them with anything. Shifty as a pack of . . . (*He looks at* **Hirsch** *and stops himself.*) . . . shifty things . . . Now. If that's all, you must excuse us, Mr. Hirsch. We have an appointment. Nice of you to drop by, let us get a taste of each other's brains, as it were.

The two Brits show **Hirsch** *to the door and all exit.*

Scene Seven

Yusef *and* **Tariq** *sit on opposite ends of their cell.* **Tariq** *continues to draft his letter.* **Michael** *enters with food and the newspapers.*

Michael   Scraps off the master's table. And an old Arab out front told me to give this to you. Said to tell you the Arabic edition sold out.

He hands the newspaper to **Yusef**.

Yusef   Front page: "The Fork in the Road."

As he reads, **Anbara** *appears elsewhere, at her typewriter.*

Yusef/Anbara   By Mohammad Ali Baybars . . .

Anbara   "This, people of Palestine, is the decisive moment, our fork in the road . . ."

Yusef   "Our cry for freedom is once again threatened by the terrible sound of silence and servitude . . ."

Anbara   "Our leaders have been exiled, killed, imprisoned, or co-opted. And the Arab kings are far too comfortable under the tutelage of their Western masters to be of any use. Soon we will find ourselves / strangers in our own land,"

Yusef   "Strangers in our own land." My line / .

Anbara (*out*)   My line.

Yusef   "The question then, is this: Why should we believe our British overlords who promise us morsels of a state that is not theirs to give or take?"

Tariq *rips the paper from* **Yusef**'s *hand.*

Tariq   Cheap words printed on cheap paper. People need food on the table. They need stability not your "revolution" with its funerals and famine and anarchy in the streets.

Yusef *pushes* **Tariq** *and* **Tariq** *pushes back. The paper falls to the ground.* **Michael** *picks up the paper and reads on as they fight, which they do, off and on, throughout the scene.*

Michael   "The British promises of independence are empty: Their declarations and delegations; their mandates and solutions are nothing but the crude tricks of magicians. And as long as they rule, they'll play the Arab and the Jew like so many chess pieces."

Yusef *subdues* **Tariq**.

Yusef   See! You're a pawn, being played by the Brits and the Zionists. Resist, boy, it's in you. I can see it in those beady eyes /.

Tariq *breaks free.*

Anbara   "When the British leave we will find ourselves out-gunned. Our Jewish cousins see their prize and they are ready to take it. In the meantime, the British will promise us the moon to keep Palestine and to ensure our help in the coming battle with Germany."

Tariq *pulls* **Yusef**'s *mustache.*

Tariq   That's for burning down my store!

Yusef *subdues* **Tariq** *again.*

Michael   "So let us look to the opponents of England elsewhere for guidance: To the brave Irish strikers and to the mass movement of non-violent resistance led by Mr. Gandhi and Badshah Khan in India . . ."

Anbara   "And yet what of our leaders neutralized by British foul play and violence?"

Michael   "Most recently, Yusef al-Qudsi . . ." Hey, he's talkin' about you! ". . . thrown back into British dungeons despite his advanced years."

Yusef   What?!

Michael   "It is our duty to free him and the others from their chains as we march towards freedom."

Yusef   Advanced years?! Let me see that.

He takes the paper from **Michael**, *who keeps reading over his shoulder.*

Anbara   "The British believe that they have made us into a defeated people, but we are only defeated if the flame of revolution recedes into fear and doubt, subservience and subjugation."

Yusef   "If we are reduced to such a state then we are nothing but walking ghosts."

Anbara   "So let us march to the gates of every British compound and show them that the resistance of the people of Palestine is eternal and just. Our day of liberation approaches!"

Anbara *fades back into the darkness.*

Michael   Jesus. Give me a pitchfork and a torch and let's burn this fucking prison down, ey.

Tariq Rhetoric and drum-beating. We can work with the British to achieve—

Yusef *shoots* **Tariq** *a threatening glance.*

Tariq (*to* **Michael**) Please, just get this letter to Mr. Samuel Hirsch.

Yusef *intercepts the letter.*

Yusef Ah, here we have really cheap words on cheap paper!

Tariq Careful, don't get too worked up at your advanced age!

Rajib (*interrupting*) Settle down. You're needed on the court today, and it's hot. Save your energy.

Michael *takes* **Tariq***'s letter as they are led out of the cell towards the tennis court.*

The **General** *and* **Duff** *stand doing their stretches as the prisoners enter the court.*

General So which one is the rebel Yusef al-Qudsi?

Tariq *points to* **Yusef** *and* **Yusef** *points to* **Tariq**. **Duff** *points to* **Yusef**.

General Ah. Welcome back.

Yusef Thank you, sir.

General Maybe this time we'll send you to rot in Sarafand prison instead of the Seychelles. It'll make you miss those days of tropical bliss.

(*To* **Tariq**.) And *you* must be the financier? Definitely not the rebel type in any case.

Tariq That's precisely it, General. There's been a grave misunderstanding. I would happily / explain—

General —Soldier, have these men shackled together at the feet.

The two men are chained together by their feet as the **General** *and* **Lt. Duff** *retreat, rackets in hand, to their playing positions in the wings.*

Lt. Duff (*offstage*) It's love-all, sir.

The tennis balls start flying back and forth across the net center stage.

Yusef What do you barbarians know about love?

Tariq Just keep your mouth shut, Yusef.

Lt. Duff Excellent shot, sir.

Tariq *jumps up and runs for the ball but runs out of chain and falls flat on his face. The balls start flying again.*

General (*from offstage, as they play*) I wonder if that Hirsch fellow has an ulterior motive, Lieutenant. A kind of hidden agenda.

Tariq (*offstage*) You know Sam Hirsch, sir? Sam is a friend and business partner. He'll vouch for my cooperation with the British—

Yusef *pulls the chain,* **Tariq** *falls hard.*

Lt. Duff   Balls!

Yusef *sits in protest, while* **Tariq** *obediently collects balls as far as the chain will allow him.*

Yusef   Look what they've turned you into. Their pet monkey.

Tariq *is out of breath.* **Yusef** *begins laughing.*

The stage darkens and the rumbling of thunder is heard, followed by lightning. It starts to rain.

General   Teatime, Douglas.

General *and* **Lt. Duff** *exit, soldiers carrying umbrellas above their heads.* **Tariq** *and* **Yusef** *remain. As lights fade their laughter is heard mixing with the storm.*

Act Two

Prologue

The dark cell. Steady rain outside. A scream pierces the cell. **Tariq** *is startled awake. He looks around.* **Yusef** *is not there.*

Tariq   Yusef?

Another scream from a close-by room. **Tariq** *moves around the cell trying to determine where it is coming from.*

Yusef?!

Silence. After a moment, he picks up the newspaper with **Anbara**'s *article. He begins to read it.*

After several beats, the door swings open and a bloodied **Yusef** *is thrown in. The rain outside slows as dawn breaks.*

Scene One

Anbara *in her house practices jabs with the sword. She stops and writes something down. This is her writing routine.*

Waleeda *enters with a small sack in her hands.*

Waleeda   Soap, fresh from the factory . . .

She pulls out a folded newspaper from the bag.

The new Baybars article. He's something else, that man.

Anbara   I know.

Waleeda   I bought all the copies I could.

Anbara   I thought the British raided the newsstands?

Waleeda   That's why the grocer sells the papers now. Hidden under his produce. I passed out copies for free on the way home . . . as discreetly as possible, of course. Listen to this: "Brothers! Have we still not realized that in order to truly liberate Palestine we must also liberate and elevate the Palestinian woman?" . . . Ah! And here it is, the second to last paragraph: "If the High Commissioner is a buffoon, and he certainly is, then our leader the Mufti is marked by the signs of a man prone to mediocrity and poor decisions." It's true, I've met him.

Anbara   What news on the streets?

Waleeda   There's a British warrant for Baybars' arrest. And apparently the Mufti has sent orders from Beirut that he wants Baybars "reined-in."

She draws her finger across her throat.

And the word from Tel Aviv is that the Jewish Agency fellows are looking for Baybars as well.

Anbara To . . .?

She draws her finger across her throat in a question.

Waleeda No. Rumor is they just want to pay him to stop writing against the Zionists.

Anbara Really? Shameful! (*Beat.*) How much?

Waleeda They did the same thing with the editor of *Filastin*. A couple years back. He refused the money. Just like he refused to agree with the Mufti. Now he's exiled as well.

Anbara Maybe he should have taken the money.

Waleeda Anyone low enough to take such money would have to disappear and start over, with a new name, a new everything.

Anbara And you believe Baybars wouldn't stoop so low?

Waleeda Well they can't even find the man. The money will surely sit uncollected, gathering dust in Tel Aviv.

Anbara What if Baybars took the money but used it for a worthy cause?

Waleeda His ideas, my dear, are worth more than a thousand rifles . . . And it would be a shame if a bag of gold silenced his tip-tap-typing in the middle of the night . . . Unless he had a *really* good plan.

A moment. **Anbara** *disappears into the bedroom.* **Waleeda** *prepares a bag.*

Anbara *re-enters and* **Waleeda** *seamlessly hands her the bag.*

Anbara Watch the house.

Waleeda I take it you're off to Tel Aviv?

Anbara Yes, I hear they've made it look like Europe.

She exits . . . lights fade down on **Waleeda**.

Scene Two

Lights up on **Tariq** *and* **Yusef** *in the cell while unseen, from offstage, a tennis game is heard.*

Lt. Duff (*offstage*) Fantastic shot, General.

General (*offstage*) Thank you, Duff . . . Deuce.

Yusef (*to* **Tariq**) I prefer football: more of a people's sport.

Tariq This tennis is still a rather new game. Give it time.

Yusef It can have all the time it wants.

Lt. Duff Balls!

General (*offstage*) Pick up the pace, Paddy!

Yusef (*calling to the court through the small window of their cell*) Hey, General! Can you send us up some *kunafi*? It's a Nablus specialty. Hot cheese with a crispy layer of pastry –

Tariq (*to* **Yusef**) Semolina.

Yusef (*to* **Tariq**) Not wheat?

Tariq Semolina.

Yusef (*off to the Brits*) Semolina! All soaked in warm orange blossom syrup. Better than your lemon curd or your Bedfordshire clanger! Yikh!

Lt. Duff (*offstage*) Balls!

Yusef Empire Biscuits are also predictably depressing!

Lt. Duff I'm going to count to three, O'Donegal. One! Two . . .

Rajib *enters and shouts offstage towards the tennis court.*

Rajib (*off*) General, there is a telegram just arrived from London.

General (*still off*) What does it say, Dipankar?

Rajib I don't know what it says, sir. While I am fluent in Hindi, Bengali, Tamil, Urdu, Punjabi, Malyalam, Gujarathi, Telegu—and Dutch, written English is beyond my grasp. Perhaps you should read it yourself, sir.

General We have to do everything around here.

Rajib *exits.*

Tariq (*to* **Yusef**) Perhaps I owe you an apology . . . for . . .

Yusef Turning me in?

Tariq I hope when we're old men we can laugh at all this.

Yusef If I don't hang, why not.

Tariq You won't / hang.

Yusef I've seen men hanged for less.

Tariq I heard you screaming—

Yusef I wasn't screaming . . . I was laughing.

Tariq I thought they were going to kill you in there. And then all of a sudden I felt . . .

Yusef Guilty?

Tariq Different. Awake. /

Yusef Stop. I was wrong. You were right. It's too late.

Tariq What?

Yusef The revolt. Maybe it's time to . . . give up. Change / strategies.

Tariq After all your grand speeches you're going to surrender?

Yusef No.

Tariq So?

Yusef But a revolt, Tariq, it's a reaction; a stand against something, Right?

Tariq Sure.

Yusef But we forget that it also has to be a step towards something. We want independence, *fine*, but what's next? And until we are sure, and everyone is united, then we just end up fighting to forget, to survive, to resist. But we are easily divided and distracted.

Tariq You don't sound like yourself.

Yusef I haven't been myself for years. All this, the jailings, the running, the death, the fear . . . it changes you. (*Beat.*) What if we can't get back what we've lost?

Tariq Maybe a well-executed rebellion can scare the Brits into concessions. /

Yusef That is what I mean! Why must we be feared in order to be free? What does it do to you to become something that is feared?! (*Beat.*) In any case, as long as the Brits fear the Jews more than us, we will always be at the bottom, fighting over the scraps.

Tariq They don't fear them.

Yusef Oh, they look down on them and fear them at once. They actually believe Jews plot to rule the world. (*Beat.*) I don't fear them, Tariq, why would I? No. It pains me, what is happening to our long lost cousins at the hands of the Europeans. They are changed by Europe, of it and yet not, the tribes of Berlin and Odessa, Vienna and Warsaw. But Zionism scares me. For it is a solution infected by Europe's diseases, by colonialism and slavery, even fascism. And they arrive in Palestine, relieved to be rid of their Christian overlords but not rid of them, not in their minds. And they are intrigued by this place, it's beauty, it's harshness. But also repulsed by it. And repulsed by us. So they change the land, mold it in their own image to make it theirs, just like the Europeans do, and plot to make us invisible one way or another. *That*'s what scares me.

Tariq Not all of them think like that.

Yusef The ones that matter do.

He lies down and closes his eyes.

Tariq Oh come on, you don't know how this will end.

Yusef No. And yes.

Tariq Nonsense!

Yusef (*calmly, almost drifting off*) What if I told you I know because the bananas told me? Or because I read the coffee grounds every morning; because I was forced to steal an orange from what had been my own family's grove. Because there is a European city that's appeared on the coast of Palestine that wasn't there thirty years ago. Because the trees speak to me at night and tell me they're scared. Because it rains in the summer! Because I dream of vultures and I wake up with the urge to run and keep running! Because . . . Because . . .

Tariq Yusef . . .

Yusef Because I dream of my unborn children and they don't speak our language. And because the wind has told me secrets: . . . we will soon be the new Jews; wandering, hated, nostalgic nomads with anger and sadness in our prayers.

A beat. **Tariq** *laughs. Then realizes* **Yusef** *was serious.*

Tariq Fine. Well, what if I told you that I have hope, Yusef? Me. Your worthless, traitorous nephew.

Thunder rumbles then turns into the sounds of protest outside. It grows. **Yusef** *sits up.*

Tariq They've come to get us. They're calling our names. There must be thousands.

Yusef They've answered Baybars' call.

Tariq I've never heard so many people saying my name at the same time!

Yusef You're guilty now, Tariq.

Tariq No! Yes. Fine. Give me a cigarette.

Yusef *hands him one.*

Tariq So this is what it's like, huh? To be a rebel?

Yusef No need to get drunk on their love, eh. Sip it. There's work to do.

Tariq You're right, you're right. You know, these people,

Yusef They're our people. Your people.

Tariq Those people out there, they—

Yusef They're resilient, / yes.

Tariq They admire me! Yusef, I'll put my money behind the revolt. With certain caveats.

Yusef Caveats?

Tariq Stipulations, / requirements—

Yusef Yes, I know the meaning, I / meant—

Tariq I can unify us. I can convince others!

A raucous cheer from outside.

I can't let them down, Yusef, not now. They came for us.

Yusef You have to love them back. I mean really love them.

Tariq So what now?

Outside, shots are fired—screaming, chaos, more shots. The sound of a riot.

Yusef (*calmly*) Just promise me something.

Tariq What?

Yusef That you'll always come back to them.

Tariq But I won't leave them. I'm here!

Yusef *clocks doors opening and closing in the distance, footsteps approaching.*

Yusef Don't forget how they cheered for you today.

Tariq I won't.

Yusef *is suddenly pulled violently out of the cell. The crash of thunder brings darkness.*

Scene Three

Yusef *is thrown back into the cell as* **Tariq** *sleeps. Another figure stands in the darkness.* **Yusef** *sees him and removes a folded picture from his pocket. He looks at it and then the man, as if to compare. It is the shadow of* **Emiliano Zapata**. *The shadow hands him a bottle.*

Zapata Have a sip, *hermanito*. It dulls the pain.

The two men drink in silence. **Yusef** *smiles. Church bells ring in the distance as morning breaks. After a moment, it is just* **Tariq** *and* **Yusef**. **Zapata** *is gone.*

Rajib *and* **Michael** *enter.*

Michael Rise and shine. Word is, your trial's been set for tomorrow morning, boys.

Tariq Trial? Where's the evidence? What about habeas corpus?

Michael *and* **Rajib** *stare at* **Tariq**.

Rajib (*to* **Yusef**) He's serious?

Yusef Until yesterday he thought he was equal to any Brit in the Empire.

Rajib Ah yes, one of those. (*To* **Tariq**.) You'll adjust.

Michael And if you ever doubt it, just remember hopping around picking up tennis balls for those two gobshites.

Yusef Michael, Rajib, I need a favor. You'll have to go to the old city.

Michael We're fond of mingling with the riffraff, sir. /

Yusef My house is at the end of Khalil Street, white stone, three arches and a fig tree in front. Give this to my wife.

He writes something on a piece of paper, hands it to them.

She must tell Baybars to think of something. Today. Time is running out.

Rajib Anything else, sir?

Yusef Tell her I'm sorry.

Michael Do you want me to demonstrate to her the depths of your affection, sir. Humbly, of course, and with your permission?

Rajib *smacks* **Michael** *across the back of his head.*

Yusef You Irish boys can fight, but I hear you're not much as lovers.

Michael British lies and propaganda! They're threatened by our virility and romanticism, sir. They're quite insecure, you know.

Michael Simpson (O'Donegal), Demosthenes Chrysan (Yusef), and Jim Sarbh (Rajib) in the Alliance Theatre's 2009/10 world premiere production of *Tennis in Nablus*, winner of the 2010 Alliance/Kendeda National Graduate Playwriting Competition. Photo by Greg Mooney. Photo courtesy of Alliance Theatre.

Rajib It's true. You should see how they turn red when they flip through the *Kama Sutra*.

Michael Which also explains the British obsession with conquest and plunder, does it not.

Rajib We'll go as soon as we can, sir.

Rajib *and* **Michael** *salute and exit.*

Tariq So the costume parties?

Yusef The stripping and whipping. All related. Makes sense when you think about it.

Duff *and* **Soldier** *enter.*

Lt. Duff (*to* **Tariq**) You have a visitor.

Tariq *exits with* **Duff**.

Scene Four

Hirsch *sits waiting in the prison holding area. He bounces a tennis ball, which he loses at the sight of* **Tariq**.

Tariq I'm not picking that up.

Lt. Duff You've got five minutes.

Duff *exits.*

Hirsch My God, what have they done to you?

Tariq They've made me a ball boy.

Hirsch I came as soon as I heard. I've already talked to the High Commissioner and the General /

Tariq How are you, Sam?

Hirsch Smoking too much. Nightmares, an ulcer . . . the usual . . . but good.

Tariq From here it looks . . . different. Out there. Worse, you know. /

Hirsch Of course it does, but when all this calms down a bit, some sanity will return and we / can—

Tariq I think we both know it's not going to end the way we said it would.

Hirsch But two men like us. We can make a difference.

Beat.

Tariq You really look like shit, you know. How about one of those cigarettes?

He takes one and **Hirsch** *lights it for him.*

Tariq It helps me wipe away a little of the bourgeois shine. I'm a rebel now.

Hirsch Yes, you're quite the star in the casbah. You look well. Alive. Alive is good when you've been thrown in a British prison.

Tariq I'm not out yet.

Hirsch Not quite. I've arranged for you to be released, Tariq. By the afternoon. It's a matter of paperwork at this point.

Tariq And Yusef?

Beat.

Hirsch No.

Tariq I see.

Hirsch Not him.

Tariq Tell me, Sam, can we both live here, or is it only going to be one of us in the end?

Hirsch You're being released! Say something.

Tariq You say something.

Hirsch I want to live in Palestine, as a proud Jew. Alongside the Arabs. Safe. You know / that.

Tariq Well I don't feel safe, Sam.

Hirsch That's why I want you out of here.

Tariq And what about your leaders? The Ben Gurions, the Begins, and the Sterns, what do they want?

Hirsch There are always reactionaries as well as sensible folks, Tariq.

Tariq You're building an army. With British weapons. An army that will fight anyone in the way of an all-Jewish state, including the Brits.

Hirsch (*hushed*) The British are limiting our immigration now, so, yes, there is talk of a break with the Brits. What does this have to do with anything?

Tariq It's everything, Sam. I just ask us to talk, as friends, honestly, while it is still possible.

Hirsch That way of thinking is winning. It's stronger every day. And every blow struck against the Arab Revolt, the stronger the hardliners get. On all sides!

Tariq I'm asking about *your* side.

Hirsch I'm not represented by those who dream of war and conquest.

Tariq   And yet, do you oppose them? Do you oppose them when they speak of us as trash to be disposed of?

Hirsch   When I can, I do. But as their strength grows our population grows, our economy grows, our land / grows!

Tariq   Ah and you have to take the good with the bad.

Hirsch   We all do.

Tariq *erupts into laughter.*

Tariq   And I just gave it away to you! I sold off the land. Like it was a crop that could be re-grown the next year.

Hirsch   Listen, all of Germany is / mad!

Tariq   And what do I have to do with Germany?!

Hirsch   There is talk of the Germans invading Poland by the end of the summer. There will be war and there will be nowhere for us to hide, Tariq. It's become intolerable for Jews, for anyone who thinks differently or looks differently. People are being shipped off in trains they say, a trickle now, but perhaps a flood tomorrow.

Tariq   I am sorry for that. I am. I / wish—

Hirsch   And it's going to make Palestine look like paradise. Even to the non-Zionists.

Tariq   Yes. But then what if your paradise turns into our hell, Sam? (*Beat.*) I don't think I can help you anymore. Not like before.

Hirsch   Yes. I suppose that is how it must be.

Tariq   I've been a fool.

Hirsch   It's an age made for fools.

He hands him a newspaper.

Like this Baybars.

Tariq   He's no fool.

Hirsch   You're right, he's smart. Fiery. He's awoken the Arabs.

Tariq   And terrified the Brits.

Hirsch   Not to mention the Ben Gurions, Begins, and Sterns. Though between us, I don't think you'll be seeing any more articles from him.

Tariq   How come?

Hirsch   He was paid. Heftily. By Tel Aviv. To shut his mouth. So I've heard. I find it a bit disagreeable, throwing money around to silence opponents. But if he can be bought, well it's his burden to bear.

Tariq *is silent.*

Tariq   I should get back.

Hirsch   You'll be released. It's the least I could do for a friend.

Tariq   Thank you, Sam. But I'll find my own way out of this. Goodbye.

Hirsch   Tariq, / please.

Lt. Duff (*entering*)   Time's up!

Tariq *exits with* **Duff.** **Hirsch** *stands alone, then exits.*

Scene Five

Anbara *sits at the table with several stacks of bills. She shifts the piles into different arrangements as she speaks.*

Anbara   Run. A ticket to Beirut. A villa, just me and Yusef . . . No.

She shifts the piles.

Rifles, ammunition and . . . Or . . .

She shifts it again.

Buy back land. Yes. Buy it back . . . Plus a new typewriter and some books.

Shifts the money.

A massive citrus grove hugging the coast. An orange-scented wall against the spread of Tel Aviv. No, God, how sentimental . . .

Again.

A car. Like the British generals. And a sailboat to zig-zag between Greek islands, sunbathing nude . . . Or . . .

Shifts the money again, into one huge stack.

A typewriter, fifty rifles, a small sailboat, thirty olive trees, thirty orange trees, a bicycle, books, and a weekend in Alexandria.

She knocks over the stack of money.

Damn it, Yusef, I'm no good with money! . . . (*Beat.*) . . . Yusef . . .

A knock at the door. **Anbara** *covers the money with the tablecloth, leaving a noticeable bulge. She grabs the sword from the wall.*

Who's there?

Michael   We're looking for Yusef's wife. We're friends, ma'am.

She opens the door to reveal **Michael** *and* **Rajib** *in Arab garb.*

Michael I have a feeling our disguises are not entirely convincing, ma'am.

Anbara No. Come in.

She ushers them in with the raised sword.

Rajib You have a lovely sword, miss. And a beautiful house.

Michael (*noticing the bulge in the tablecloth*) And a unique table as well.

Anbara Do you have a message from him or not?

He hands her the folded-up piece of paper from **Yusef**.

Michael Well, what does it say, ma'am?

Anbara A picture of the rebel Zapata. From Mexico. My husband tore it from the newspaper years ago. He's written his name on it.

Michael Perhaps it's a secret message ma'am.

Anbara More of an autograph. He has a tendency to make a martyr of himself. How is he?

Rajib Holding up. We're fond of him. He asks that we tell you that / he—

Michael That he loves you very much, ma'am. And that you're drop-dead bloody gorgeous—

Rajib *kicks* **Michael**'s *foot.*

Rajib Their trial is tomorrow. He said perhaps Mr. Baybars could help.

Anbara Can he escape before then?

Michael Oh, it'd be difficult ma'am. /

Anbara Could you help him? /

Michael Perhaps . . . but . . .

Rajib We'd / be . . .

Michael Done for, ma'am. It'd be the gallows for us. /

Rajib We'd need to disappear, for our own safety, and one needs resources for that.

Michael Funding, you know.

Rajib And unfortunately, our Irish friend here is unlucky at the card table and in serious debt. With everyone. From the officers' corps to the mess hall. You see, he keeps drawing kings, ma'am. In pairs.

Anbara I thought that was a good thing.

Michael Not in Bolshevik poker, ma'am. /

Rajib Different rules. /

Michael Long story.

Anbara *uncovers the money.*

Anbara   What if I were to say that half of this was yours?

Michael   I'd probably say I could lose that in one night.

Rajib   Ma'am, have you thought this through?

Anbara   Not really. Half. If you can get him out. Tonight. I'd say this would take you as far as . . .?

Rajib   Calcutta.

Michael   Monte Carlo.

Anbara   What do you say?

Rajib   I'd say you have a deal.

Scene Six

In the cell. **Yusef** *prays as* **Tariq** *is let back in.* **Tariq** *watches him finish.*

Tariq   I didn't know you prayed.

Yusef   Good for the soul. And my back as it happens.

Tariq   We certainly could use God's help.

Yusef   Come on, what does God have to do with all this? It's about the pounds and dunams, acres and hectares. Land leases, population registries and business ownership ratios.

Tariq   Numbers?

Yusef   A complicated, dirty real-estate deal.

Tariq   I want to make it right.

Yusef   I know you do, boy.

Tariq   Then help me. Give me orders.

Yusef (*not hearing* **Tariq**)   You know, I can almost see myself disappearing sometimes. Just now when I woke up, I couldn't even see my right arm.

Tariq   Sam Hirsch came . . . to have me released. Everything is arranged. Later today, he said. /

Yusef (*half to himself*)   It flickers in and out of sight like a mirage on the horizon of my body.

Tariq   I said no. I'll stay / here.

He snaps out of it.

Yusef Are you out of your mind?! Get out. Go!

Tariq I won't leave you. /

Yusef I'd leave you!

Tariq In here I'm a hero. Out there, I don't know, I don't know, but I'm not that. I'm scared.

Yusef Scared?! Listen, like I said, it's about numbers. And you're good with numbers.

Tariq They've paid off Baybars.

Yusef What? What do you mean?

Tariq He's taken money. From the Zionists. To shut up. Hirsch told me.

A beat. **Yusef** *paces, his head in his hand.*

Tariq I'm sorry. /

Yusef How much? I mean, how much do you think a bribe like that will get you?

Tariq You're missing the point.

Yusef No, she's got something up her sleeve, I know her.

Tariq Who?

Rajib *and* **Michael** *enter, handing* **Yusef** *a note.*

Michael From your wife, sir.

Yusef *opens it.*

Yusef It's signed Abdel Qader Salah al Din.

Tariq Who the hell is that?

Yusef If I'm not mistaken, he's the newest reincarnation of Mohammad Ali Baybars.

(*To* **Rajib** *and* **Michael**.) I assume there's a plan, so let's hear it.

Rajib (*quietly*) During the ball tonight, at midnight, while the General drinks and dances /

Michael Wouldn't call it dancing, really, / but—

Rajib We, well-armed with cash for bribes, will unlock your gate and slip you out unnoticed / . . .

Michael Into the serene Palestinian night, full of gunshots and distant explosions /.

Rajib Then . . . we all disappear. Each his own way. There's enough to pay off two guards and get me and my Irish friend as far away from the Britishers as possible.

Michael Be ready at midnight.

Rajib   The signal is three knocks and a sneeze . . .

Michael   And then another knock.

Yusef   How did she look?

Michael   A stunning specimen, sir—

Rajib *shoots* **Michael** *a glance to silence him.*

Yusef   Yes. I know. Stay! Have a drink.

Michael *complies but* **Rajib** *stops him.*

Rajib   On the other side. In the meantime, we must prepare.

They exit.

Scene Seven

On the balcony. The same evening. **Lt. Duff** *stands dressed as an Italian-style clown.*

General (*offstage*)   Ready.

Lt. Duff   Ladies and gentlemen. Fraulines and . . . monsieurs. I now present to you the man with the plan, and perhaps the most peculiar facial hair in the free and fascist worlds: the mad Chancellor, the freaky Führer, Mr. Adolf Kraut-Hun Hitler.

The **General** *enters in a Hitler costume.*

Lt. Duff   Oh bravo, sir. You've really captured the gravitas, the stern, demented energy of the man. Bravo, tut-tut, well done.

General   And you're supposed to be . . . ?

Lt. Duff (*proud*)   A clown, sir. Of the commedia dell'arte genre. I had it sent from Florence.

General   I thought you were going to be a Nazi thug with me, Douglas?

Lt. Duff   Well, sir, yes. But then I thought one of our sharp and alert guards might spot my convincing outfit, mistake me for a German infiltrator, and shoot me. I figured you wouldn't want to lose me over a misunderstanding like that.

The **General** *doesn't respond.*

Lt. Duff   Right, sir?

General   I suppose not, Doug.

Lt. Duff   I also got to thinking, sir, that the Nazi theme might upset some of our Jewish guests at tonight's party and that / perhaps—

General   Oh nonsense! It's a witty piece of political satire and nothing more. And if all else fails they'll laugh to please us and keep us on their side.

Lt. Duff   Right, sir. Of course.

General   Not that it matters much, since London will court the Arabs for the war effort now that the revolt has been crushed. You know what I tell people, Douglas? I say that I'm neither anti-Arab, nor anti-Semitic. I am simply, utterly, and eternally pro-British.

Lt. Duff   Well said, sir.

General   Though that's a bit of a lie too. God help them and their wicked ways if the British Empire leaves Palestine and they're left to fight over it. But in the meantime, we have work to do. In the meantime—

Lt. Duff   The Mandate is here to / stay!

General   In the meantime, Lt. Duff, we have a party to attend and a busy day ahead of us tomorrow. Orders to execute, tennis to play, and a trial to get on with.

Lt. Duff   Yes, sir, the case of Al-Qudsi.

General   Right. Now, remind me how they do their little thingy, Douglas.

Lt. Duff   Oh, no. I don't know, sir . . .

General   It's an order. Get me in the mood.

Lt. Duff *does a half-hearted Nazi salute.*

General   Good. Now don't let me see you do that again or I'll have you shot for treason . . . Shall we?

He exits off the veranda with **Lt. Duff** *following behind.*

Scene Eight

Lights up on a soldier in the prison holding area. **Rajib** *brings* **Tariq** *in.*

Soldier   Sign it.

Tariq   What's this?

Soldier   You're being released.

Tariq *hesitates.* **Rajib** *nudges him to get on with it.* **Tariq** *signs the paper.*

Soldier   Your things. And a note. You're lucky to have friends like Mr. Hirsch.

Rajib *shakes his hand and* **Tariq** *steps forward, out of the prison. After a moment he opens the letter. As he does,* **Hirsch** *appears elsewhere.*

Hirsch

Dear Tariq

I hope you don't mind that I went against your wishes. It seemed the right thing to do. I hope to never see your freedom taken away, and hope that all this ends well. But perhaps that's naïve.

In my life I've seen capitalists turn to socialists, socialists to capitalists and far too many people turn into fascists. I've seen men quoting the Torah in one hand and holding their still-warm rifles in the other. I've seen a whole country fall into line behind the devil dressed in a well-ironed uniform. I've moved in and out of dozens of apartments on three continents. I've learned Hebrew, the few words of Arabic you've taught me, and now, I've fallen in love with Palestine, its past and its future. And yet I hope that none of us love it so much that we would smother and strangle it just to keep it to ourselves. I am not that kind of lover and I don't think you are. That is not true love but possession.

So it is my hope that this little place is big enough for us all.

Either way, I will find solace in the knowledge that I have a friend who wished it otherwise before our future was stolen by men who follow a violent God. And I will remember that you welcomed an exile to these shores and made me feel at home when perhaps you had every right to do otherwise.

Take care of yourself, friend.

Samuel

Tariq *folds the letter and puts it into his jacket. The lights shift.*

Scene Nine

The cell. **Yusef** *plays cards. Across from him sits* **Emiliano Zapata**'s *ghost. They drink as they play their hands.*

Zapata   It was smart to let the boy go.

Yusef   I know.

Zapata   You never know. Or maybe you do.

Yusef   It's a shame. What they did to you.

Zapata   The world is full of shameful things. But beauty, too. So much beauty.

Yusef   They hunted you down.

Zapata   Such people, they do such things. *Siempre ha sido así.*

Yusef   Stabbed you in the back.

Zapata   I went to Jerusalem today. It's a sad sort of city, eh. Stones cry and shadows whimper in corners. But the sky. Man, it's a special color when you're inside those walls. Jesus was a lucky bastard. To die with a view of that sky.

Yusef   You know what Jesus was? A Palestinian-Jewish freedom fighter; an anti-imperialist leading a spiritual rebellion against the occupiers.

Zapata That's good. I'm gonna use that one.

I was riding today, you know, just south of the walls of the old city, and for a moment, you know, for one moment, I could swear I was riding across the plains of Northern Durango. (*Beat.*) Then I saw a camel.

They laugh. Church bells in the distance.

Yusef It's almost time to get out of here. You think I have some fight left in me?

Zapata Why not. But, *ojo* . . . the land is full of hunters these days. Beware how the prey can turn to predator, the hunters into the hunted and back again, until we don't know predator from prey, right from wrong, up from down.

They play their cards. **Yusef** *loses.*

Zapata That's three straight for me, *compadre*. You keep losing your hands.

Yusef *slides the chips to* **Zapata** *and then looks at his own hands.*

Yusef Yes. They flicker. On and off.

Zapata *whips his head towards the door and watches it. It is silent for a beat.*

Yusef Is it time?

Zapata *turns to* **Yusef** *and nods. A loud knock and then darkness.*

Scene Ten

The prison holding area. **Rajib** *waits. He has a small duffel bag. Suddenly* **Michael** *runs up out of breath, holding several bags.*

Rajib You're late! It's almost midnight.

Michael Got caught in the market. /

Rajib What the hell were you doing in the market?

Michael Souvenirs. For me mum and me family.

Rajib Souvenirs?

Michael You know, crosses, olive-wood virgins.

Rajib I know what souvenirs / are!

Michael It took an hour to find an open store at this hour. Then, you know, we sat for tea, and . . .

Rajib *stares at him in disbelief.*

Michael Listen, I can't come back from the Holy Land empty-handed.

Rajib We have a job to do. It's time.

They quietly make their way to the cell.

Rajib *knocks three times then sneezes, and knocks again. No response. After a moment they unlock the door.*

Michael   Yusef... Yusef... Hello?

From behind them a **Soldier** *appears.*

Soldier   What you fellas up to?

Michael   Nothing. Nothing at all.

Rajib   Where's the prisoner?

Soldier   I was looking for you two. You missed the show.

Michael   Was the General doing his belly-dancing routine again?

Soldier   No, no, thank God. I mean the trial.

Rajib   What trial?

Michael   You mean tomorrow?

Soldier   No. General decided to get on with it a bit early. Apparently the high commissioner's coming tomorrow, and the trial was scheduled when the General wanted to play tennis with him. So he pushed the proceedings up a bit. Wouldn't have made much of a difference anyway, tonight or tomorrow.

Rajib   It might have.

Soldier   Well, at least you didn't have to clean up the mess. I was at it alone. So you owe me a pint.

Michael   Mess?

The **Soldier** *turns and looks upstage and we see, in the dim light, the twisting silhouette of a limp and bloodied body hanging from the balcony.*

Soldier   He wouldn't go easily. (*Beat.*) Tell you what. You two can have the job of taking him down tomorrow after the tennis match, and we'll call it even.

Rajib   *After* the tennis game?

Soldier   The General insists the Arab watch his match. From the balcony.

Scene Eleven

The sound of protests and rain outside. A knock at the door. **Anbara** *opens it.* **Rajib** *and* **Michael** *stand in the doorway, their hats off.*

Michael   They took him before we could get to him.

Rajib   Secret trial.

Michael   You're not at the funeral? It's massive. You should see all the / people –

Anbara   I hate funerals. (*Beat.*) He used to play the oud for me, you know. He wasn't great, but the notes. They fit perfectly into the arches of windows. He sold that oud. To buy a gun.

Michael   They say he fought to the end.

Rajib *hands her the money.*

Rajib   We can't take it. Not now.

Anbara   It's yours. Go home . . . And give them hell.

Rajib *and* **Michael** *bow and exit. After a moment there is another knock at the door.* **Tariq** *enters carrying a bag.*

Tariq   It's started to rain again. Unusual this time of year.

Anbara   Did you come to talk about the weather, Tariq?

Tariq   I'm sorry. For / everything

Anbara   Quiet. No need to say it /.

Tariq   Your writing. You should be . . . careful.

Anbara   I should. (*Beat.*) But I won't. And I won't hide anymore.

Tariq   I suppose if anyone can handle the times, it's you, Anbara.

Anbara (*calmly*)   That's nice of you.

Tariq   I went to the rally. After the funeral. I walked up to the front of the crowd. I was pushed. Carried even. I got up on the fountain and I . . . spoke. I felt . . . intoxicated. I was holding something, a flag maybe, or a rock, a gun, I don't . . . even remember. It was as if . . .

Anbara   As if Yusef was speaking.

Tariq   And they cheered me, Anbara. They roared, and we marched. Moving like a sea.

Anbara   And then the shots.

Tariq   Yes.

Anbara   Always the shots.

Tariq   We scattered in every direction. Blood and shoes on the ground. I ran. Like a boy escaping a beating, not seeing or hearing a thing. Just the explosions echoing in my head. I was lost. In Nablus; lost in my own city. I made my way back. To where the shots were fired, and it was empty. I was sure it was a dream, Anbara. I told myself that it was a dream the whole way home. And when I got there, it was in flames. The house of my great-grandfather. And I felt empty. On fire.

Anbara   Who did it?

Tariq   The British . . . the Zionists. Does it even matter anymore?

Anbara   Yes. And no.

Tariq   I don't want my hands to disappear in all this blood. I have to leave. At least until things die down . . . I can't . . . I can't live like this.

Anbara   None of us want to live like this.

Tariq   I'm going to Beirut. I came to say goodbye.

Anbara   Go.

He hands her a ring of three old iron keys.

Tariq   The keys for what's left. What I haven't sold or seen burn. Take them. Until I return.

She nods. **Tariq** *turns to leave.*

Anbara   Don't forget how they cheered for you.

Tariq *pauses then exits without looking back. From the back door,* **Waleeda** *enters.*

Waleeda   Who was that who just left?

Anbara   No one.

Waleeda *puts a small sack of vegetables on the table.*

Waleeda   Imagine, perfectly good vegetables. They were throwing produce at a pair of British soldiers. People have no sense anymore. No sense at all.

Anbara *goes to the back wall and takes the sword down. In its place she hangs the keys.* **Waleeda** *sits by the window and looks out. A kind of sunlight peeks through the windows.*

Waleeda   The sky is clearing. That strange rain has stopped. Perhaps things will start looking up.

Blackout.

End of Play.

Final Status

Time: 1993, 2008.

Place: Act One takes place in a Washington, DC hotel circa 1993.
Act Two takes place in the Gaza Strip home of Edriss in the last days of 2008.
Prologue takes place in Madrid in 1991.

Characters

(second age corresponds to the characters' Act Two ages)
Ibrahim, *twenty-eight/forty-three*
Edriss, *sixty-three/seventy-eight*
Mazen, *(fifty-five/seventy)*
Faisal, *(forties)*
Hala, *(forties)*
Motti, *(fifty-five)*
Uri, *(thirty-five)*
Denny Martin*, *(forties)*
Moose**, *(thirties)*

Set

Act One should have a minimalist nineties hotel vibe with a center table of some sort, perhaps with rolling chairs around it. A couple simple pieces in other parts of the stage could represent the lobby. On the side wall (stage right) there might be a mirror and perhaps the simple suggestion of a lobby bathroom. The stage-left entrance/exit could be represented by a kind of elevator door.

Act Two takes place in a simple Gaza living room.

Act One especially calls for a screen of some sort on the back wall.

---

*   Denny is never seen, only heard over the phone. His voice can be played by one of the offstage actors.
** The actor playing Faisal or Uri in Act One can play Moose in Act Two.

Prologue: 1991, Madrid

Edriss, *mid-sixties, stands at a podium. There are flashbulbs going off. A sign or screen reads "Madrid Peace Conference, 1991, Round 1".*

Edriss I should start by thanking you all for finally recognizing the Palestinian people at an international summit. But I won't . . . One shouldn't ever have to thank another for his inalienable rights.

He takes a sip of water. A flashbulb and a shift from **Edriss** *at the podium to* **Motti**, *elsewhere, who is addressing an unseen group of colleagues. On the back screen behind* **Motti** *is a black and white surveillance picture of* **Edriss**. *There is a shift from one to the other as each speaks.*

Motti Dr. Edriss Abul Hajj. From Gaza. Well-respected. And no one's bitch . . . Not yet.

Edriss We've come here to Madrid to make peace. /

Motti Lived through the revolt against the British in the thirties, fought in '48, a medic in '67. /

Edriss But as we speak, thousands of our brothers and sisters languish in Israeli / prisons . . .

Motti Imprisoned twice. /

Edriss Most detained without evidence or trial. /

Motti Twice exiled.

Edriss Many tortured. Repeatedly. /

Motti Tortured. On one occasion. Officially. /

Edriss And for nothing more than daring to defy a military occupation. /

Motti Unofficially, more than / once.

Edriss Simply for daring to proclaim our mere existence. /

Motti Arafat knows this guy has support on the ground, and that scares the shit out of / him.

Edriss The sole representative of our scattered nation—the Palestine Liberation Organization—long exiled in Tunis—has been excluded from direct participation in these talks.

Motti But he also knows Edriss is the smartest one he's got to lead the delegation. So Arafat will be keeping an eye on him from Tunis.

Shift back to **Edriss**.

Edriss The group assembled here in the absence of the PLO is made up of committed individuals from every corner of occupied Palestine and the diaspora.

The lights shift back to **Motti**.

Motti Next slide!

The slide changes to a picture of **Edriss** *with* **Hala** *and* **Faisal**.

Motti Next to him are Hala 'Adnan and Faisal Khallaf, both academics and activists originally from the West Bank. Both studied in England. Mr. Khallaf stayed in the West and has lived much of his adult life there. Ms. 'Adnan returned and has a following in the territories. She was an effective spokesperson during the Intifada. Feisty. And very smart.

Shift back to **Edriss**.

Edriss We are untested, yes, but we find strength in the knowledge that the Palestinian people are fused by centuries of history and a collective memory of shared sorrows and joys / . . .

Motti Our orders from Rabin: Keep the negotiations on our terms. /

Edriss To our people, who have sent us to this appointment laden with their trust, their love, and their aspirations, we say that the load is heavy, but we shall be true. /

Motti They're learning on the spot.

Edriss There will be obstacles, as there are on any road to peace. /

Motti So we can take advantage of / that.

Edriss But we are confident that we will soon celebrate on the day of our / liberation.

Motti We're not here to make war. That is true. But we're also not ready to jump in bed with them either. And if we do decide to make love, we want to make sure we're on top. Understood boys?

The stage goes black . . .

Act One

Scene One

The screen—in the form of a nineties overhead projector—reads: "Two years later, Washington, DC Round 10 of negotiations." **Edriss** *is on the phone. He is disheveled, tired, and yet totally together.*

Edriss   I don't give a shit what you think the Israelis will say! I refuse to turn in this proposal. Why? Because it's shit! Give me Abu Ammar. I said give me the old man!

He waits.

Brother . . . Yes . . . No. Well, they want to wear us down . . . Yes, we've been reading the faxes you're sending from Tunis. I'm listening . . . Yes, Chairman, understood. Ok, ok. Goodbye.

He slams the phone down repeatedly, then sits at a small table . . . Lights shift to **Ibrahim** *who stands in front of a mirror straightening his tie.*

Ibrahim   Hi, I'm Ibrahim . . . Abu Eid, sir. First name Ibrahim. (*To himself.*) Jesus, who speaks like that? Ibrahim, sir. Ibrahim Abu Eid. That's much better, Ibrahim. Brilliant, really brilliant, dude. Ok, ok, man, get your fucking shit together.

A deep breath and then.

I'm honored to be invited to be part of the delegation, sir. I hope I can be helpful. Yes, Georgetown Law . . . Yes, I remember my dad. I was a kid but . . . Of course I know he was a martyr. For the cause. Yes. The mouth and the eyes. That's what everyone says. Thank you. So where shall we start? (*A pause and then, to himself.*) This is gonna be a fucking / disaster.

Shift back to **Edriss** *looking over documents.* **Faisal** *enters, nervous, worked up, caffeinated.*

Faisal   This is going to be a bloody disaster, Eddie. Look at this fax.

He puts a piece of paper on the table.

Faisal   They're sending Mazen. From Tunis.

Edriss   I can read. So what? Ignore him. I've been doing it for twenty years.

Faisal   He's the boss's right-hand man!

Edriss   Please don't call Arafat "the boss." Abu Ammar. Old man. But not boss.

Faisal   Look, I expected we'd have an assortment of morons calling us to get updates, / but—

Edriss   But you figured we'd just give a call or two to Tunis a day, do it all by fax and that would / be it?

Faisal   Yes. And preferably no Mazen breathing Johnnie Walker fumes down my neck.

Edriss Then you don't know the PLO. Why do you think I wanted to stay in Gaza when the negotiations got underway?

Faisal They're gonna blitz, Eddie, I can feel it.

Edriss Remind me what a blitz is?

Faisal It's when the defense charges in American football. They all run at your team; a surprise attack.

Edriss And who is it that's going to "blitz" us?

Faisal I don't know; the Israelis, that American, what's his name, the suspicious little shit?

Edriss Denny Martin?

Faisal Him! Denny. What kind of name is Denny, anyway.

Edriss Let's just hope there's no blitz. And that we can work as a team with Tunis.

Faisal The old man hasn't listened to a word we've said for the past year.

Edriss (*calmly*) He's vulnerable, Faisal. He's isolated in Tunis. He walks like a rooster but he feels like a mouse.

Faisal And the Israelis can smell it. That's what worries me.

Edriss We can handle the Israelis. I assume the old man's smart enough to realize that.

Faisal You know he's suspicious of Hala. Because of her support in the West Bank. Same goes for you in Gaza. The Intifada / showed—

Edriss —Showed him he's not as relevant as he thought? I know. I read your article in the *New York Review of / Books*.

Faisal *London Review of Books*.

Edriss Look, they can fax and phone all they want, but in the end we're still the ones at the table.

Faisal *gives him a look.*

Edriss And if the Americans are serious about peace, and if international law means anything, then we have a chance.

Faisal Sounds to me like we're waiting for the perfect storm of "maybes" and "ifs"!

Edriss *stops what he's doing again.*

Edriss Faisal, everything about our existence over the last forty-five years has been a "maybe." But here we are.

Faisal Here we are.

Lights shift back to **Ibrahim**, *still in front of the bathroom mirror.*

Ibrahim (*to himself*)   Alright, just play it cool and do you, man. Be a solid legal adviser. You studied contracts and treaties and international law for *this* moment. This is your chance to do something meaningful. To make your old man proud.

He grabs his briefcase and lights shift as he enters the space where **Faisal** *and* **Edriss** *are.*

Faisal   Hello.

Ibrahim   Hello.

Faisal   You must be Ibrahim. Come in.

Ibrahim   Hi. Yes. Hi.

Edriss   A spitting image of your father, boy. *Allah yir Hamou* ("God rest his soul"). Welcome, welcome.

Ibrahim *steps in and they all shake hands and kiss on the cheek.*

Ibrahim   I'm so . . . happy. . . . I mean . . . I'm honored . . . Really.

There is an awkward pause and before **Ibrahim** *can continue, he is interrupted by the phone ringing.* **Faisal** *answers.*

Faisal   Hello . . . Yes . . . Zayna Abu-Eid?! It's been ages. No, it's Faisal Khallaf . . . Yes, Edriss is right here . . . And your son just walked in . . . Oh yes, a lot like his father. . . . Oh yes, *very* handsome. . . . Don't worry, Zayna, we'll take care of him. Here he is. (*Whispered to* **Ibrahim**.) Your mamma.

Ibrahim (*mortified, almost whispering into the receiver*)   Hi . . . Yes, I'm *here* . . . Ma, how'd you get this number? Never mind. . . . What? Yes, I ate breakfast . . . No, the blue tie. I told you, I don't like the purple one. Fine, lavender, whatever! Listen, I gotta go, Ma. Bye. Ok, thanks. Bye.

He hangs up the phone quickly.

Ibrahim   My mother. She's . . . I don't know how she got the number. Sorry about that.

Faisal   Mine called me twice a day . . . on my *honeymoon*. That particular marriage ended in divorce. Unsurprisingly, in retrospect.

Edriss   Number one or two?

Faisal   Number one. My mother never said a word to number two. Like a mean Marcel Marceau, right to the bitter end.

Edriss   Sit, Ibrahim. Please.

Ibrahim   Thank you. It's a pleasure to finally meet you both.

Faisal   Think of it like this, kid; you're a reliever. Brought in to stop the bleeding in the bottom of the eighth.

Edriss   No more hockey analogies, Faisal, please / .

Faisal Baseball / .

Edriss (*to* **Ibrahim**) You're Salim's son and that goes a long way with me. I loved your father. But you're here because you're a good lawyer and you come highly recommended. You were a foot-in for this job.

Faisal A "shoe-in."

Edriss Faisal insists on using English, to stay sharp for negotiations.

Ibrahim What happened with the last lawyer? If you don't mind me asking.

Faisal Faris Bamyeh was a very nice man.

Edriss But a terrible lawyer.

Faisal Not very good, no.

Edriss Counselor Bamyeh also had a rather poor command of the English language as it happens.

Faisal Which, *incidentally, is the* language of negotiation . . .

Edriss Not to mention a feeble grasp of the issues.

Ibrahim Well, I hope I can be of help.

Faisal Avoid the mines and you'll be fine.

Ibrahim Mines?

Hala *enters and jumps in seamlessly.*

Hala Faisal, that's my speech. Don't steal it.

Faisal Hala, you know that the "mine" speech / is mine.

Hala (*ignoring* **Faisal**, *speaking to* **Ibrahim**) The trick, Ibrahim, is to know when the Americans are speaking for the Israelis and when they're flying solo. In other words, don't trust anyone or it'll blow up in your face. Hala 'Adnan. Pleasure.

Ibrahim I know who you are, auntie. The pleasure's mine.

Hala Oh dear lord, drop the "auntie," please. And don't mind Faisal. He's been in love with me for years. His failure to impress me has left him rather infantile and unattractive.

Faisal The lady doth protest too much, methinks.

Hala (*to* **Ibrahim**) Did they fill you in on Bamyeh?

Ibrahim Yes.

Edriss (*to* **Ibrahim**) As you know, Faisal is the best cartographer in the Occupied Territories and Madame Hala here is a scholar and a tireless advocate for human rights. Faisal, please show Ibrahim the maps.

Faisal *turns on the overhead projector. Both maps appear on the back wall.*

Faisal So here are the maps which I have termed *el Kharaayet ezbaleeyeh* or the "bullshit land-grab hog-wash, super-swindle" maps.

Hala As proposed by Rabin's team and endorsed by the Americans and their envoy, Denny Martin.

Faisal On the right you will see is the map of all the illegal settlements along with water sources and agricultural land. On the left you will see where they propose to hand over some sort of control to us in the territories. Now, when I superimpose these two images you will see that under this proposal, we would ostensibly be cut off from both the water and our best lands.

He superimposes the two maps on the projector.

Hala In other words, the occupation remains intact, as do the majority of settlements. We would get some islands of control, but no sovereignty. We've rejected it, of course.

Faisal But they just keep re-packaging it and trying to re-sell it to us.

Hala It's been going on for months. Since we got to Washington.

Faisal The Americans won't pressure the Israelis, / so—

Edriss So, we are putting together another counter-proposal.

A loud knock on the door.

Faisal I bet you that's our neutral American third party.

Hala / Edriss Israelis.

Edriss Only Israelis knock that hard, Faisal.

Faisal *calmly removes the maps as* **Motti** *Brenner (sixty) and* **Uri** *Ayalon (thirty) enter.*

Motti Gentlemen. Madame.

Hala Your team is looking a little thin today, Motti.

Motti Ariel and Yigal have flown to Europe for important matters. But I have permission to go ahead. This is Uri. He'll be filling in as counsel in their absence.

Faisal And the Americans?

Uri Denny informed us that we are to be left to our own devices for today while he bangs out the bridging proposal.

Motti There you have it. I take it you've replaced counselor Bamyeh. Shame. I was a fan.

Edriss I'm sure you were. This is Ibrahim Abu-Eid, our new legal adviser.

They shake.

Motti You look very . . . American.

Ibrahim Is it that obvious?

Simultaneously:

Motti	**Hala**	**Faisal**
It's the hair.	Your shoes.	The way you walk.

Edriss I like to think the only reason he doesn't look like the rest of us, Motti, is that he hasn't spent his entire life with the heavy boot of occupation pressing down on his neck. Colonial occupation ages you.

Uri So, he's your secret weapon?

Edriss No, no, that would be *me*, Motti.

They look at their watches, papers, etc. and then almost in unison take out cigarettes. All but **Ibrahim** *and* **Uri** *light up and puff away. Lights dim and table melts behind a blanket of cigarette smoke.*

Scene Two

Faisal, **Ibrahim**, **Hala** *and* **Edriss** *are alone again and stand around the table.*

Faisal They're stalling.

Hala Allow me to introduce a curious Israeli-American concept termed: "Final Status."

Ibrahim (*taking notes*) Which means?

Hala "Final Status" is a framework they're pushing that puts a bunch of issues into a folder.

Faisal Not to be discussed until later.

Ibrahim When's later, exactly?

Hala No one / knows.

Faisal Two years, three years. / Unclear.

Hala Basically, until some unforeseeable date in the future.

Faisal And only after a vague interim period of so-called "trust-building."

Ibrahim So, we have to gain their trust in order to talk about—?

Hala Anything /

Faisal Everything.

Ibrahim Jerusalem?

Edriss Yes. And / refugees.

Faisal Water /

Edriss   Borders /

Hala   And airspace. *All* off-limits.

Ibrahim   What about sovereignty?

Faisal   That too. We're also discouraged from evening mentioning international law. Imagine /

Hala   Everything delayed until "Final Status" talks . . . . In the interim, boys, I'm off to my room. Call if you need anything.

He exits.

Edriss   Ibrahim, you ever hear the story about Faisal and Hala when they were kids?

Faisal   Ok, *back* to final status!—

Edriss   It was right before '67 and there was a talent show for the junior high students—

Faisal (*ignoring*)   As you can see, Ibrahim, the Israelis are trying to negotiate a deal in which they do not make any commitment to a Palestinian / state—

Edriss   And young Faisal and Hala were both performing in the contest that night. Tell us, what did Hala do, Faisal?

Faisal *shakes his head.*

Edriss   Tell him!

Faisal   She sang a song.

Edriss   Some standard fare. Fairuz, Oum Kulthum, something like that. Now, tell us what you did, Faisal.

Faisal (*mumbles*)   A poem. I read a poem.

Edriss   A love poem. To Hala.

Faisal   The recipient was *never* specified.

Edriss   What was the line, Faisal?

Faisal *complies, playing along.*

Faisal   "I dance my way into the cave of your beauty, only to find that there are stars and universes in the sky of your soul."

Edriss   "I dance my way into the cave of your beauty." Very edgy stuff.

Faisal   That translation is misleading . . . The Arabic was more . . . subtle.

Edriss   You should've seen how hard your father laughed when we heard that story for the first time, Ibrahim. Your dad had the best laugh, the best.

Ibrahim   I don't remember it. But my uncle Ramzi does an imitation.

Edriss   Salim was the only one of us who could blow perfect smoke rings!

Faisal *begins to pack up his things.*

Edriss Faisal. Tell me: what do you think has kept us from disappearing all these years?

Faisal Stubbornness probably.

Edriss Yes. What else?

Faisal I have a feeling you're going to enlighten me.

Edriss Laughter!

Faisal There's nothing to laugh about. I'm sick of these negotiations.

Edriss What about the time I tripped and landed in Gorbachev's lap at the UN in '88? *That* was funny.

They both laugh. **Faisal** *exits . . . After a moment, an enormous stack of papers is slid onto stage, just as a phone rings.* **Edriss** *answers, putting it on speaker phone.*

Denny (*his voice heard over the speaker*) Ed-riss . . . .

Edriss Denny. Hello.

Denny I'm great, thanks. I know it's late. So listen, you should have gotten the, uh, bridging document. Sorry it took us so long. President Clinton looked it over himself this time. It's a bit long, so skim it if you have to. We'll talk tomorrow? Ok. Good. Great. Night.

Edriss Denny, I want to introduce you to / Ibrahim—

Denny *has already hung up.*

Edriss . . . I hate the way that guy says my name.

Ibrahim Shall I take a look at it tonight?

Edriss I'll look it over first. Study the latest Israeli proposal for now. Give us a legal briefing on it, tomorrow morning. 8:30.

He exits. **Ibrahim** *is alone. He sits at the table and starts studying his files. Lights fade down.*

Scene Three

Ibrahim *asleep at the same table with the papers spread about. He wakes up, startled.*

Ibrahim Shit.

He starts to gather his things. As he does, **Mazen** *(fifties) enters sipping a glass of whisky.*

Mazen You're here late, Ibrahim.

Ibrahim Sorry, I don't think we've met.

Mazen Mazen Haddad

Ibrahim Oh! Abu Thowra. I'm sorry, sir, I didn't . . . recognize you. I've seen pictures but . . . How are you? I mean—

Mazen I've gotten fatter, I know. I was very photogenic once upon a time.

Ibrahim I didn't know you were in DC. I thought—

Mazen Arrived from Tunis this evening. You look exactly like your father, you know. A little shorter but . . .

Ibrahim (*nervously*) That's what everyone / says.

Mazen And I hear you're the new legal adviser. Too bad they didn't get along with Faris. Those guys from the inside, like Edriss and the rest, sometimes they look down on those of us who've lived and fought in exile. I bet they call you "the American," huh?

Ibrahim *doesn't respond.*

Mazen Sorry, I've interrupted. Please, don't let me keep you from your work.

Ibrahim No, no. I was just going to my room. Will you be around tomorrow, sir?

Mazen The PLO is still a dirty acronym around here, Ibrahim. So I'm technically not allowed at the table. How about a drink?

Ibrahim Thanks, but I shouldn't.

Mazen It's dawn in Tunis now so I need someone to keep me company. Scotch? Good.

He exits and comes back with two fresh glasses of whisky and sits.

Your father was a scotch drinker like me, you know . . . Nothing fancy. Always humble. Even when we were meeting the French ambassador in Beirut, he wouldn't dress up. Didn't try to hide the fact that he was a poor kid from the camps . . . The rest of us, we tried. To hide it. But there was always a give-away. Our shoes were always too big, or too small. Or our suits. You could just see those French assholes with their Yves St. Lauren laughing behind our backs. But your father, he was at home in his own skin . . . (*Beat.*) . . . Enough about the past! How does it feel, heh, to be in the big leagues?

Ibrahim Good. Overwhelming but / good.

Mazen All this banter over maps. Maps and zones, charts and deeds, wells and bones. It's tiresome.

He takes a gulp of whisky.

Ibrahim Well, there are a lot of fine points to be worked out.

Mazen (*confiding*) You know, I've been PLO since it existed. I survived the hell of Jordan, then Beirut and now the boredom of Tunis. But imagine, after all that, when it's finally time to sit down with the Israelis, we're locked out and thrown to the side?! Why? Because the Israelis and the Americans want to divide us and to weaken Arafat! But the key to all this is a deal with the PLO, directly. *We* represent the Palestinian people.

He moves closer to **Ibrahim**, *sits in the seat next to him.*

Mazen Ibrahim. Listen. And this is strictly between us . . . No, never mind. Forget it.

Ibrahim No. I'm listening. You can. I'm . . . You can trust me.

Mazen *stares at him, sizing him up for a long beat.*

Mazen You know your father, he used to be my eyes and ears, when he was your age. He started out with me. Did you know that?

Ibrahim *nods.*

Ibrahim What did you want to tell me just now?

Mazen Between us?

Ibrahim Client–attorney confidentiality. Of course.

Mazen Arafat believes Edriss and the others have their own agenda. They're patriots of course. But they're ambitious. They want their own power in the West Bank, in Gaza. But we are not at the table so we can't always know what is being said and done. And this serves the Israelis, it divides us. You know, divide and conquer!

Ibrahim It's not ideal, tactically, for you. Us, I mean.

Mazen Which is why I need someone here who I can trust totally. Someone who's committed to the struggle of Palestinians everywhere, not just for the ones on the inside. The old man and I need someone sharp, from the outside. Like you. (*Beat.*) Your father and I, we went through a lot together in Beirut.

Ibrahim My mother mentioned that she knew you in the old days.

Mazen Well, she always complained I was a bad influence on your father but . . .

He laughs and cleans the last drops from his empty glass.

But he turned out fine, your dad. A damn hero.

Ibrahim A dead hero.

Mazen You'll make your people even prouder than your old man. You'll make it far, I can see that already. Another drink? I insist.

Lights down.

Scene Four

Back in the negotiation room, the next morning.

Ibrahim It's simple. What I am suggesting is that we ask for jurisdiction over *all* territory handed over. Legally, our strongest position under the limitations they're imposing is to get jurisdiction.

Hala Meaning what?

Ibrahim Meaning we're asking to be granted the practical authority to deal with and make pronouncements on legal matters and to administer justice within that defined area. That's it.

Edriss Including the Israeli settlements?

Ibrahim Precisely. Listen, if we let the settlements, or any occupied territory, remain outside of our jurisdiction in this agreement, then we're overlooking the inherent illegality of the occupation itself. As your lawyer, I don't think you can afford to contractually or even implicitly condone that illegality.

Edriss Or else it ceases to be illegal?

Ibrahim Exactly!

Hala So if they want these illegal settler towns to remain, which they insist on, then they have to be a part of what will become a Palestinian state?

Ibrahim Yes, ma'am. Or at least something along those lines.

Hala (*to* **Edriss**) It makes sense.

Edriss It's our strongest position.

Ibrahim To be clear, jurisdiction is a compromise on our part. But what's important for us here is that it draws its substance from international law. That means we have legal claim over any land transferred to Palestinian control in the deal. It's legally sound.

Edriss Let's get this to Tunis, let them know what we're thinking.

Everyone gets back to work. **Ibrahim** *stretches, then leaves the table . . . The lights shift to* **Ibrahim**, *now in the "men's room" taking a piss.* **Uri** *leans on a wall near* **Ibrahim**, *watching him.*

Uri Why do you do that?

Ibrahim Excuse me?

Uri Standing there with your chest puffed out. The posing doesn't suit you.

Ibrahim And you know what suits me?

Uri I know you are a sensitive guy. With some sadness in him

Ibrahim Every Palestinian has some sadness in him, Ari.

Uri It's Uri. And you're Ibrahim Abu-Eid . . . BA University of Michigan, JD Georgetown Law. Born in Beirut, 1965, came to the US as a kid with your mother to escape the war in '76. New York. Then bounced around the Midwest with mom as a kid. Detroit, Chicago, Columbus. Your father, the infamous Salim Abu-Eid, originally from Gaza, stayed behind in Beirut with the PLO, only to be neutralized in 1982 by an Israeli hit squad.

*He points his fingers at **Ibrahim**'s head as if a gun.*

Uri "Bam" . . . And here you are.

Ibrahim Here I am. As of yet "un-neutralized."

Silence.

Uri But you don't seem boastful, you know. That's what I like about you. In our part of the world you don't see that humility in men very often.

Ibrahim *Our* part of the world?

Uri I mean the Middle East.

Ibrahim Funny, I always thought you had a disdain for our part of the world, what with your looking towards the West, a beacon of democracy in the barbaric darkness of the Orient.

Uri Well said. And interesting that I commend you on your sensitivity and you become threatened, take the opportunity to berate / me.

Ibrahim I'm not threatened, Uri, you just seem like a bit of a dick is all.

Uri You want pleasure and joy, I think. And comfort . . . And peace of course. I can tell by your eyes.

Ibrahim Are you hitting on me, Uri?

Uri No. I'm a soldier. And you're an Arab.

Ibrahim Of course. You forgot "home" by the way. That's what I want. That's why I'm here.

Uri In the bathroom?

Ibrahim At the negotiations. And I should get back. Thanks though. Do I owe you for this session?

Uri Tell me more about "home."

Ibrahim I thought you knew the Palestinian mind inside out?

Uri Maybe that's why *I'm* here. To master it.

Ibrahim "They lived on the margins or in the nooks and crannies of their respective nations. Each of them was in society and yet not in it, of it, and yet not of it . . ."

Uri I know it. It's about us. The Jews. Not you.

Ibrahim But it could just as well describe us, Uri. Because we're becoming more and more like you, and ironically enough, *because* of you.

Uri *laughs.*

Uri Well, you still have a couple thousand years to go to be us, so pace yourselves.

Ibrahim I don't want to be you, Uri. That's the point. That's why I'm here.

He exits the rest room and re-enters the negotiation table, followed by **Uri**. *The Palestinians watch the Israelis in silent anticipation as they read over a document. This lasts for some beats and then—*

Motti It's a non-starter, Edriss. You can't have jurisdiction over the settlements!

Hala *Illegal* settlements, Motti, the operative word, which you omit, is *illegal*!

Motti They're Israeli citizens! No way.

Edriss So, you don't want to discuss sovereignty at all, you want to put it off until *later*, correct?

Motti *nods.*

Edriss And no UN resolutions either, right? Right! Fine. We'll do it your way. So how is it so hard to give us jurisdiction in return? Over Palestinian land for God's sake! Otherwise your offer is rubbish and you know it!

Motti No.

Hala We're not asking for jurisdiction over Tel Aviv here, come on.

Motti So, on land handed over to the Palestinians in the West Bank and Gaza, your police force, untested and trigger-happy, will protect Jewish settlers? My God, it's like foxes in a chicken coup.

Edriss Cut the victim shit with me, Motti. We've both been around long enough to know it's goat shit!

Faisal (*quietly, to* **Edriss**) Bull shit.

Edriss And if you want to talk about who is trigger happy or who is the fox and who is inside a chicken coup, we could—for hours!

Motti My response is just a reflection of what Rabin and the government will and will not allow. You know that.

Edriss Let me tell you what I know, Motti, my dear. I know that if you insist on keeping your settlers—from Brooklyn and France and God knows where—planted in Palestinian territory, then there are compromises you must make. Risks you must take. We're crazy enough to trust you, so trust us!

There is silence. **Motti** *laughs and then* **Edriss** *starts to laugh until they are both laughing together.*

Motti (*still laughing, from his stomach*) Trust us! Ha!

Edriss Crazy?! More like stupid!

They erupt into laughter again.

Motti Chickens!

Edriss In a fox coop! Ha!

They laugh more. **Faisal** *joins in but unsure why.*

Hala You have no idea what they're laughing about do you?

Faisal No.

Motti *and* **Edriss** *gather themselves.* **Hala**, *agitated, grabs* **Motti**'s *Zippo lighter from the table but* **Motti** *instinctively grabs her hand.*

Hala Don't worry Motti, I claim no jurisdiction over your lighter. May I?

Motti *lights her cigarette for her with a smile.*

Edriss Give us something here. We're walking a balancing act, too.

Hala We need to have something to show or else Arafat gets nervous

Uri Like a puppy?

Hala And there's no knowing what rug he'll shit on to prove his point. We need results.

Motti Just be sensible and we can talk.

Uri (*to* **Hala**) Was that a threat?

Hala No. But even if it was, what would you do about it?

Edriss Hala, drop it.

Uri I guess we'll see.

Hala Don't bother, I know. When all you have is a hammer, Uri, everything looks like a nail, doesn't it.

Uri I have no shame in the strength of Israeli resolve.

Hala Strength? Resolve? Slapping around kids and old folks in refugee camps is something to be proud of?

Faisal Hala, save it.

Hala I know who you are, Uri, dime a dozen at every checkpoint and every raid—just another insecure dickless fascist wearing the mask of a liberal.

Uri *is about to respond, but* **Motti** *stops him as* **Faisal** *takes* **Hala** *aside to cool down for a moment.*

Motti Edriss. Let's just be realistic here. Please.

Hala (*jumping back into the fray*) You want to be real? We've seen how *"real"* your buddies can get in the field: arms broken, genitals smashed / with rubber bullets, with pipes and bricks and fists.

Uri Rioters and / terrorists.

Hala Ask Edriss, he's a doctor, he's seen what your troops do to teenagers in / Gaza.

Uri Jew-haters. /

Hala And for what crime? Flying a flag? Throwing stones and burning tires?!

Uri (*to* **Motti**) We don't have to listen to this / Motti.

Edriss The Geneva Conventions are "real" aren't they? But you wouldn't know it from the way you—

Uri You think the army wants to do these things!?

Motti What's the point of this outburst, Edriss?

Uri (*to* **Hala**) They are forced to!

Faisal How about a break? Who wants coffee? We have doughnut holes. "Munchkins" they're called. Everyone have a / munchkin.

Ibrahim (*calmly*) The point Motti, if I may call you that, is that we are here, ostensibly, to talk about coming to an agreement towards a sustainable peace, no?

There is a silence; all heads turn towards **Ibrahim**.

Ibrahim And by even agreeing to negotiate with you outside of the parameters of international law and without even the *mention* of sovereignty for the Palestinians, we're making a *huge* compromise . . . And not only in legal terms, but in that we are conceding land for which we have titles to, which is ours under every law except the law of your holy books. So don't think it is you and only you who are making concessions.

Uri And which concessions are those?

Hala Don't play dumb, you know better than anyone how we've had no choice but to watch you for the past four decades as you took what you wanted, *when* you wanted!

Edriss We can walk away from these talks just as fast as you can, Motti.

Motti My God, you're stubborn, Edriss.

Ibrahim With all due respect, sir, you can't just make up rules and follow the ones that suit you. We're simply asking you to adhere to the laws which were created precisely because of what was done to your people in Europe.

Faisal *stands holding the plate of doughnut holes in silence as* **Edriss** *and* **Motti** *light cigarettes.*

Motti (*to* **Edriss**) I see why you fired Bamyeh . . . (*Beat.*)

Motti *turns to* **Uri**.

Motti This is when I should storm out of here, right, Uri?

Uri *nods*.

Motti Edriss, let me have a word with you. Alone.

Edriss *nods to the others who exit, along with* **Uri**.

Motti He's smart that one.

Edriss Like his father.

Motti Is that so?

Edriss I won't bother to ask if you know who his father was. I assume you have files on all of us, especially the kids of ones you've assassinated.

Motti Edriss . . .

Edriss In fact, weren't you there, Motti?

Motti Watch yourself.

Edriss A spring morning in Beirut, soft breeze off the sea, after a night of rain? Salim's door swings open and two men disguised as Arabs fired twenty-seven Israeli bullets that ended him before he could even get out of bed, before he could put his glasses on or smoke his morning cigarette. Wasn't that your handiwork?

Motti No.

Edriss For some reason I thought that was your squad.

Motti I was more involved in the car bombs side of things. You're thinking of Ehud.

Edriss Ahh, yes. Ehud. And remind me what post he holds these days? Chief of . . . ?

Motti Chief of the General Staff.

Edriss Right. You know, another friend of mine, a poet, he had the pleasure of running into Ehud one morning too. Ehud was dressed as a woman that time to get through our lines unnoticed. I'm sure you've heard what happened next.

Motti Stop this petty game or I / walk.

Edriss Shot him in the mouth. No more rhymes out of that ungrateful refugee's mouth.

Motti *and* **Edriss** *stare at each other. The following exchange is somehow calm.*

Motti You know, I could pull out the files of the people you answer to, as well.

Edriss Don't compare the acts of the occupied and the occupier, Motti. That said, I have no issue condemning the mistakes of my comrades, especially once you and your buddies are all in The Hague.

Motti Why are we doing / this?

Edriss I wonder, when you go into a cabinet meeting or into the parliament, and they surround you on all sides, these assassins and war criminals and religious zealots . . .?

Motti Enough. / It's . . .

Edriss Do you condemn them? Or do you just smile at them, pat them on the back? Have a laugh and plan an outing with the wives? Perhaps a picnic in one of the parks you planted over a village you "cleansed" in '48?

Beat.

Motti Listen, I don't know what they'll say in Tel Aviv about this jurisdiction offer. Actually, I do. They'll say no. Most likely. But I'll see what I can do. Put it in writing. But let's keep it between us.

Edriss We'll get it to you tomorrow.

Motti The sooner the better. Rabin and Peres are restless these days.

Edriss Arafat too. Politicians . . .

They get up and start packing up their stuff.

Motti Speaking of politicians, I hear Mazen Haddad is in town.

Edriss *bristles but smiles and shrugs.*

Motti So, from now on, it's the future? We let the past go, yes?

Edriss I don't think so. But we'll get you that proposal. And I'll keep Hala from knocking out your young colleague.

He offers him the doughnut holes. **Motti** *takes one. They eat doughnut holes in silence for a moment.* **Motti** *excuses himself, exits. After a beat,* **Mazen** *enters.*

Mazen Avoiding me, comrade?

Edriss Just been busy, Mazen.

They shake and kiss on the cheeks, cordially, but coldly.

Mazen You know, I went to the Smithsonian today. Saw a painting. By some depressing Dutch master. It reminded me of you, Edriss. It really did.

Edriss How's the old man?

Mazen Chairman Arafat is fine. Fine.

He picks through the doughnuts as he talks.

Made it to the Space Museum too. Always fascinated by astronauts. During the siege in Beirut, sometimes I'd stare up, past the flares and tracers into the great beyond. Imagine myself up there.

Edriss They've already sent a monkey to outer space, Mazen. Sorry.

Mazen *laughs heartily, from his gut.*

Mazen Well, I'm more gorilla-sized these days. Have they sent a gorilla to the moon yet?

Edriss What news from Tunis?

Mazen You haven't been calling as much.

Edriss We try to be in touch when there's something of importance to pass on.

Mazen There's always something to pass on as far as the old man is concerned.

Edriss Well, it's the same dance as before. Israelis won't discuss much of substance. We've just put together / a proposal—

Mazen (*cutting* **Edriss** *off*) We've been hearing that you and the rest have been stubborn with them.

Edriss Isn't that what we are supposed to do?

Mazen Oh come on, Edriss, the Israelis won't budge because you gave them a good lecture. Just go easy on the legal talk for now, build trust. The Israelis are scared to talk about these things as you word them. So word them a bit differently and see what happens.

Edriss Scared? They have hundreds of nuclear weapons! They're not scared of us, just scared to say sorry.

Mazen Time is running out, Edriss, quicker than you know. And the pressure is on *us*, not them. If we have to take out a word here, a word there, who cares! We need a deal. This is it, man. We trust you. The people do. But their patience will run out, too. It doesn't always pay to be stubborn.

Edriss Mazen, if you want to sign a deal that isn't stubborn, why was I dragged from Gaza to Madrid to bloody DC? I hate this place.

Mazen I'm only saying we can't afford to be stalled like this. We have to keep in mind our people's expectations. Their suffering. That is our ticking clock.

A beat . . . **Mazen** *pops a doughnut in his mouth and cleans his fingers off.*

I like the boy, by the way.

Edriss Me too.

Mazen *and* **Edriss** *exit in opposite directions.*

Scene Five

The next morning, back at the main negotiating table. A phone rings. They put it on speaker and **Denny***'s voice is heard.*

Denny   Edress.

Edriss   Hello, Denny. It's actually Edriss. "Ed-reese."

Denny   Sorry. Lot on my mind.

Edriss   That's OK, Denny.

Hala   After all, why would we expect the man tasked with forging Mideast peace to have a grasp of the Arabic language, Denny?

Denny   Touché, Ms. Adnan.

Hala   That's French, Denny, not Arabic.

Denny   Listen, Ed-reese, I just wanted to ask about the bridging proposal. What'd you think?

Edriss *takes out the enormous binder* **Denny** *handed him the day before and puts it on the table.*

Edriss   We were . . . intrigued.

Denny   Good, good.

Edriss   We all agreed it was a fresh take on bridging the gap between us and the Israelis.

Denny   That's what we hoped. What about it specifically did you find intriguing?

Edriss   Hala.

Hala   Well, we were intrigued by the fact that this document, which was put together by you, the "neutral third party," offers us *less* than the Israelis already offered us two months ago.

Denny *is silent.*

Edriss   What Ms. Adnan is suggesting is that it seems to bridge nothing, Denny. Except the Labor and Likud positions in Israel.

Denny   We took into account all the sides on this one, Edriss.

Hala   You did manage to bridge their latest offer, which was unacceptable, to the offer before that, which was even more unacceptable.

Denny   That's an exaggeration.

Hala   We're beginning to think the term "honest broker" is an exaggeration, Mr. Martin.

Denny   We're doing the best we can here. You people should be able to understand that.

Edriss   Let's just move on. Keep working. I'm sure we can / find a way to—

Denny   The President wants this to happen. If you have some edits here and there, I'm open to that.

Edriss All of it, Denny. Edit all of it.

There is a beat.

Denny Well, I think you should know that you're gonna have to bend a little to make a deal. One way or another.

He hangs up. As soon as he does, **Edriss** *throws the binder in the trash.*

Edriss We've been bent to the point of cracking.

Hala These people are all out of their bloody minds!

Faisal We have to be a bit more diplomatic with the Americans.

Edriss Faisal, get up to Mazen's room, see if there's any word from Tunis?

Faisal *exits. Lights shift to* **Ibrahim** *in the "lobby" working.* **Uri** *enters.*

Uri Counselor Abu-Eid. Just the man I wanted to see.

Ibrahim Ah, Uri Ayalon. Born in New York, 1958, moved to Israel with your family when you were eight. Grew up in a kibbutz then later an illegal settlement. Military service, then re-upped, excelled, and wound up in military intelligence.

Uri Not bad.

Ibrahim Saw action in southern Lebanon in '82, which must have been great. We certainly appreciate your service.

Uri You're welcome. Done yet?

Ibrahim Marched back home to Tel Aviv and cleaned up nicely. But only after attending a couple protests and some soul-searching sessions with a good liberal shrink in Tel-Aviv. That last part is just a guess, of course. Then on to law school at Stanford before heading back to the Promised Land to become one of the baddest and brightest defending the Israeli Defense Forces.

Uri I am impressed.

Ibrahim Now. How may I be of service to you, counselor?

Uri (*in a low voice*) I was wondering maybe if you've you been hearing anything about a back channel, in Europe or something? It's probably just a rumor but . . . Anything like that ring a bell?

Ibrahim Cashing in on our budding friendship so soon, Uri? I'm surprised. I think we're moving a little too fast for my taste.

Uri Perhaps we got off on the wrong foot.

Ibrahim Or perhaps this is you trying to turn me into your snitch? Isn't that how you guys operate in the territories?

Uri Please, Ibrahim. I would have to have something on you to turn you. A secret. A weakness. But I don't have a thing. Not yet.

Ibrahim   Keep digging, Uri. One day, if you're lucky, maybe you'll get me in your web.

Uri   Forget you heard anything from me. That said, if you hear anything from anyone else, let me know.

Ibrahim   You'll be the first person I tell.

Uri   Well, it was worth a try.

The two men walk in opposite directions and **Ibrahim** *returns to the table, just as* **Faisal** *enters.*

Faisal   I knock and knock and knock. And nothing.

Edriss   Probably he's out.

Faisal   No. I can hear the TV, blaring bloody Road Runner cartoons with the "beep-beep, beep-beep" . . . And I swear I could hear Mazen in there, laughing and then coughing then laughing!

Edriss   Ibrahim, you go up and try.

Ibrahim *exits, the lights dim on the round table.*

Scene Six

Lights shift to **Mazen** *upstage. He sits with his back to the audience on a lazy-boy chair in front of the screen on the backstage wall. As Wile E. Coyote falls off a cliff,* **Mazen** *roars with laughter and lights another cigarette. A knock on the door.* **Mazen** *ignores it.*

Ibrahim (*offstage*)   Mazen. It's Ibrahim.

Mazen *turns the volume down then rises and lets* **Ibrahim** *in.*

Mazen   More like his pops every day. Come, come in. Excuse the mess.

He notices **Ibrahim** *noticing the cartoon. He lights a cigarette.*

Mazen   There's a backstory to this, really. (*Beat.*) When I was young. They lined up the men between the church and the mosque. I remember that well. When they came to our village in '48, the Zionist militias. I was twelve. I ran north with my grandmother and my sisters, my mother too. We didn't stop until we were in Lebanon. A week later my uncles made their way. But not my father. He had fought the British in the '30s, you see, so he was a threat to them. We thought he was dead. He should have been. But one day several years later he showed up at the refugee camp where we had been stuck since we left our village. He was missing an eye. And when people asked my father how he escaped and how he lost his eye, he would only smile and say, I can't tell you . . . but you should see the other guy. Anyway, one evening they brought a projector to the UN school in the camp and showed the kids a cartoon. Bugs Bunny. I stood in back with the older kids and watched, and the bird, this Road

Runner. He reminded me of my father, you know. Always outrunning this crazy coyote on his tail, surviving. So whenever I find it on TV now, I watch. Think of my father. Running, running, all his life.

He is silent for a beat. He then puts out his cigarette.

So, son. What can I do for you?

Ibrahim Edriss sent me to see if there's been any response to the jurisdiction proposal?

Mazen Jurisdiction? No. Nothing today. Sit, sit. Tell me how it's going down there?

Ibrahim Slow. But I think we might be onto something.

Mazen Cigarette?

Ibrahim *declines.*

Mazen I'm expecting a call from the old man any minute now. I told him about you . . . I told him "that Ibrahim, he might be a leader one day soon, he's got it in him."

Ibrahim Thank you. (*Beat*.) Look, I figure it's nothing, but I wonder if you knew anything about a back channel of some sort? In Europe?

Mazen *takes in* **Ibrahim**.

Mazen No. Why?

Ibrahim Nothing. I was just thinking that I might have inadvertently gotten more information out of one of our Israeli colleagues than he got out of me. I figured I'd come to you first about it.

Mazen Smart as a whip aren't you. And Edriss hasn't heard anything of this . . . rumor?

Ibrahim Not that I know of.

Mazen Good. It *is* just a rumor of course.

The phone rings.

Like clockwork . . . You answer it.

He picks up the receiver and gives it to **Ibrahim***, who replies in Arabic.*

Ibrahim Hello? . . . Chairman Arafat . . . Ibrahim Abu Eid speaking . . . Salim's boy, yes . . . Thank you, sir . . . Yes I'm doing as Mazen says. Of course . . . Yes, that's right . . . My mother's fine, thank you . . . Well we're proposing the idea of jurisdiction, as you know . . . We're trying to hold out for the best terms . . . Yes, I know, sir. I agree . . . Yes I understand . . . Oh . . . No, I won't say a thing. I'm simply happy to be helping the cause, in any way I am asked . . . God willing, sir.

He passes the phone to **Mazen***. He listens, nodding.*

Mazen (*to* **Ibrahim**) Excuse me a moment.

Mazen *unwinds the phone cord and stretches it to the back of the stage or perhaps to another room, unseen, only the cord visible. He speaks quietly, mostly unheard.*

Ibrahim *stands alone. He looks around the room, perhaps at some papers, a half-empty bottle of whisky.*

After several moments **Mazen** *returns.*

Mazen   We'll look over them on the way there.

He hangs up.

Ibrahim   On the way where?

Mazen   Tunis . . . The old man insists you accompany me there and then on to Oslo.

Ibrahim   When?

Mazen   Tonight. You'll be an adviser to me and Chairman Arafat. If you want to, that is?

Ibrahim   Yes. I . . . Yes. And the talks here?

Mazen   The talks are no longer in Washington, Ibrahim. Not the real talks. Oslo is where it's happening. A direct line between Israel and the PLO. That means they've recognized us. This is our moment.

Ibrahim   Shouldn't Edriss be there?

Mazen   These are at the highest levels. Rabin sent his big shots. Edriss would understand the significance, trust me. But he mustn't know. No one must know for now. Edriss has done us all a great service over the past two years, and everyone is grateful, and now it's time to make history.

Ibrahim *nods.*

Mazen   Hey, I'm proud of you, kid. I'll call your room in an hour. Be ready.

Ibrahim *exits.* **Mazen** *sits down, lights another cigarette, and turns up the volume of the cartoons.*

Scene Seven

Motti *and* **Uri** *sit at a table downstage.* **Motti** *is looking over documents.* **Uri** *hangs up the phone.*

Motti   So?

Uri   Same thing Peres told you.

Motti   To stall?

Uri   And get on the next plane to Norway. We're close, Motti. Peace. It almost sounds surreal, that word.

A knock. **Edriss** *enters with several files.*

Edriss Gentlemen, I've brought the jurisdiction proposal, as we discussed.

Uri *reaches to take it from* **Edriss**, *but* **Edriss** *makes sure to put it directly into* **Motti**'s *hands.*

Motti Thank you, Edriss.

Edriss Wait until you read it.

Motti I just hope it's not too late.

Edriss Too late?

He reads **Edriss**, *who clearly has not heard.*

Motti Nothing. You know how impatient politicians can be.

Uri You must excuse us, Edriss. We were in the middle of something important. But we'll look at this.

Edriss Of course.

He turns to leave but stops.

Have you heard the joke about the Mossad agent?

Motti *shakes his head.*

Edriss There's a Mossad agent, a KGB agent, and a CIA man, and they decide to find out who is the most skilled intelligence agent in the world. So they go to a forest and release a hare, and whoever can track the rabbit and bring it back the fastest is the superior spy. So the KGB agent goes after the rabbit first and is back in 20 minutes. Not bad. Next is the CIA agent, who returns in ten minutes! Hard to beat. But the Mossad agent is confident. He goes off after the rabbit and five minutes pass, then ten, fifteen, twenty, and after a half an hour he's still not back. So the CIA and KGB man go looking for him. They hear shouting ahead and finally come upon the Mossad agent in a clearing where he is punching the hell out of a donkey and shouting: "Admit you're a rabbit! Admit you're a fucking rabbit! Admit it!"

He laughs and **Motti** *too, though* **Uri** *is not amused.* **Edriss** *nods and exits.*

Motti He doesn't know.

Uri Maybe it's for the better, Motti . . .

Motti Maybe. But . . . Yes, perhaps it's better.

He exits. **Uri** *picks up the document* **Edriss** *gave them and tosses it in the trash as he exits.*

Scene Eight

Edriss *stands at the table with* **Hala** *and* **Faisal**.

Edriss Well, where the fuck have they gone, then?

Hala Something's not right. It's been two days.

Edriss And we're sure Mazen is not in DC anymore?

Faisal He checked out of the hotel, Edriss, just like Motti. Gone.

Edriss And Ibrahim?

Hala Off the radar. Even his mother doesn't know where he is.

Faisal And if she doesn't know the precise location of her only son . . .

Edriss Something's very wrong.

Hala All he said to her was that he was traveling.

Edriss Mazen.

Hala Denny doesn't know what the hell is going on either. Maybe it's nothing.

Faisal I think we just got blitzed.

The phone rings. They all freeze . . . **Edriss** *answers.*

Edriss Hello. Yes. We've been calling for days. Did you get the jurisdiction proposal? . . . I understand you've been busy, sir . . . mmmhm. . . . What?

He sits down and listens for some moments.

Yes . . . Fine. Please . . . Fax it right away. Thank you.

Edriss, *pale, lowers the phone.*

Hala What's going on?

Edriss They've made a deal.

Hala What deal?

Edriss I don't know.

Faisal When?

Edriss Last night, in the middle of the night, he said. In Norway.

Faisal Let's not jump to conclusions. We have to wait and see what this is all about.

The fax machine starts spitting out sheets of paper. They all turn and stare at it.

Scene Nine

Several days later, a Washington, DC press conference.

Hala Mazen Haddad, the PLO rep from Tunis, who was involved in the details of this agreement will be arriving shortly and he will take questions. At the moment we are still being briefed on the details of these secret negotiations. That will be all for now, thank you.

She steps away from the podium as **Uri** *takes her place. As he arranges his papers,* **Hala** *and* **Faisal** *exit stage with their suitcases in tow.* **Uri** *is alone at the podium.*

Uri The Israelis and the PLO have reached an historic compromise. And while Israel has reached her hand in peace, we are still committed to ensuring our security and the integrity of a Jewish state for generations to come. The Palestinians will now be on the spot to prove their willingness to make similar compromises for peace. We are confident, though, that we have taken the first step.

The lights shift to **Edriss**, *walking with a suitcase.* **Mazen** *enters, also with a suitcase, going in the opposite direction. They stop in front of each other.*

Mazen Big day.

Edriss Big deal.

Mazen Off already?

Edriss Flight to Cairo in three hours. Then the bus to Gaza. Long trip for an old man.

Mazen You should be here with us. It's a big day, for all of us, Edriss.

Edriss I bet I still get strip-searched at the border by the Israelis.

Mazen It's just a first step. It's not perfect, I know.

Edriss As far as I can tell it's the same deal we've been saying "no" to for over a year now.

Mazen You should be happy. Everyone else is!

A beat.

Edriss Let Ibrahim go. He's smart. Too smart to work for you.

Mazen He is smart. Ambitious.

Edriss He's young. Too young to see it maybe.

Mazen We did what we thought was best under the circumstances, Edriss. Ibrahim understands that.

Edriss Just do one thing for me. Tell him I'll smack him across his pretty face the next time I see him.

He exits the stage pulling his suitcase behind him.

Mazen (*calling offstage*) You'll see we were right. Time will prove us right.

Blackout.

Act Two

Scene One

Fifteen years later. The first days of 2009. A Gaza home. It is the middle of the night and **Edriss** *sits smoking a cigarette in the dark. There are the thuds of massive explosions in the distance, the whine of ambulances. A knock on the door.*

Edriss   Who is it?

Ibrahim   Ibrahim.

Edriss   Ibrahim who?

Ibrahim   Ibrahim Abu-Eid.

Edriss *opens the door, ushers him in.*

Edriss   Watch your step.

Ibrahim   Hello, Edriss

Edriss   Electricity went out. No gas for the generator. I would offer you tea . . .

Ibrahim   Water's / fine . . .

Edriss   Water's been cut too.

Ibrahim   Don't worry. Nothing at all / I'm fine.

Edriss   I need to save it for brushing my teeth, shaving, the / toilet

Ibrahim   I understand. Of course, '*ammou*. How are you? It's / been . . .

Edriss   Johnnie Walker? That I have. Hamas turns a blind eye for me. I suppose I've earned it.

He goes to the cupboard and takes out a bottle and pours two small glasses.

Ibrahim   Where are your kids?

Edriss   Just me and the Apaches overhead. Their lullabies tuck me in every night.

They touch glasses.

My sons are in Amman, working for NGOs. My daughter is in London. They're the lucky Gazans.

Ibrahim   So why don't you go, get out of here?

Edriss   You don't think they've tried, begging their old father to go? Why should I leave?

Ibrahim   Because it's not safe and you're alone. Come with me. Until it blows over.

Edriss   Until what blows over?

Ibrahim   The Israelis will invade any minute now. These airstrikes are just the beginning, Edriss.

Edriss   They come and go, come and go, since I was a kid. So when will it "blow over"? I'd rather be alone now than have to deal with their border bureaucracies and humiliation from a coffin. I don't want to die in some horrible hospital in Cairo or London. God forbid in Amman. I hate that place.

Ibrahim   Come on, you look well, no talk of death.

Edriss   Oh shut up. You've always been a flatterer, Ibrahim. I look like King Tut *after* they dug him up.

His laughter turns into a cough, after which he lights a cigarette and puffs away.

I assume you are gonna get out of Gaza before they move their tanks in and flatten us? Which reminds me of a joke: Devil shows up at a bar, night after night, and the man next to him says, "Satan, you've been in this bar every night for the past month? Why don't you go back to hell?" The devil turns to him, finishes his glass in one sip, and says: "Don't you know? The Israelis have closed all the borders of Gaza, so I can't go back."

Ibrahim *doesn't laugh.*

Edriss   Get it? Gaza's hell. They won't let him back into hell. Never mind.

Ibrahim   I got it.

Edriss *pours another couple shots.*

Edriss   So when are you going to get the Gaza out of hell?

Ibrahim   In the morning. I wanted to come here first, before I left. Pay you my respects.

Edriss   I'm old, but I'm not dead yet.

Ibrahim   That's not what I meant. It's just that I haven't seen you since . . .

Edriss   Since you eloped with Mazen?

Ibrahim   Since '93, yes.

Edriss   Fifteen years since Oslo. Jesus.

Ibrahim   I should have called.

Edriss   I've seen you though. On the news, from Ramallah, at the press conferences. Heard you started your own NGO.

Ibrahim   A law center. I spend half the year in Ramallah and half in the States.

Edriss   Good for you. American money?

Ibrahim   Some. Mostly European. Foreign aid is the gas that Ramallah runs on.

Edriss   And the NGO is the vehicle everyone's driving through the streets.

Ibrahim   Ramallah is booming, yes.

Edriss   So is Gaza . . .

A dull thud then a large boom in the distance, a shell or a missile falling.

What timing, eh. I'm telling you, we read each other's minds, their aircraft and me. That was the police station they just hit again. Good thing too, because traffic cops are dangerous. What with their whistles.

Ibrahim   I know what you must think of me.

Edriss   What I think of you? You're a brilliant young man. I hear you've been doing good work too, so presumably you stopped working for Mazen, who inspires fetid mediocrity in the people around him. And God knows we need all the lawyers we can get fighting for us, to dig us from this grave.

Suddenly the electricity kicks in.

And then there was light!

He gets to his feet when another loud thud is heard, this time closer and the windows rattle. The electricity once again cuts off. Back in darkness.

But the IDF said, "No, God! No light is better for them! Let them grope!"

Edriss   I was going to make you a cup of coffee / but . . .

Ibrahim   Whisky's fine.

Edriss   So, let's cut to the chase: How did you get into Gaza? That's no easy feat these days.

Ibrahim   Pulled some strings.

Edriss   And why exactly are you here?

Ibrahim   To convince you to come with me, Edriss.

Edriss   I still love the way you say my name, with a hint of American in your tongue when you roll that "r."

Another series of thuds / explosions. The windows shake again.

Ibrahim   We can't stay much longer, day is going to break soon.

Edriss   We're near the UN building. It's no guarantee, but in theory it should be safer here.

Ibrahim   Ramallah is much / safer.

Edriss   I must get a bit of sleep now. I have to look my best for the morning. You know their smart bombs have cameras on them.

Ibrahim   There's a car. I've arranged for it to take us across. Just until the fighting's passed. And then you can return.

Edriss   Fighting doesn't pass. It stays. It settles into the air, the concrete, the dust, the kids. Even the animals. The animals are changed. No. It never leaves. (*Beat*). Fifteen years and *now* you want to save me?

Ibrahim   Come to Ramallah. There at least you can talk to the press, be of use.

Edriss   A car you said? Coming here?

Ibrahim   The border will be opened at dawn. We want to be there then.

Edriss   I wish you had told me a car was coming. Ferdinand hates cars.

Ibrahim   Who's Ferdinand?

A long beat, **Edriss** *deep in thought.*

Edriss   You know what? There's no reason to die here alone. I'll come! But I'll need an office. And a car. And some kind of title, something to make an old man feel important. I can help you. Deal?

Ibrahim   Of course. Yes. Of course. Anything. Can I help you pack some things?

Edriss   I'll buy a new suit there. The clothes in Gaza are all second hand, donated by the Scandinavians. Half of the men here are walking around in worn out suits two sizes too big. It's not fair, really. Make yourself comfortable, I'll be right back.

He exits. **Ibrahim** *paces for several beats as the electricity flickers on and then off. He stops in his tracks.*

Ibrahim   You're not really coming with me are you?

Edriss *walks out in an old two-piece pajama suit, brushing his teeth.*

Edriss   You always did believe anything. Any flattery, any praise. Now I know how Arafat and Mazen seduced you. Ferdinand is my pet fox by the way.

Ibrahim   Please reconsider, Edriss. The car will be here any minute.

Edriss   And who would feed Ferdinand while I was gone? Who would dust my Fairuz records? Who would talk to my books? Who would count the bombs falling from the sky?

He spits out his toothpaste and then rinses his mouth.

Ibrahim   What do you want me to say?

Edriss   Say goodnight, Ibrahim, goodnight and goodbye. And smile. You have your father's smile.

Ibrahim   I'm not my father!

Edriss   I know.

A car horn is heard outside.

Edriss   Your Mercedes has arrived.

There is a knock at the door. **Edriss** *opens it to reveal a man with a rifle slung over his shoulder.*

Moose   Good evening, sir.

Edriss Evening. Pleasure to meet you . . . And you are?

Ibrahim His name is Mustafa. Could you give us a second, Mustafa.

Moose I prefer Moose, actually. I go by Moose.

Ibrahim Edriss, we can talk in the car. Please.

The car horn honks again, repeatedly.

Edriss Whoever is in that car is gonna get an Israeli missile through the roof if he keeps honking like that.

Moose Well, you know Abu Thowra, he's always impatient to get moving.

Edriss *freezes. He shoots a look at* **Ibrahim** *who looks away.*

Edriss . . . Hey, Moose, give me your radio thing.

Moose Official business only, sir, sorry.

Ibrahim Just go, Mustafa,

Edriss Moose! He likes to be called Moose, Ibrahim! Respect the man's wishes. Now give me your walkie-talkie, damn it.

Moose *gives it to him.* **Edriss** *speaks into it.*

Edriss Mazen! Abu Thowra himself! How the fuck are you, man? Edriss here. Haven't seen you in this ghetto for years. I've seen you on TV. You've gained weight. And your mustache looks stiffer.

He listens, there is no response but quiet static, and perhaps the sound of someone breathing.

I know you're there. Quit honking that horn and come in, have a drink. No ice but you'll make due . . . You can't come here and not say hi! I know you're there so get your fat ass out of the car and come in! You have plenty of time to make it to the border. Just one last handshake, to put it all in the past. I'll be leaving this world any day now. C'mon, you old jackal. I'm in my pajamas for God's sake, I won't hurt you.

A beat. . . . then the sound of a car door slamming. **Edriss** *shouts offstage.*

Edriss There he is! Mad Mazen himself! Listen, brother, go through the garden and the back door and then the kitchen so you don't track in mud through my living room. And watch out for my thyme bushes.

He closes the window. After a moment a commotion is heard and then the sound of **Mazen**'*s screaming.* **Moose** *reaches for his gun and cocks it in alarm . . .* **Mazen**, *wearing a fake beard, stumbles in, his pant leg torn.*

Mazen You have a wild animal in your garden, Edriss! Moose, go shoot that fucking thing.

He moves immediately in the direction of the back door.

Edriss Don't you dare lay a finger on Ferdinand! He's been through enough.

Mazen That crazed beast is yours?

Edriss He's not crazed. He just doesn't like cars. Here, throw a bit of scotch on your leg and it'll be fine.

He slides a bottle to **Mazen**.

Ibrahim Why the hell do you have a fox in your backyard, Edriss?

Edriss There used to be a zoo in Gaza. A little park. Nothing much, really. But the Israelis bulldozed it a couple years back. Half the animals were killed, maimed, left for dead, half-deranged. Ferdinand escaped. Ended up here. I let him stay.

He walks over to **Mazen** *who is dressing his wounds.*

Edriss No hard feelings?

Mazen Go fuck yourself, Edriss.

Edriss It seemed so fitting. A chicken and a fox. And now a moose. Moose, go get a glass for your boss. He's thirsty.

Moose We should go, sir.

Mazen Let me rest a moment. Glass.

Edriss I told you he was thirsty.

He pours him a full glass of whisky. **Mazen** *tries to sip it but the beard is in the way.*

Edriss Nice beard by the way.

Mazen *tears the beard off.*

Mazen Well, I never thought I'd stoop to this, but now that Hamas has turned Gaza into bloody Afghanistan.

Edriss Oh come now. I'm no fan of Hamas but you sound just like the fucking Americans, you know. Do they write your lines for you now, Mazen?

Mazen That's unfair, damn it. Why do you think we're here, Edriss?

Edriss I have no idea. But I bet the beard has more to do with the fact that here the name Mazen Haddad reeks of American money and a place called Oslo.

Mazen For your information I'm here to save Gaza.

Edriss How's that?

Mazen By getting Hamas to agree to a truce!

Edriss I knew it. There's always a dotted line needing to be signed when you appear. Ibrahim, I'm surprised you agreed to such a mission.

Ibrahim Edriss, please.

Edriss Let me see the terms you've got in your pocket, Mazen. Let's see what deal you're pushing on your people this time.

Ibrahim I came for you.

Mazen We are on the brink of a massacre here and I want to stop it before it's too late!

Edriss It *is* too late. Because the past is now. That deal you signed sealed our fate and that dotted line reaches from Oslo to Gaza, from then to this moment, in one zig-zag of barbed wire and walls, checkpoints, settlement blocks, and bomb craters; little dots leading to this madness. And you're one of the authors of all this, whether you like it or not.

Mazen The Israelis and the Americans didn't hold up their end of the deal, that's why we're here, not because we signed a bad deal. They didn't hold up their end!

Edriss But you held your end way up in the air didn't you, Mazen?

Ibrahim Edriss, please, uncle. Enough. We don't have time for —

Edriss Let us. It's been a while . . . And that reminds me.

He walks over to **Ibrahim** *and slaps him across the face.*

Edriss That's for going off in the middle of our negotiations without telling me.

Mazen You always said you weren't a politician, so let it go, it was our decision to make.
It's so damn easy to judge and to criticize from the outside, isn't it, Edriss?

Edriss Outside! I *was* the one on the inside and you were the ones on the outside in Tunis.

Mazen We were and still are committed to the people, Edriss, you have no right to question that!

Edriss I have no rights at all, anymore. We were the ones who knew what was going on on the ground, inside Palestine. We knew the occupation, inside out: where the settlers were, where the water was, we knew the land, which was what we were negotiating after all.

Mazen Negotiations that were getting nowhere! We saw our only chance and we took advantage of the will to make a deal. There was only so much we had the power to do, and so we ran with it, man!

Edriss Right into a trap.

Mazen Well, you know what a famous historian once said? "The greatest acts of statesmanship were made by people who did not know what they were doing."

He laughs as he finishes his glass of whisky.

Hindsight is 20 / 20, friend, so spare me.

Edriss And here we are, fifteen years on, less land, besieged and bombarded, a giant wall around us, and no state in sight.

Mazen And this is all our fault?

Edriss Tell me something, Mazen, 'cause I've always wanted to know if it's really true: did you have proper maps when you signed Oslo?

Silence.

What about English? When Arafat made the final touches, who was translating for him, or was he conducting the negotiations in English himself?

Mazen Yes, in English, over the phone. We were in Oslo, he was in Tunis.

Ibrahim I tried to help, I was trying to tell them everything you had been / saying—

Edriss (*ignoring* **Ibrahim**, *still to* **Mazen**) So you're telling me that the fine points of the future of the Palestinian people were worked out over the phone by a man, God rest his soul, who spoke terrible English, all with no proper maps?

Mazen They had all the cards.

Edriss Cards?

Mazen What should we have done?

Edriss Cards. That's it. A game. We can see who had the better hand. I love games.

Mazen We have no time for fucking games! But if you can help us talk to Hamas . . . they'll listen to you, Edriss.

Edriss So that's why you came? To use me as a puppet to convince Hamas to capitulate?

Mazen *is silent.* **Edriss** *laughs.*

Edriss Oh, I love it! You know what chutzpah is?

Ibrahim We don't have time for this.

Edriss Of course you do. Of course you know what chutzpah is. Because you've got it, man. Got chutzpah coming out your ears.

Mazen I've taken a chance coming here. I trust you'll do the right thing.

Edriss Now that you've squandered every ounce of credibility, Mazen, now that we're walking the steps to the bloody guillotine, *now* you trust me? And you, Ibrahim?

Ibrahim The deal was that if I helped him, we could get you out of here. I thought you'd want to.

Edriss I want to play a game. That's what I want. Who wants to play a game?

Moose I love Texas hold 'em. I learned it when I lived in Cincinnati.

Mazen Moose, shut up and wait outside, keep an eye out.

He exits obediently. **Mazen** *turns back to* **Edriss**.

So you won't talk to Hamas for me? For us?

Edriss   What would you say if I told you that I'd rather die tomorrow than peddle your deal. Excuse me.

He exits.

Mazen   Thinks he's better than everyone. This madness goes back to Beirut.

Ibrahim (*in a whisper*)   There's no more time, Mazen. This was a bad idea. We have to convince him.

Mazen   Yes, yes, I know.

Edriss (*from offstage*)   The cabinet under the photos is full of whisky, help yourself.

Mazen *looks at his watch.*

Mazen   We have a bit more time to kill.

He goes to the cabinet and takes out one of the ten identical bottles of Johnnie Walker.

It's like he knew I was coming.

Edriss *re-enters, still in his pajamas but with a tie around his neck, a suit jacket on, and a briefcase in his hands.*

Edriss   I'm ready.

Ibrahim   Are you serious, Edriss?

Edriss   Dead serious, my boy. Excuse the slippers.

Mazen   So what's this game of yours? Make it quick.

Edriss   No rush. Hamas won't sign anything anyway.

Mazen   In that case.

He pours himself a drink.

Edriss   Moose!

Moose *comes in, his gun at the ready.*

Moose   Sir?

Edriss   Put that thing away and join us.

Moose   Yes, sir.

Mazen   Sir? I'm "sir"! He's "uncle"! Stay outside, you're on duty.

Edriss   No one in Gaza will touch you while you're under my roof. And I'm guessing the Israelis know about your trip here, anyway. Ok, listen, we're gonna play a game, Moose, and we need you . . . Who do you want to be?

Moose   Barack.

Mazen Ehud or Obama?

Moose Obama.

Edriss Try again.

Moose Wolverine?

Edriss How about you play Bill Clinton?

Ibrahim What the hell is this, Edriss?

Edriss (*ceremoniously*) We're playing a game I call "Final Status." Good ole Faisal, eh! Where is he these days?

Ibrahim He left Ramallah a couple years ago.

Edriss Luckily for us, Hala is still at it, fighting the good fight. (*Beat.*) So, the game starts now! I am no longer Edriss. Now I am Mazen. Mazen Haddad.

Mazen In that case, have a drink. (*He laughs at himself, drinks more.*)

Edriss I will, thank you.

Mazen Here you go "Mazen", you handsome dog, you!

He pours **Edriss** *a glass.*

Mazen He's in Paris by the way.

Edriss Who?

Mazen Faisal. He's in Paris, teaching. In fact, "Mazen," you and him fought a couple years back. I remember. I heard that you kicked him out of your office.

Edriss Why would I do such a thing?

Mazen Because he was always after you, Mazen. Always suspicious of you. Always resentful and disrespectful. But you showed him.

Edriss I did didn't I?

Mazen (*getting worked up and blustery*) You told him: "Get the fuck out of my office and don't ever talk to me like that! I'm Mazen Haddad! Abu Thowra! Foreign Minister of the Palestinian Authority! And you're nothing but a goddamn elitist mapmaker with a fancy degree and a fancy accent. Yet you think you can come into my office and demand I step down on false accusations and lies?! I'm not corrupt! The world is corrupt! The Americans are corrupt! The Israelis are corrupt! I am a survivor!"

Edriss I told him that right to his face!

Mazen You sure did "Mazen." Roared. Like a fucking lion.

Moose The whole office heard it.

Mazen And like a good little boy he scurried off to write rude little pieces in the papers about me.

Edriss   You mean me. I'm Mazen.

Mazen   Right. You. About you.

Edriss   God, I can be such an ass can't I?

Moose   You sure can.

Mazen   Boy!

Moose   I'm confused now.

Mazen   So who do I get to play in your game?

Edriss   Let's see, I'm Mazen, Moose is Clinton. So you can be . . . the Israelis.

Mazen   I was hoping I'd get to be you, Edriss, and lecture everyone for hours. (*He laughs, a bit drunk now.*)

Edriss   Well, I would let you but we're playing "Final Status Oslo Edition" and I wasn't at Oslo was I.

Mazen   Fair enough. I'll be the Israelis.

Edriss   Ok . . . And you, Ibrahim, you can be . . .? You can be your father. Salim Abu Eid.

Mazen   He definitely wasn't at Oslo.

Edriss   Yes he was. You just refused to hear him. You ignored him, Mazen.

Moose   My mother used to tell me that Salim Abu Eid was a better speaker than Arafat, Mazen, and even Habash. She said losing him was a huge blow to the revolution. She memorized all / his speeches!

Mazen   I gave some pretty fantastic speeches in my day, / Ok!

Ibrahim   I'm waiting outside in the car, this is . . . a waste of fucking / time.

Edriss   Sit down!

Ibrahim   This is madness, Edriss!

Edriss   If you think this is mad then stick around to witness what the Israelis have in store for us.

Ibrahim   Exactly. They're about to invade and you want to play games! Come. We can hash this all out once you're out of harm's way.

Mazen   Fucking Hamas! If they weren't so goddamn pig-headed!

He slams back another drink.

Edriss   They halted the rockets to barely a trickle. If you can call those pathetic fertilizer-powered projectiles rockets. And look where that got them. Anything short of total surrender would lead to the same result.

There is a tense silence. **Mazen** *pours himself another drink.*

Mazen I think you've mistaken me for someone else. My name is Uri Ayalon. Now. Shall we get on with the negotiations?

Edriss That's the spirit!

Ibrahim Fuck it, give me a drink.

Moose Can I be Arafat?

Edriss But if you're Arafat, you have to be on the phone with us, since Arafat wasn't in Oslo in person.

Moose *has taken a seat on a chair far from the others. He picks up a phone receiver and* **Edriss** *picks up the other, they are on the same line.*

Moose Is this good?

Mazen Perfect.

Edriss Can you hear me, Chairman Arafat?

Moose Loud and clear, "Mazen."

Edriss Good, good.

Moose (*whispers*) Edriss . . . I have a question . . .

Edriss Time out, time out. Yes, Moose?

Moose *talks through the phone, still in a whisper.*

Moose Do you have a keffiyeh?

Edriss Right. Good. Yes. Behind you there, on the bookshelf, right near the encyclopedias.

Moose *turns around and grabs a checkered keffiyeh scarf. He then puts it on his head in the best impersonation of Yasser Arafat's style.*

Moose Ok, time in.

Ibrahim What should I do?

Edriss Whatever your father would have done. Just be here. Watch. Listen. And talk when something needs to be said. I'll listen.

Mazen This is boring. What about me?

Edriss That is, if I can hear you through the incessant barking of my ego.

Mazen What am *I* supposed to do?

Edriss Whatever you want, you're an Israeli now. No rules apply; no laws, no conventions.

Mazen Right. Right.

He lights a cigarette, puts his feet on the table.

Ibrahim   So?

Edriss   Ok, now you pass me the deal, sell it to me.

Mazen *grabs a piece of scrap paper and a pen and slides it across the table to* **Edriss**.

Mazen   Well "Mazen Haddad," here's the deal. We're giving you mutual recognition, immediate withdrawal of IDF troops out of most of Gaza, save for some settlers, and we'll throw in Jericho . . . Plus, we are letting the PLO into Palestine.

Edriss   But you promise we'll talk about all the important stuff later? You promise? Pinkie promise?

Mazen   That's not what happened.

Moose (*on phone*)   Hey, what's going on over there in Oslo?

Edriss (*on the phone*)   So we don't get Jerusalem, no talk of refugees nor about the dismantling of settlements, all of that for something called "Final Status," later, but they promise, they pinkie promise, sir.

Moose   I don't trust pinkies.

Edriss   Trust me. Here, ask the others.

He passes the phone to **Ibrahim**.

Moose (*to* **Ibrahim**)   Ibrahim, what do you think?

Edriss   No, he's not Ibrahim! He's the ghost of Salim Abu-Eid, Ibrahim's father.

Moose   Then who's playing Ibrahim?

Edriss *looks around.*

Edriss   The lampshade. That's Ibrahim. Ask him.

Moose *is stumped.* **Mazen** *sits up.*

Mazen   Time is running out. You say no to this deal, we start from scratch, we go home, you get nothing. Nada. This is the only chance you get. The window is closing.

Moose (*to the lamp*)   Ibrahim, what do you think?

Edriss   Wait! I forgot to tell you the most important part of the deal they're offering.

Moose (*genuinely excited*)   What? No. Let me guess . . .

Mazen   You're Arafat, not Moose, remember.

Moose (*suddenly back in character*)   Oh yes. Ahem. So, what's the best part of the deal?

Edriss   We get to move our offices from Tunis into Palestine! After all these years, we get a foothold, not much, but something, and they'll give us flags, too. Exile ends.

Mazen Yes! For the first time your flag will not be outlawed, and children will not have their arms broken for carrying it on the streets or hanging it on rooftops.

Ibrahim That's something.

For the first time, he lights a cigarette.

Mazen It's profound, it's symbolic. It's a start, no?

Edriss Yes, that's right, Chairman Arafat, we can fly the flag. We'll have our own security force, with uniforms, nice green matching uniforms.

Ibrahim *starts blowing smoke rings.* **Edriss** *notices.*

Mazen Not the old tattered, patchwork discarded uniforms from Yugoslavia and Algeria that were an embarrassment to any army. No more sets of two left boots sent from China. No fourth-hand Russian pistols.

Ibrahim I liked those uniforms; their asymmetry was their poetry . . . a patchwork revolution.

Edriss *stares at* **Ibrahim**.

Mazen Shut up, Salim, you were always an idealistic poet with no pragmatism. Romantic and sentimental.

Edriss Excuse me, "Uri" but I'd appreciate it if you didn't speak to the ghost of my friend Salim Abu Eid. Anyway, you can't see him.

Moose What else is in the deal they're offering, "Mazen"?

Edriss Some light arms, Chairman Arafat, and cars, and maybe a helicopter or two. And lots of European and American aid. To build a country, one villa, one police station, one Mercedes at a time.

Moose But the settlements stay?

Edriss Yes. But guess what we get if we sign this piece of paper?

Moose What?

Edriss A post office. Our own stamps! And maybe one will have your face on it, Chairman, imagine that!

Mazen Don't get carried away.

Ibrahim Was I sentimental? Unrealistic?

Edriss (*to* **Ibrahim**) So much so the Israelis had to kill you, Salim. You imagined something after the fighting. Sang it to us and they silenced you for that. Knew you had ten times the imagination of me or Arafat, or any of the others.

Mazen Wait, are you saying that as Edriss or Mazen?

Edriss Sorry I forgot I was "Mazen." Let me try again. (*To* **Ibrahim**.) I was jealous of you, Salim, because you had the balls to stand up to Arafat when I didn't, even when we all knew he was wrong. The old man respected that. I was threatened by it. Because you had the nerve to go it alone, Salim, to take the revolution on your back when all I could do was cower in the chief's shadow and tell him what he wanted to hear. And when they assassinated you, Arafat cried. But not me, not Mazen Haddad. And I outlived the old man didn't I?! So we'll never know if he would have cried at my funeral.

Beat. **Mazen** *stares down* **Edriss** *then gulps his drink.*

Mazen   Back to the deal, then. What's it gonna be?

Moose   What does Ibrahim think?

They all look at the lamp. Silence.

Mazen   That's a yes.

Ibrahim   Maybe it's a no. Maybe he's too scared to say no.

Edriss   The son of Salim Abu Eid, scared? I don't believe it.

Mazen   He's more practical than his father was, he's a politician, not a poet.

Ibrahim   Maybe he's in over his head. Not scared but intimidated. And young.

Edriss   And deferential in the presence of leaders who he grew up hearing about,

Ibrahim   Old men who knew his father,

Edriss   Who use his name, tell him he can become a real Palestinian hero, like his dad.

Ibrahim   Maybe.

Mazen   Will you sign it or not? Last chance!

Edriss   And if we don't?

Mazen   If you don't, it's back to unrecognized, invisible, untouchable lepers in exile. To build a state piece by piece, slowly, but surely; or to die. To die as withering, bent trees in Tunis.

Edriss (*to* **Moose**)   What do you think, old man? Is it a deal?

Moose   Sounds tempting.

Mazen   Ten seconds!

Edriss   Salim, old friend, what do you say? To sign or not to sign? I say we do it.

Edriss *and* **Ibrahim** *share a moment.*

Mazen   Five seconds!

Ibrahim   I can see the future, Mazen.

Edriss   And what does it tell you?

Mazen   Time's up!

Ibrahim Damned if you do, damned if you don't.

Mazen Exactly!

Edriss Sad but true.

Ibrahim But we are a patient people.

Edriss Yes. We are.

Ibrahim No. /

Edriss (*to* **Mazen**) The answer is no.

Moose I agree. Close call.

He turns to the lampshade.

And what about Ibrahim, what does he think?

Edriss/Ibrahim He agrees.

Edriss *rises to his feet.*

Edriss (*to* **Mazen**) Now watch closely. I'm about to illustrate something you should've learned following your mom around the *souq* as a kid.

Mazen And what's that?

Edriss *rips the paper in half and then in half again and again.*

Edriss How to walk away from a shitty deal. Even if the salesman has sworn on his mother's grave that it's the best you'll ever get. Call his bluff and keep walking until he calls you back and you get the deal you want.

Mazen And if they never call you back, huh? If they never offer you the deal you think you deserve? What then?!

Edriss Then at least you go home knowing you didn't get ripped off.

Mazen What bullshit.

Moose *looks out the window into the pre-dawn light.*

Moose They're in formation now. They're coming. Soon, sir. You can hear the drones above, and the armor to the east. It won't be long.

Mazen *is slumped with the drink in hand, unresponsive, gloomy.*

Edriss Game over. Time to get up. The sun is almost up and there will be a line to get across the border.

Ibrahim It would make me feel better to know you're out of harm's way, that you aren't alone.

Edriss Don't worry. Ferdinand will protect me. And your father will keep me company.

Moose I'll start the car.

He shakes **Edriss'** *hand and exits.*

Mazen What is it you want from me, Edriss?

Edriss Nothing, Mazen. Nothing anymore.

Mazen I'll stay. That's what you want, isn't it?

Edriss Not at all.

Mazen No. I'll stay with you, just the two of us, two wash-outs who failed their country but sacrificed their blood in return.

Edriss It's not about blood.

Mazen Then what?

Edriss It's about having some pride, Mazen.

Mazen So that's your plan? To die a martyr! So you can't be blamed for anything? That way those of us strong enough to survive in this fucking jungle, we get all the blame?

A car horn. **Mazen** *rises, lifts his glass, bows, and exits, leaving* **Ibrahim** *alone with* **Edriss**.

Edriss You better get going.

Ibrahim I'm going to stay.

Edriss No way, my boy.

Ibrahim I'm not a boy anymore.

Edriss So stop following us old men around, waiting for your orders. Clean up the mess we've made. You and the *shabab*. And the women. Too many men onstage for fuck's sake.

The car horn honks again, frantically.

Ibrahim Goodbye.

Edriss For now, my boy. For now.

They hug. **Ibrahim** *starts to leave but* **Edriss** *speaks and he freezes.*

Edriss I ever tell you the one about the CIA agent, the KGB man, and the Mossad operative looking for the rabbit in the woods?

Ibrahim No.

Edriss Another time perhaps. Another time.

Ibrahim *exits, leaving* **Edriss** *alone.*

Edriss (*to himself*)   So it ends . . .

Rhythmic, thunderous explosions in the distance but building. He looks up.

. . . and so it begins.

The electricity flickers on for a moment and then cuts out to black.

End of Play.

Foot
An Encounter in One Act

Time: 2007, between World Cups.

Place: A bare room/space with the hint of a refugee camp—i.e. concrete, metal, dirt, graffiti, a poster—but just a hint. There is the simple rectangular outline of a soccer goal spray painted onto a wall, around which dates are written in chalk. A stool sits somewhere and perhaps a simple locker-room bench. A bag is placed on the ground toward one of the wings, but is hardly visible. Inside it are three footballs/soccer balls.

Character: A young person* (twenties), in shorts and an undershirt. S/he is athletic but also a thinker, a person whose imagination takes their tongue on tangents. Their mind moves fast and sometimes they do too, but it is never manic.

---

* While the stage directions are written with he/him/his pronouns, this play is equally suitable for a female footballer and would require only minimal adjustments of language/direction.

A man stands breathless, without his shoes. He looks at his feet, pokes them, and then brings them close to his face and inspects them before speaking.

"Walking with a light foot."

He takes a step.

"Getting off on the right foot" . . .

Another step.

or the wrong foot.

"Let's foot it all night," meaning to dance . . .

He gets up and does a jig, then stiffens, regains his concentration, and continues, picking up speed.

"Foot the bill."

"Put your best foot forward."

"To be at one's feet," meaning enchanted or subservient.

"To get one's feet wet."

"Get a foot in the door."

"To have one's feet on the ground."

"To have cold feet . . . itchy feet."

"To find your footing."

"To think on your feet."

"Stand on your own two feet."

"To sweep them off their feet."

"To have one foot in the grave" . . .

Beat.

The foot itself is an incredibly complex mechanism, with hundreds and hundreds of bones and muscles intertwined and fitted like puzzle pieces. Tarsal and metatarsal bones; intrinsic and extrinsic muscles; arches and joints; sesamoid bones and . . . "sesamoid". . . . Note to self: Find out if these bones are related to the sesame seed?

He walks in tight circles and then with a piece of chalk writes some of the following numbers and stats on the wall or ground.

A fact: Your feet log approximately 1,000 miles per year. Even if you are prevented from going very far.

Another fact: As shock absorbers, feet cushion up to one million pounds of pressure during one hour of exercise.

A quote: Leonardo da Vinci: "The human foot is a masterpiece of engineering, and a work of art."

I wonder if Mister da Vinci ever saw Ronaldo or Messi or Maradona cut through defenders, effortlessly riding their own feet? Or if he ever imagined a set of sketches detailing the trajectories of Zinedine Zidane making the ball hover so close to his feet during a dance of the most precise poetry, before threading the ball across the field through pairs and pairs of opposing feet to finally meet a set of friendly feet and into the gooooooooooooooooooooooaaaaaaaal!

Beat.

Yes. I wonder if he ever imagined the mechanics of the foot put to use to fire the ball to the back of the net at breakneck speed? A masterpiece of art and science indeed.

He dumps the balls from the bag. They are worn and have words and shapes written and drawn all over them.

The ball. Utterly simple. It's really all you need. The rest can be improvised.

He effortlessly balances one on the top of his foot, flips it into the air, and catches it between his shoulders and neck, then bows his head and catches the ball in his hands.

I like to see the ball as a globe. I write on the ball. For example, on this one I drew all of the continents, so that every week I can visit a different one. Kind of an exercise . . . in wishful thinking. In imagination. But more than that, an exercise in foot–eye coordination. The only rule is that I can only take shots on goal from one continent of my choice. Well, on the word for that continent. Not the actual continent. Allow me to explain.

He measures out seven paces between him and the stool.

I'm a professional footballer, but I can't even get to the playing field seven kilometers away. I can't even get to the village where my great-grandmother was born, in the next valley over.

He starts walking in tighter and tighter circles, as if encaged.

Checkpoints! And closures. And curfews . . . curtailed, cut-off, camps, cockroaches, crescents, crosses, craters, carcinogens, cracks, croaking, cauterized, incarcerated, quasi capitals . . . and of course, cannons . . . Copious quantities, cleaned, coddled and cocked! Yes. Too much preventing me in the end . . . Too much shit between me and the rest of this archipelago of ghettos passing for a homeland that my feet have to forgo the pleasure of getting to . . . including *that* village, the village where my great grandma is from—the village whose name even I sometimes forget, as *you* would, as you *have*, as you will . . .

That village is also the village where my uncle Iyad got chased by the goat he was supposed to bring to slaughter on his ninth birthday. It fell on the 'Eid . . . His birthday, not the goat. The goat never fell. He lived. My grandfather spared him for his valor. Kept him as a pet. And as a reminder of the comical sight of a boy in his birthday suit running from a bow-legged goat. Named him Shamir . . . like the Israeli prime minister. Because he was stubborn. Stubborn and ugly. My grandfather made Iyad watch Shamir the goat until he was almost twenty years old. (*He shouts offstage in a deep, smoky, older voice, as if to someone else.*) "Ey, boy! You gotta feed Shamir and clean Shamir. Then you are to walk Shamir around town! He needs exercise."

He used to play in the leagues in Jordan before 1967, my grandfather that is. Not the goat. He was a defender. His nickname was *el raa'ee ma'az*, or the "Goat Herder," because they say he had a way of containing the other team, leading them where he wanted them to go, always in control. His favorite player was Pelé, then Socrates, from Brazil. He always just called him *el doctoor* . . . Because Socrates was also a physician. He said, that's how you play revolutionary football, with elegance and with political awareness . . . and with a medical degree in case you get injured and need a proper job.

That's right, my grandad played in the Jordanian leagues. It was actually one of the only places to play against the *living*, since, after 1948, many of the Palestinian football players were exiled or killed, or exiled and then killed. But with those that remained, teams re-formed in the West Bank and played in the Jordanian leagues. Until the West Bank and Gaza were occupied by Israel in . . . 1967, and all organized sports activities ceased. No more fun and games for the natives! I studied journalism in university, you know. Before the university was shut down. And before most journalists stopped coming here.

He sets a ball up and starts positioning himself, judging angles, adjusting his feet as if for a penalty kick.

Right, so I kick the ball, top of the foot to the chosen continent.

And once you see Europe, for example, you can time the exact moment when it is right smack in the middle of the rotating radius, *the striking point*, where your foot has to land in order to hook the ball in a perfect arc to the top left corner of the goal. I personally like to aim for England. Because that's what the old folks say I should do, something about the bastard Balfour . . . They're my fans, the elders, they watch me practice and sell their cucumbers and eggplants, and the olives that didn't rot on the trees on the other side of the wall; that didn't fall with the centuries of twisted turning wood they clung to until their demise by fire or the metal maws of some monster. My fans are the old timers, the traders of our rotting but resilient agricultural heritage; mourners over the corpses of our fallen sustenance. (*A pause.*) I studied some poetry too.

The old folks know their poetry. And their football. They remember the games played outside the walls of Jerusalem, during the British occupation. There were lots of clubs then, and even a Palestinian star, Jabra al Zarqa, who played in the British League in Haifa. They say Jabra was so good they even asked him to join Arsenal . . . But that's another story. All I know is that the Palestinian national team was not recognized by FIFA until 1998. In the interim, absence. Non-existence.

He scans the writing on the ball as if it is a document . . .

My files tell us, however, that the Israelis count international matches in the 1930s as part of *their* record. But no Palestinians. Absence, non-existence. Of course, in the Holy Land, football . . . is just like falafel! It is appropriated, cleansed, and exiled. It's easy. Just sweep away the rubble, annex it, rename it, re-package it and you have a mythology on which to plant your feet; the mythology of a sandwich, a bean dip, a record, a war, a game . . . and finally a state to promote on the international stage.

He gets his socks and shoes and starts putting them on.

Our team played in the Arab Cup in '99. We won the bronze there, and when we arrived back home, 60,000 people came to meet us at the airport in Gaza. That was when we had an airport, before it was destroyed. And so it was there that we started—at the bottom, at 191st place in the world rankings in 1999!

By 2006, we were ranked 70 places higher, at 121st place, and boasted players plucked from a pool of 10 million Palestinians spread throughout the world.

As he speaks he points to the appropriate continent on the ball.

We have players from the US, Lebanon, Kuwait, France, Germany, and Chile, a country at the bottom of the world. Some of my teammates don't even speak Arabic. Their grandparents left long ago and walked across deserts and even the seas on foot and landed in Brooklyn or Santiago. But now, we've all answered a call to play for an idea . . . For a team full of phantoms suddenly back from the dead. What can I say? The football Gods have their methods. And I know.

He sits and begins to put on his socks and lace up his cleats.

Because I hear them sometimes. In the whispers, hints, and puzzles they leave for me in my dreams. Some are darker than others. Like the dream I had of bullets entering the feet of one of our players; which is a bit like shooting a singer or a poet through the tongue, or breaking the hands of a guitar player. But I didn't see the face that went with those feet . . . And then there is the song I heard the other night about the perils of playing or watching football on the beach in Gaza. To do so, I am told, is worthy of a missile or a shell that puts such insolence to a fiery end. But I hear good things too from time to time: that we will climb in the rankings and go to the Asia Cup soon and then maybe to the big one . . . but who knows?

As a team, as a whole, we can't all communicate in any one language, but we still manage to cook a kind of dysfunctional diasporic stew on the field. No recipes. No hands. All in the head . . . and the feet.

He speaks in a gruff, hoarse coach's voice.

"It is a call to arms. No! A call to feet!" That's what our coach told the media once before a match. He was trying to be poetic. He's no Darwish, but it was a hell of a lot sweeter than his fucking whistle.

A whistle sounds from offstage. It is deafening, screeching. He covers his ears and then starts doing drills up and down the stage.

121st place! Room for improvement, but not bad! I would call that getting one's foot in the door, while getting one's feet wet, by putting one's best foot forward, all despite getting off on the wrong foot!

We might have qualified for the 2006 Cup, but a travel ban was put on the players from Gaza in the middle of a tournament, our goalie was arrested, and our midfielder was killed. Boom, bam, snap!

Beat.

I have one good football, but three overall . . . One has the names of Israeli leaders written on it . . . and another with Palestinian leaders.

He looks around to make sure he is alone and lowers his voice.

But only the living and the free of the Palestinian leaders make it onto that ball . . . That's because the good ones have all been assassinated or incarcerated, or incarcerated and then assassinated.

A story! Once, one of the living and the free—and the especially mediocre—of our leaders came by to congratulate me for making the national team. He came in a fur hat and a long black British pea coat . . . that's what they are called, no? Pea coats? A question: Why not a "bean coat" or a "zucchini coat" or an "okra coat"?

So he arrives in his Mercedes with his guards and a film crew. And he steps over the sewage running through the lot where I train . . . He hops over it and almost falls in a puddle of rain and garbage and shit, which swells and stinks since the sewage system was destroyed by the occupation. And this leader and his brother in construction are too busy making money selling concrete to the Israelis who are building the wall around our reservations to bother actually fixing the sewage. That would be too much to ask. As would the simple pleasure of seeing him fall in a puddle of shit . . . As fate would have it, two of his bodyguards caught him. He shook my hand and the photographer took a picture.

Then he noticed my ball and then he noticed his name written on it, alongside the names of some of his colleagues. Like his chief of police, who's especially fond of applying electricity to the testicles of his opponents, or whoever the Americans or the Israelis tell him to slap around. And he's prepared of course, seeing as how he's backed by the same heroes who funded death squads, dictators and drone strikes . . . (*He puts his finger to his mouth and looks around again.*) But you didn't hear it from me.

He stood for a moment and scoured the ball, and before he could ask, I lied! Told him: "Your Excellency, this is to honor the leaders of . . . the revolution," and his smile widened, and he said: "The revolution . . . yes, God grant the revolution victory."

But it was with his mind somewhere else that he said it, like the way you say good morning to your wife of forty years—the wife you forgot why you married, and whose body looks like a sack of potatoes compared to the woman whose skinny legs wrap around your flabby back in the hotel in the foreign capital where you finalize deals for your cars, your helicopter the Israelis won't even let you fly, the weapons, trinkets and uniforms, the bags of money, and your British pea coat! But I didn't say that. And, he didn't sing the word "revolution" the way the dead ones did, the way they still do. I can hear them now . . .

He puts his ear to the ball and listens, eyes closed for a beat, perhaps then offering the ball to the audience to listen. The hint of voices sweep through the space and disappear.

No, of course he didn't sing it like them, that's why they're dead and he's able to go to the next village, and to foreign capitals without getting harassed by the very system he professes to be revolting against; the very system he solemnly swears—upon Korans and Bibles, road maps and resolutions—that he is liberating us from. And that's why his name was on the ball, exposed to mud and shit and the power of my left foot slamming into his laughable nom de guerre day after day.

He wished me luck and walked back to his plush leather seats. The engine roared and the tires skidded as he made a quick exit from the camp.

But led by old Abou-fattoush, who was balancing on his prosthetic right limb, my fans met the man's departure with eye-rolls, head shakes, and an eggplant waved inappropriately in the direction of the fleeing entourage. Like I said, all the good leaders are dead or in jail. And football is a kind of hope that no leader can own. It is ours, even on broken fields, it is whole.

He writes something onto the ball, then stands atop a stool with two balls in hand.

A date: On March 30, 2006 the Israeli Air Force bombed the Palestinian Football Stadium in Gaza.

He climbs to the highest point in the space and throws one ball up into the air and lets it drop while making the whistling sound of a bomb.

. . . Leaving it with a massive crater in its center.

Another ball is dropped.

Like a moonscape. Imagine: football on the moon! The moon has fallen. Plummeted like a bunker buster, right smack in the middle of Gaza! And if your feet are up to it—or if you are a trained and sure-footed astronaut like me, or even if you are half goat—you can play soccer in this crater.

He jumps down as if onto the moon, and bounces, floats in slow-motion lunar leaps for a couple beats before stopping to speak.

No. We didn't qualify for the last World Cup. And no, we usually can't practice or play home games in Palestine. We are eternally away, on the road . . . Maybe one day we'll even be exiled up up and away. To the moon. (*Beat.*) We speak five languages. We all like Arabic music. Some like rap. Others smoke cigarettes and can't stop. Guilty. Some of us have orange hair, others black, some light eyes, others dark; some have brown skin or black, others pale. Some of us . . . (*Beat.*) . . . But the only thing all of us could think of that day was:

How did he die? How did our midfielder, Tareq, die?

The news said: "blah blah blah, two goals to nil, blah blah blah . . . while Palestinian midfielder Tareq al-Quto was killed in the violence." Period. End of report. Pretty vague. But at first we didn't know, we just thought he was late that day . . . or held up . . . checkpoints! And closures. And curfews . . . curtailed, cut-off, camps, cockroaches . . .

We didn't know . . . until we knew. But then what do you do? How do you play? How do you concentrate on practice when your midfielder gets a bullet from 200 meters, 100 meters, 53.3 meters . . .

After "measuring" 53.3 meters he draws in chalk on the ground the outline of a man's body. He takes it in and then circles it as he speaks.

Was he juggling a football at that moment? Shooting a gun? Tossing a rock? Skipping a stone? Hoisting a flag? Taking a piss? Maybe he was hanging the laundry? Or just having a smoke.

He takes a bent cigarette from his sock, lights it, and takes a drag.

Or maybe our midfielder Tareq was caught making a bomb . . . with his sweaty practice shorts, cracked shin-guards, and the shoelace from his left cleat?

How does a team go on when it can barely stand on its feet?

He puts out the cigarette.

Maybe the same way we had to tell Roberto that he had had too much to drink at the hotel bar and that the Russian lady for hire was *not* his ex-girlfriend Cristina from Santiago, and that he should *not* ask her to marry him before we left for Egypt the next morning! Or the way we continued on after we watched Nasser's house get demolished on TV, sitting in the hotel room three hours before a match. We won 3-1 that night . . . Nasser was all over the field all game, but I swear, he didn't sweat a drop. How the fuck did he do that? Probably the same way he had practiced alone against the wall of that same house for all those years. Alone. Because sometimes there is no one to practice against in Nablus under military curfew. Another fact: Organized sport is considered organized crime under occupation.

How do you go on? Because you have no choice . . . Because your feet tell you to and you listen.

He looks at his feet and then does a flurry of exercises before freezing, out of breath.

I was warming up alone before the match when we got the news: Tareq wouldn't be there . . . Tareq was . . . I heard it from the other end of the field and I froze. And then it hit me, the future, all of it, at that moment: Tareq would never play

Constantino Marzuqa (Young Man) in Ismail Khalidi's *Foot*, directed by Ismail Khaildi, produced by Teatro Amal, 2016. Photo by Carolina Villar. Photo courtesy of Teatro Amal.

football again; he wouldn't practice with his teammates, share jokes and sprints and stories. He wouldn't face Taiwan, or Egypt, Chinese Taipei or Guam that year. He wouldn't face England in the quarters in a future World Cup, or Brazil in the semis, or Italy in the finals one day . . . He wouldn't return home with the team to Palestine, holding in its possession the proof that we still exist. That we've always existed. Millions of people will see that match, I thought . . . but they won't see Tareq. He'll be invisible.

And those thoughts, to know the future then, suddenly brought the past back in shots: My mamma making *ful,* garlicky lemon-doused beans with hot bread and eggs in the morning; the day the leader came to take his picture with me; the smell of my father's subtle cologne, and how it lingered in the house, after he left for work . . . Even after they took him for good. I remembered the first time I kissed Selwa Abu-Eid, right behind Abdullah Asfour's pigeon coop . . . The second time and the 63rd time we kissed . . . and that very morning . . . outside her backyard . . .

He hastily fills the bag with the balls and other items and slings it over his shoulder.

How I was late but needed to kiss her anyway; went out of my way, on foot, to see her. How I ran to catch the bus afterwards, my bag under my arm so it wouldn't beat against my thighs as I sprinted across town, still tasting Selwa's saliva on my teeth, like cardamom; the taste of her voice on my tongue as I took the shortcut . . .

And then the jeeps, the tank, turning its turret to face me, moving closer: 200 meters, 100 meters . . . 53.3 meters . . . my heartbeat . . . A shot. . . . Ice ripping through my neck, the sound of it cracking . . . my spine, split by metal, the ball in my bag, hitting the ground . . .

He gently puts the bag down on the ground and bends down and sits near it. He opens it, slowly.

A new ball, with new things written on it. Every team in the last World Cup . . . in tiny calligraphy.

He removes on of the balls and sits cross-legged on the ground.

And the poem I'd added that morning, in Arabic and English, French, Spanish and Hebrew. My knees hitting the dust . . . the sky . . . the names of my teammates on my lips. And my name: Tareq. Tareq Al-Quto, who would not be seen on the field again . . . And my feet, melting into blackness, into the words of one of our poets; words written in the five languages of my team:

"On the day you kill me

You'll find in my pocket

Travel tickets

To peace,

To the fields and the rain,

To people's conscience.

Don't waste the tickets."

He starts to write on the ball but stops and rises. The light becomes bright, as if at the center of a stadium. The song of a large crowd envelops the space. Tareq places the ball on the ground and measures the distance needed to take his penalty kick. The call of the crowd increases as he prepares to take the shot. He stops. Silence. A moment's glance at the audience. He then turns away from the ball and the audience and picks up his bag. He takes a step and stops.

Don't waste the tickets.

He exits, leaving the ball on stage as the light fades.

End of Play.

Sabra Falling

Characters

Sofyan, *fifties, a refugee. The father of Hani and Eyad.*
Leena, *fifties, a refugee. The mother of Hani and Eyad.*
Dalia, *twenty, the fiancée of Sofyan's and Leena's late son Eyad.*
Hani, *early twenties, a PLO fighter.*
The Pilot, *mid-twenties, an Israeli pilot.*
The General, *an ageless Israeli general.*
Uli, *twenties, The Pilot's girlfriend in Tel Aviv.* *
Mira, *fifties, The Pilot's mother.* **
Eyad, *a vision.* ***

Time: August and September of 1982.

Place: A home in the Sabra refugee camp in West Beirut.

Set: A simple living room with doors leading off to two other rooms and one to the street. Minimal furniture. The roof has hole in it, which can be suggested by lighting if needed.

Here on the slopes of hills, facing the dusk and the cannon of time

Close to the gardens of broken shadows, We do

what prisoners do,

And what the jobless do: We

cultivate hope.

. . .

The siege is a waiting period

Waiting on the tilted ladder in the middle of the storm.
—Mahmoud Darwish from "Under Siege"

---

*   Uli is played by the same actor playing **Dalia**.
** Mira is played by the same actor playing **Leena**.
*** **Eyad** played by the same actor playing **Hani**.

Prologue

The clack and tap of a typewriter in the near darkness. A figure, smoking a cigarette, can barely be seen in the dim light, typing with his back to us. As he does we hear many voices whispering, from all directions, overlapping.

The figure types to their rhythm.

A knock on a door. He ignores it, keeps typing. A louder knock. Urgent. He looks up. The voices stop. He rises and opens the door. BANG! A crack and a flash of light and then complete darkness.

Act One

Scene One

It is night. The thunder of bombing can be heard.

Then, the sound of something falling to earth from a great distance. It gets closer, screeching, whistling, louder, closer and then a CRASH!

Dust. Moonlight shines through a fresh hole in the ceiling, illuminating a large object in the middle of the floor.

Leena *enters with a gas lamp. She studies the object.* **Dalia** *and* **Hani** *enter behind her.*

Dalia *is in pajamas.* **Hani** *wears nothing but his underpants. He holds a rifle.*

Leena Hani, put that thing away. You remember what happened last time.

Hani It could be a shell.

Leena It's not. It's not a bomb.

Dalia Don't get close.

Hani Where's Babba?

Leena That man sleeps through anything. He hasn't heard half of this fucking war. I envy him for that. Leave him.

She takes another step towards the object. She is about to poke it but **Hani** *stops her.*

Hani Let me call the guys.

Leena No.

Hani They'll know what to do.

Leena Dalia's in her nightgown.

Hani She can change!

Leena I won't have a bunch of fighters obsessed with their guns barging in my house to tell me what I already know.

She reaches towards the object.

Hani Don't!

Leena It's not a bomb.

Dalia How do you know?

Leena Bombs don't breathe.

She lifts the tattered remnants of a parachute to reveal a man in a pilot's jumpsuit and helmet.

Dalia He's . . .

Leena A soldier.

Hani An Israeli.

Dalia A pilot.

Leena My God.

Hani Son of a . . .

Dalia He's alive.

Hani Not for long.

He points his gun at the unconscious pilot but **Leena** *shoves it away.*

Leena Dalia, help me lift him.

Hani He's the enemy, Mamma.

Leena Yes but he's a man, and none will be executed under my roof, or what's left of it. Not while I'm alive. Understand?

They remove his helmet to reveal a bloodied face. **Hani** *exits.*

Leena (*to* **Dalia**) Get the bottle of whisky and the cloth and scissors.

Dalia *exits.* **Leena** *is alone with the pilot.*

Leena A human bomb. An enemy human.

She unbuttons his shirt to reveal more blood.

I swear, if you ruin my carpet with all this blood, I'll let Hani kill you.

Dalia *re-enters with supplies.* **Hani** *re-enters behind her, dressed in mismatched fatigues.*

Hani We'd be shot as traitors if anyone in the camp saw this.

Leena I suppose that's true. Dalia, lock the door. Hani, give me a hand.

Hani They hunt us from the skies and you tend to him as if he were a tiny bird fallen out of his nest.

Leena He's fallen, so I tend his wounds. Yes.

Hani He's a vulture, not a dove, mother. A killer.

Leena Not a human?

Hani This piece of shit dropped the bombs that wiped out half the city.

Leena You don't know it was him.

Hani Of course it was him!

Dalia He wasn't just passing over Beirut in a fighter jet.

Hani It was him and his friends. They push the buttons.

Leena Don't lecture me, boy.

Hani He can't stay here.

Leena So take him. Drag him through the streets, treat him as an animal, the way the Israelis would treat you if they caught you.

Hani Exactly!

Leena Exactly!

Hani Yes! Exactly!

Leena Good!

Hani What?

Leena It's settled. He stays.

Hani They'll come for him.

Leena Who?

Hani Them. He has a tracking device on him.

She starts stripping **The Pilot**, *searching him.* **Leena** *tries to stop him but* **Hani** *tears off* **The Pilot**'s *uniform so that he is in his underwear.*

Sofyan (*offstage*) What the hell is going on in there?

Hani Nothing, Babba.

Sofyan Tick tack tick tack, bang boom, like a goddamn silversmith in my own house!

Leena Go back to sleep, Sofyan.

Sofyan (*offstage*) I wouldn't have to go back to sleep if you hadn't woken me to begin with.

Leena Either get up and help us or and go back to sleep!

Dalia Why do you shout at him like that?

Sofyan (*offstage*) Because a hammer only knows how to do one thing, that's why.

Leena Because I cook, and I sew and I chase the roaches. Because I follow the news and watch the skies to stay one step ahead of this war.

Dalia We all do.

Leena He sits and reads and writes, twiddles his thumbs and fiddles with his balls.

Sofyan (*offstage*) I would if you'd left me any, woman!

Dalia   He's working.

Sofyan (*offstage*)   That's right! I'm working!

Leena   Of course! He prepares to direct his next play! With actors that have either been killed or fled; in a theatre that's been shelled, for an audience too terrified to leave their houses!

Not to mention incapable of understanding Beckett.

Sofyan (*offstage*)   They understand! And when I do Molière or Shakespeare they understand that too!

Leena   What about when you made me play Pozzo! Half the audience took their cigarette break in the theatre and talked over me. Never again!

Sofyan (*offstage*)   Maybe it was you who didn't understand Pozzo!

Leena (*to* **Hani** *and* **Dalia**)   Don't touch him!

She exits. **The Pilot** *moves groggily.*

Dalia   I think he's starting to come to.

Hani   What do we do?

Dalia   He's a prisoner of war, no?

Hani   Yeah, I suppose. So?

Dalia   So, if you'd listened in training instead of studying Zaynab al Kurdi's ass then maybe you'd remember.

Hani   I do remember.

Dalia   So let's hear it.

Hani   Fine . . . When Zaynab's right leg crosses over the left, the back of her shirt slides up just enough to see that space where the small of her back transitions to the top of the peach-shaped entity that is her miraculous ass.

Dalia   I should slap the ass-shaped entity that is your face.

She takes a cigarette from **Hani**'s *sleeve.*

Dalia   You know, the way you and your friends drool over her like a pack of hyenas, I'm not surprised Zaynab prefers women.

Hani   You're full of shit.

Dalia   I really don't blame her.

She exhales smoke in **Hani**'s *face. She then takes the gun and points it at* **The Pilot**.

Dalia (*to* **The Pilot**)   You're now a prisoner of war in the custody of the Palestine Liberation Organization. Your wounds will be attended to and you will henceforth be treated according to the guidelines for combatants captured in war.

The Pilot *does not respond.*

Leena I decide his fate. Now either help or get out.

Hani He's a prisoner now. You can treat his wounds, but then he's gone. We turn him in.

He storms out. **Dalia** *stays. The two women bandage* **The Pilot**'s *head as the lights fade.*

Jawdy Obeid (The Pilot), Adlyn Carreras (Leena/Mira), Adri Mehra (Sofyan), and Michael Karadsheh (Hani) in Ismail Khalidi's *Sabra Falling*, directed by Dipankar Mukherjee, produced by Pangea World Theater, 2017. Photo by Meena Natarajan. Photo courtesy of Pangea World Theater.

Scene Two

The Pilot, *with his head bandaged, sleeps.*

Hani *tiptoes into the room, ties his hands together with rope, then exits, leaving* **The Pilot** *asleep and bound.*

The light of dawn creeps through the hole in the roof. **Sofyan** *enters without noticing the sleeping man on his floor.*

He starts making coffee and puts a record on. It is Fairuz singing "Habaytek bel Sayf." As **Sofyan** *mixes his coffee over the small gas burner on the floor he sings along.*

Dalia (*offstage*)   Babba, please, it's barely light out!

Sofyan   In Abu Shusha we'd wake up and sing as we tended the flocks in the dark.

Dalia (*offstage*)   There aren't any flocks here. And there's no grass either.

Sofyan *sings another refrain. A neighbor's voice from offstage is heard.*

Neighbor One (*offstage*)   Goddamnit, man, there's people trying to sleep in this camp!

Sofyan (*shouting through the window*)   Sleep is the last thing you need, Abu Ali. Get off your ass and do something instead of playing backgammon all day with that pipe stuck in your face!

Neighbor Two (*offstage*)   There's a war going on! No time for bloody love songs!

Sofyan   War is the best time for love songs! It's our best defense against that donkeyfucker Begin and his friend The General!

He turns back to his coffee then freezes. He looks up, studying the hole in the roof, seeing it for the first time. He then looks directly down from the hole and sees **The Pilot**, *who is awake. They stare at each other.*

Sofyan *slowly circles* **The Pilot** *several times. He inspects his hair, then his chin. He looks closely at his nose, his eyes, and then his hands. This goes on for several beats.*

Suddenly, **Sofyan** *mimes a cowboy walk, à la John Wayne, turns and draws his finger as a gun on* **The Pilot**. **The Pilot** *is still.* **Sofyan** *turns his back and repeats the action. This time,* **The Pilot** *has made his finger into a gun and "shoots"* **Sofyan**, *winning the "duel." The old man mimes an ornate death, eventually collapsing to the floor.* **The Pilot** *laughs.* **Sofyan** *looks him over.*

Sofyan   Eyad?

The Pilot *smiles at* **Sofyan** *and then darkness.*

Scene Three

Leena, **Dalia**, *and* **Hani** *speak in hushed tones on one side of the stage. On the other side, just out of earshot,* **Sofyan** *changes the bandage on* **The Pilot**'s *head.*

Hani   Is he fucking serious?

Dalia   Be quiet.

Hani   Why? Is it a secret that this is totally crazy? I want him to hear me.

Leena   He hasn't been like this for years, since . . .

Dalia   Look how he's smiling.

Hani He's lost his mind!

Leena Don't say that!

Hani You say it all the time.

Leena I'm allowed to! Not you. And I don't mean it. Your father's not a mad man.

Hani He's playing house with an Israeli soldier!

Dalia Look at him, Hani.

Hani I am!

Dalia Not your father, the other one. Eya . . . The pilot.

Hani You too?

Dalia No! But . . . .

Hani But what?! Just say it!

Dalia Look at his eyes.

Hani He's got two of 'em. So what?

Dalia The nose.

Hani What about it?

Dalia The slope of it. How it's slightly bent to the right.

Hani So?

Leena The scar on his chin.

Hani It's a wound, not a scar. Fresh.

Dalia He's a dead ringer for Eyad.

Beat.

Hani Dalia. My brother is gone.

Leena You think we don't know that?

Hani The question is whether Babba knows! Listen, I'm taking the pilot to my commander. He'll decide how to handle this.

Leena And what about your father?

Hani Tell him the truth.

Leena He thinks that's his boy. He thinks /

Hani He doesn't think. That's the problem.

Leena He thinks Eyad's come back to us. That he's escaped from some Israeli dungeon and made his way across the border.

Hani   And what about when that pilot realizes where he is and who he is? Or when their death squads come to rescue him and execute us in the process? Is that a better ending?

Leena   There are no happy endings. Not here. So what's the difference?

Dalia   He must know.

Leena   He knows what he sees and that boy /

Hani   Soldier!

Leena   That soldier looks like my Eyad.

Dalia (*whispers*)   My Eyad.

In the other space **Sofyan** *exits and re-enters with a pile of clothes. He hands it to* **The Pilot**.

Leena   Until now. For the past three years he talked about Eyad as if /

Hani   I know!

Leena   . . . as if he was going to walk through that door any minute. So imagine how he felt when he saw . . . Him.

Hani   The pilot goes.

He takes out his pistol again.

Leena (*calmly*)   You're not going anywhere while they're hitting the camps, it's not safe. And he'll harm no one in his state.

The thud of a bomb dropping. The lights flicker and then go out. Darkness.

After a moment **Dalia** *has lit a gas lamp, illuminating the center of the room.* **The Pilot** *now stands between them dressed in trousers and a button-down shirt, his eyes to the floor . . .* **Sofyan** *enters, followed by* **Hani**.

Sofyan   I need a smoke. I can't work with all this bloody boom boom, doom and gloom.

Hani (*nodding towards* **The Pilot**)   Ask him when it will stop.

For a moment all stare at **The Pilot**.

Sofyan (*to* **The Pilot**)   Eyad, go rest your head. And you shouldn't be standing on that leg of yours either.

The Pilot *starts to exit but* **Hani** *grabs his shoulder. He is about to say something but stares at him for a beat and then lets go.* **The Pilot** *exits, unsteady on his injured leg.*

Sofyan (*quietly*)   Your brother escapes an Israeli prison and makes his way back through enemy lines, injured, confused—God knows what they did to him—and you treat him like a stranger?!

A beat.

Hani So which play are we in now, old man? Lear? Oedipus? Hamlet? Just tell us so we can learn our lines and you can move us around your stage.

Leena Enough, Hani!

Hani No. I want a part in my father's next play.

Sofyan I might have a part for you. A non-speaking part.

Hani I assume my brother Eyad has the lead?

Sofyan He was never much of an actor. No. I've asked him to write it for me. I mean, I've been searching for a play. To shake the camps. Who better to pen it then Eyad Akawi, "young literary light of the Palestinians"?!

Hani Of course. Brilliant. And what will this new play be about?

Sofyan The process of creation will reveal all, son.

The electricity returns, bringing light.

Sofyan Eureka! You see? Signs, boy. Signs.

Dalia Maybe it's too soon. For him.

Leena He can't write the play, Sofyan.

Sofyan And why not?

Leena Because he's not . . .

Sofyan *looks at* **Leena**.

Leena He's not . . . well.

Dalia He can barely talk. And his head.

Sofyan I know. I can see his wounds. And when he's better it will come back. And the words will flow again. But we have to help him be whole again; remember who he is. Then it will pour out of him. The poetry of revolution—revolution unlike any accomplished with third-hand rifles.

Hani Don't.

Sofyan We've been taking up arms since I was a child. Against the British we tried. My father, God rest his soul, borrowed a rifle / from—

Hani and **Dalia** From Abu 'Abbas.

Hani Yes we know. And he was torn in two.

Sofyan And he was torn in two by British machine guns at Jaddin, in front of my brother's eyes.

Hani Not the first or the last.

Sofyan Ten years later, we took up arms against the Zionists to defend our villages. With our decrepit rifles and Ottoman swords we were defeated and herded away, like so many sheep. Now look at us. Living and dying like animals.

Hani Which is why we fight. Perhaps you didn't fight well enough then. Just waited like fools, like sheep, for the Arab armies to save you.

Sofyan Exactly. They never came! And they never will.

Dalia We've fought the Israelis to a standstill this time.

Sofyan But not victory, dear. Where is your victory?

Hani All summer I've been in those trenches while you've been perched in your room scouring those yellowed plays. We've held them off for two months, on our own.

Sofyan On your own. Against all odds?

Hani Yes. We fight for ourselves now.

Sofyan And how long before their tanks and their planes overtake us? What happens in a day or a week or a month when you can resist no more?

The dull thud of shelling in the distance.

Hear that? That's the tick tock of a clock and we're running out of time. Who will come to our aid? The Syrians? Their airforce was wiped out. Those shits in Saudi Arabia? Ha! Bunch of hypocritical swine with oil pumping in their veins and cash the only cause they care about? Will they ride to our rescue? The Soviets? The French? The Americans?!

Dalia They say the Americans will control the Israelis if we hold out long enough.

Sofyan God be with you then if that's what you're relying on.

Hani We rely on ourselves.

Sofyan No matter how many of the enemy you bring down we'll never be strong enough, boy, not even with the ghosts of Marx, Mao, and Che cheering you on from the great beyond.

Hani But a play will save us, is that it? Lead us to victory? Lead us back home? Or will you crush their tanks with a poem?

Sofyan Perhaps, yes.

Hani I'll let my commanders know to stock up on couplets and explosive soliloquies before the Israelis make their next push, then.

Sofyan You make a joke out of it.

Hani You're the one making a joke out of it. People are dying. Out there. For you.

Sofyan That's why I'm telling you we can win only when we show them they can never win. By laughing at their tanks and jets. By creating beauty where they have left us none.

Hani Save them to save ourselves?

Sofyan Perhaps.

Hani And how do we do that?

Sofyan With love . . . A certain kind of love. That is all I know.

Hani *stares at his father a beat.*

Hani Well, I won't sit here waiting for them to kill me.

A jet breaks the sound barrier with a ferocious roar, shaking the house. They look up. **Hani** *then fires several shots through the hole above and exits, slamming the door.*

Sofyan We should do something about that hole, Dalia.

He exits in the other direction. **Leena** *and* **Dalia** *stand alone, looking up through the roof.*

Scene Four

Night falls on the house as the din of bombing occasionally breaks the silence. **The Pilot** *sleeps.*

Hani *sits guard nearby but is asleep.*

The sound of jets. **The Pilot** *tosses and turns. The sound of voices, some in Hebrew, over a radio frequency.*

Radio Voice One You're in too close to your targets, captain, watch the fire, pull out pull out!

Radio Voice Two Drop your load, pilot, and get the fuck out of there! Do you read? You're taking fire. Repeat. You are taking fire from below.

Suddenly **The Pilot** *sits upright. Now he wears his pilot's helmet, its visor down. He struggles to breathe and tries to pull off the helmet as the sound of jets and the radio voices reach a deafening crescendo.*

Radio Voice One Eject, man! Your wing is fucked. Eject!

The Pilot *punches the ground and with a thunderous sound is ejected upwards through the hole in the ceiling. He disappears.*

Scene Five

With morning light **The Pilot** *floats down through the hole, feather-like, and into bed.* **Sofyan** *stands over the two sleeping men.*

Sofyan Coffee. Thick and bitter with a bite of cardamom to tame its punch.

The Pilot *and* **Hani** *wake.*

Hani   The water's only for cooking and washing. Mamma's orders.

Sofyan   Well, coffee washes away the night's residue.

Hani   She's gonna kill you.

Sofyan   Yeah, but it will be a theatrical death, Hani, nothing more. I'll be alive again for the curtain call. Then we'll do it all over again tomorrow.

Hani   Not everything is theater.

Sofyan   Well, marriage is definitely a kind of theater. (*Beat.*) Just like war.

He pours **Hani** *a cup and then* **The Pilot**. *They drink, not making eye contact.* **Hani** *rises and prepares his gear.*

Sofyan   An end to all this would be a blessing. In the meantime, break a leg out there, boy.

Hani   I'll keep my leg if I can help it. Are Mamma and Dalia here?

Sofyan   The other room. They'll keep an eye on us. If that's what you're worried about.

Hani *stares at* **The Pilot** *and notices* **Sofyan** *is doing the same.*

Hani   Well. I guess I'll be exiting. Stage left.

He starts to leave stage right.

Sofyan   That's stage right, not left. You never could keep it straight. The audience would be there.

He points towards the audience and all three stare out for a beat. **Hani** *exits.*

Sofyan   Eyad, how do you feel today? Better?

The Pilot   My head. It hurts. Cloudy. Like a storm's brewing.

Sofyan *checks the bandage on his head, then produces a pile of books.*

Sofyan   It will pass. "Hungry man, reach for the book: It is a weapon." They're all yours.

He reveals an object covered in a cloth.

The Pilot   And that?

Sofyan   Another weapon. If used correctly.

The Pilot *takes it carefully, as if it is a bomb, He unwraps it to reveal a typewriter in a case.*

The Pilot   Is it mine?

Sofyan   I had Abu Ali's boy get it from your office downtown. Little shit made me pay through the nose, but what the hell. Mother Courage would have loved Beirut.

The Pilot *opens the case to reveal the machine, its keys splattered with dried blood.*

The Pilot Blood.

Sofyan Yes.

Pilot Mine?

Dalia *enters behind them carrying medical supplies. She stands unnoticed for a moment.*

Sofyan They must have wounded you when they came to take you.

The Pilot I don't remember.

Dalia *approaches* **The Pilot**.

Dalia I do. First, their commandoes slipped through the city disguised as women.

Standing over him, she checks his bandages.

Then they made their way to your office downtown.

She prods his chin upwards to look at his cut. She uses the clamps to move his head and dress his wounds, never touching him.

They knocked. And when you opened it . . .

She gently pries open his mouth, again with the clamps, and after a moment removes them.

. . . They made you disappear.

The Pilot Why?

Sofyan Because of those.

The Pilot *opens his eyes.* **Sofyan** *points to the pile of books.*

Sofyan And your articles. Do you remember now?

Dalia *and* **The Pilot** *make eye contact.*

Pilot I remember writing. Yes. Typing.

Dalia Your wounds are healing fine. Don't pick at that cut on your chin or else it will scar.

The Pilot *is about to say something to her but* **Dalia** *exits.*

Sofyan What else?

The Pilot What else? Mamma. Sometimes standing behind me while I wrote.

Sofyan That woman's always been too nosey for her own good.

The Pilot I remember a young woman. But her face, I can't . . .

Sofyan Yes. You were engaged. To her. To Dalia.

Pilot I thought . . . I assumed she was your daughter.

Sofyan Well now she is. She was orphaned. Lost her people in Tel al-Zaatar. When she was seventeen. She joined the movement right after. Tough girl. You met in some meeting. She went toe to toe with you. And won. Shut you up in front of everyone there. To your credit, you fell for her.

The Pilot I fell for her?

Sofyan Hard. Later, we took her in. As our own. After you had . . .

The Pilot And she stayed here all this time? Waiting?

Sofyan Surviving.

The Pilot Fighting?

Sofyan She's not afraid. Not of them. Out there. Up there. I know that much.

The Pilot She loved me?

Sofyan But not because your books get published or because journalists from Europe came to talk to you. She could see you, boy. From the beginning.

He removes a handkerchief from his pocket. He moistens it and carefully wipes the keys clean of the blood. He then loads paper into the typewriter.

Shall we begin?

The Pilot *nods.*

Sofyan I was thinking of one of their endless, immortal warlords. The fat general perhaps. Or the one-eyed war chief. Though he's a bit of a cliché I think. Yes. The fat one is best.

The Pilot I don't understand.

Sofyan As a character. The general. We kidnap him. Imprison him. Within the walls of the story, of your play. Oh, it will drive them crazy, Eyad, I promise. Go on.

The Pilot *moves his hands towards the keys but stops short of touching them.*

Sofyan Lights up on the fat general, in the smoldering ruins of the city he has destroyed . . . Dancing . . .

Pilot Tango.

Sofyan Good. That's good . . . I'll leave you to it.

He leaves. **The Pilot**, *alone, moves his hands towards the typewriter. As soon as his fingers touch the keys the lights shift. A flash, a crack.*

Scene Six

Lights up on **The General**, *who enters to a distant tango. He dances with a skeleton in his arms. He notices* **The Pilot** *but keeps dancing around him in circles.*

The General Name and rank, soldier.

Pilot I'm not a soldier.

The General Every Israeli's a soldier. And every Arab a terrorist. So what are you if not a soldier?

Pilot A writer, sir.

The General Nonsense. You're a soldier, but not a grunt. Air force I'd guess. A flyer. Name and rank?

Pilot Eyad. Akawi.

The General *drops the skeleton and stops his tango. He stares* **The Pilot** *over then looks at one of the books. Circling* **The Pilot**, *he sniffs him and then the book before dropping it on the ground in disgust and exiting.*

The Pilot *grabs a pen and starts writing. Hebrew letters and words appear everywhere on the walls, glowing, illuminated, filling the space. He looks at the sea of words around him, confused.*

Sofyan *enters and stares at the writing.*

Sofyan You must have learned their language in their prisons. Good. Use it to break their hearts.

In their own tongue.

He notices the discarded skeleton and gently picks it up, cradling it in his arms as he exits. As soon as he leaves, **Mira** *enters and starts tidying up around* **The Pilot**.

Mira Who was that?

The Pilot My father.

She feels his head and neck for a fever.

Mira That's not your father. Yours was a drunk who could barely rent us a flat in Tel Aviv, left when you were barely two. (*Beat.*) But I wouldn't go back to the slums where they kept all the Jews like me who came from Baghdad. Sprayed us with DDT when we arrived in Tel Aviv in '51.

The Pilot Who are you?

Mira Silly boy. But you're my silly boy. My Eyal.

The Pilot Eyad. You mean Eyad.

Mira I mean Eyal.

The Pilot Eyad.

She takes his chin in her hand and turns it towards the writing on the wall.

Mira Eyal. You see those words of yours? I can read them. You can read them. But they can't.

The Pilot   But I speak Arabic.

Mira   Because I would teach you every morning to read and write Arabic properly. The other kids made fun of you. Called you names.

She speaks as she straightens his collar.

Do you remember the day when I dropped you at school, and you told me: "Never speak to me in that language around the others"? What could I do? Soon you were just like all the other boys, and Hebrew took over your throat, your dreams. Arabic was our secret code. Our criminal tongue

The Pilot   I learned Hebrew in prison.

Mira   No. You're a Sabra.

The Pilot   We're in Sabra. In Beirut.

Mira   I mean the other Sabra, the name of the cactus. The one that grows by the side of the roads, the name given to the new Jews, to make them tough and prickly on the outside. Make them feel they belong, that they can survive in this place. (*Beat.*) Why would you want to stay in this shithole anyway?

The Pilot   I was born here. I'm from here. I—

Mira   Quiet! I washed Ashkenazi floors and stitched Ashkenazi clothes for twenty years so you wouldn't have to be from a place like this. That's why we moved to the settlements. The state paid us to move to a new house. I did that to escape. From this.

The Pilot   I need to write.

Mira   That's what I told you too. Before you went to the army. Your grandfather wrote books. In Baghdad. It's in your blood. But the sky called you.

The Pilot   The sky?

Mira   It's the price we pay to become Israelis. Every one of us must have his war to make on the Arabs.

The Pilot   I would like you to leave, please.

Mira *runs her hand through his hair.*

Mira   You always were a polite boy. And confused. So pretty and so lost. My little Sabra. (*Beat.*) By the way, your Uli, she keeps coming by the house. Come back and save me from her insufferable crying. I can't stand girls that cry.

She leaves. After a moment he begins to type. There is a knock at the door. He opens it to reveal **The General**, *in drag, with a handbag.*

The Pilot   Can I help you, miss?

The General   Are you Eyad Akawi?

Pilot   Yes.

The General *whips a gun out and puts it to* **The Pilot**'s *mouth.*

The General Bang!

A flash of light and then darkness.

Scene Seven

The Pilot *wakes in a terror, unable to breathe.* **Leena** *stands over him and pours water on him.*

Leena We don't have enough water for me to do that again. Now breathe. You slept all day.

He breathes, calming down.

The Pilot Thank you.

Leena You had a fever. It's gone down now.

She hands him a plate of food.

Up. The battles will be fierce tonight. Up now, boy. You must be hungry. I made manaqeesh to send to the fighters. You should eat something.

He rises unsteadily. He slowly dresses himself. Once he is dressed, **Leena** *is taken aback and stares at him for a long beat.*

Hani *enters from another room with his gear, preparing to leave. He too stops in his tracks and stares at* **The Pilot**.

Leena *notices* **Hani**'s *presence and falls back into motion.*

Leena (*to* **The Pilot**) Take this and go to Sofyan. He must need help fixing the shelter. Go.

She hands **The Pilot** *the bread as he exits.*

Hani He's wearing Eyad's clothes?

Leena Yes.

Hani Like a snake with a new skin.

Leena They fit him.

Hani They fit me too.

Leena I made food.

Hani I want to put a bullet through his head.

Leena I can't. Hate him.

Hani It would be strange.

Leena I want to . . .

Hani   I would do it . . .

Leena   But I can't . . .

Hani   I would.

She hands him the bag of food.

Leena   For the others.

Hani   They're working out a ceasefire. Soon.

Leena   You've been saying so for weeks.

Hani   We've been asking for one for weeks. The Israelis are buying time. To bleed us, to break our lines, hit the leadership. Every morning our position is weaker and they know it.

Leena   Trust in God.

Hani   There is no God, Mamma. Only the Phantom and the Merkava; the F-15 and the Howitzer. There's only power. And we don't have it. There's darkness and severed limbs for us. Bits of skull caked in blood . . .

Leena   There's more than that. Not now, maybe. It's hard to remember. Easy to forget.

Hani   They're looking for him, you know. They think his plane went down south of the camps.

Leena *does not respond.*

Hani   I'm not asking for him to be executed, just exchanged in return for some small victory, some safety, or time, something to hold onto in this sea of death

Leena   Would we get anything in return? Do we ever?

Hani   Maybe.

Leena   I won't stop you.

Hani   Tomorrow, then. When there is light.

They are both silent for a beat. **Dalia** *enters, also in fatigues.*

Hani   Where are you going?

Dalia   A costume ball. Where do you think?

Hani   The front is dangerous right now, Dalia.

Dalia   I know. And my job is to tend the wounded. And if I need to fight, I can do that too.

Leena   Stop pretending you can stop her, Hani.

Hani   We'll turn him in. Tomorrow. For better terms.

There is a beat with no eye contact.

Dalia So be it.

She prepares her things.

Hani (*to* **Dalia**)   I don't like the way he looks at you.

Dalia *does not say anything.* **Hani** *exits. As he does,* **The Pilot** *enters with the typewriter and sits on the floor. He begins typing.* **Dalia** *listens for a beat then approaches to look at what is written on the typed page but* **The Pilot** *hides it. She tries again and he again hides it.*

It could almost turn playful but **Dalia** *stops. She grabs her things and goes.*

Leena (*half to herself*)   Perhaps someone has some pigeons we can barter for. To stuff. I'll go before the fighting gets thicker. Those poor birds, how they've suffered with all this metal and fire cutting through their skies and over the rooftops. After tonight, who knows how many will remain.

She exits. **The Pilot** *begins to type. Lights shift.*

Scene Eight

As **The Pilot** *types in a trance,* **The General** *enters reading a file. He paces behind* **The Pilot**, *who does not even register his presence.*

The General   I'll dictate, you type . . . To the General Staff and the Cabinet: Request for more time to pound. No . . . soften West Beirut targets from the air, land, and sea. Stop. If we can delay ceasefire it is my belief, and that of my field commanders, that we can break the will of the terrorists and their left-wing Lebanese allies. Stop. Request, repeat, urgently request that grass-fed cows from the Galilee be sent to the front lines for slaughter. Stop. Feast is in order to boost troop moral and iron levels. Full stop. End of message . . . Did you get all that, soldier?

The Pilot   What?

The General   Get your head together! What's that trash you're typing?

He rips the paper out of the typewriter and starts folding it as he talks.

Now listen to me. Your comrades are in the air and positioned around this filthy snake pit of a city, risking their asses for you. And for Uli.

The Pilot   Uli?

The General   So the sooner we turn this city to rubble and drive out Arafat, the sooner you can get home to that tight little piece of ass waiting for you in Tel Aviv.

The Pilot *turns back to his typewriter, trying to ignore* **The General**.

The General (*hushed*)   I see your angle now. You're getting into the character. Going deep undercover. Good. Smart. Fine. Keep playing along with these bedouins and keep feeding us intelligence.

The Pilot   What do you mean?

The General   I mean I need you to tell me where this Hani character is going. Get me an address, get me coordinates so we can let your friends up above know where to hit once he's with his commanders. They must be taken out. If we are to survive, it must be so. It's that simple.

He has folded the paper into a plane and tosses it, making a whistling sound as it flies, and then the exuberant and childish imitation of an explosion as it lands.

The Pilot   I can't.

The General   You can. And you will. Then, look to the skies. You'll know it's time when the light of midday explodes the night. That is your signal to move.

Hearing something, he takes a step into the darkness as the lights flicker and **Sofyan** *enters from the other side of the stage carrying a leather bag.*

Sofyan   Take a break, son. I hear you pounding those keys like a madman. It does us good to hear the sound of our boy back into the house. Especially your mom. Come. Sit. The hour before dawn is the best time for a man to shave.

He sits him down, puts a towel around his neck, and lathers his face. With a razor he skillfully shaves **The Pilot**'s *face and neck as they talk.*

Sofyan   I used to be a barber. In Abu Shusha. Well, you've heard this all.

Pilot   No. Tell me. I want to . . . Tell me again.

Sofyan   I apprenticed. During the day, between tending to the flocks. I was young but I was good. Very good. I could give a man a mustache in the style of a British officer, thin and neat above the lip. Or in the Ottoman style for the old men, thick and full and twisted at the tips. Hold still.

Pilot   What about the theater?

Sofyan   Once I got to the camps . . . I was different. We all were. I saw a poster one day for a play. *Othello*. I went. And I was hooked. After that, I would sneak into the city to be in the theater whenever I could. I volunteered to hang lights at first, cleaned costumes, swept the floors. They paid me a couple pounds, something to bring home. After enough time spent in that darkness your senses adjust. Things become clear. And then people forget that you are just a nobody from the camps. So I acted, then I began directing. I was good. Do you remember when I was invited to Prague once with a delegation of artists? Well you were still young then. You wanted to come so badly.

A moment of silence as he cleans his blade.

Working with actors is not so different from being a barber. In both cases you must take care of your space of work, keep your tools sharp. And the customer is a lot like the performer. You must be gentle yet firm with him. Let him relax, but always make sure you are in control so that he allows you to move him as you see fit.

He turns **The Pilot**'s *head with one hand.*

Sofyan Both the actor and the customer must trust me, let me shape them, transform them. Because once they leave, once they cross the threshold from my space into the world and onto the stage, they're alone. And as Antipholus of Syracuse says to Dromio, "There's many a man hath more hair than wit." Boy was he right. Same is true with talent.

He stops the blade on his throat and leaves it there as he speaks.

And I know when an actor doesn't trust me, when he has his own agenda, his own plan, too much ego, too much of his old self. Same with a customer who never gives in, stays stiff and paranoid and ready to jump out of the chair at any second. I don't like working with those types. Not at all.

He continues shaving as he speaks.

Because while they're with me, whether the actor or the customer, it's my job to make them feel they're intelligent and beautiful, that they're my favorite, the one I'll always pay the most attention to. That way, they leave possessed of themselves, tranformed, transcendent. A new person. If only for a moment.

He has finished. He wipes **The Pilot**'*s face to reveal clean cheeks and chin, and a neat mustache on his face. He hands him a mirror.*

The Pilot *is lost in the image of his new face.*

A loud knock on the door. **The Pilot** *gets up and opens it to reveal, once again,* **The General** *in drag, a red wig on his head.*

The General You are Eyad Akawi?

The Pilot *is frozen.*

The General To be or not to be, man, that is the question. Are you Eyad Akawi or not?

He reaches his hand into his purse but **The Pilot** *slams the door in his face before he can draw the pistol.* **The Pilot** *looks at his face in the mirror again. After several beats there is another knock at the door.* **The Pilot** *is paralyzed.*

Sofyan It's probably your mother back from haggling with the neighbors all night like a madwoman. Go on.

The Pilot *opens it, flinching.* **Leena** *enters.*

Leena (*to* **Sofyan**, *matter-of-factly*) No pigeons. Sofyan, I traded one of your records for some meat.

Sofyan Which one?

Leena It doesn't matter.

Sofyan Which one?!

Leena The Bob Dylan one you love and I hate. Happy now?

Sofyan Damn it, woman. Ask me first! I would've given you something else.

Leena   He wanted that one. Anything else would have gotten us nothing but bone. Let it go. Get it back another time.

Sofyan   That's what you always say.

Leena   We haven't had meat for weeks now. And we can't eat Bob Dylan for dinner.

Sofyan   And we can't make a pile of bones and gristle sing like Dylan either.

Hani *enters, rifle in hand, covered in grime and lightly injured.* **Sofyan** *looks at him.*

Sofyan   Looks like the Masters of War have our number. You look like shit, kid.

He lights a cigarette and hands it to **Hani**, *then exits.* **Hani**, *in a daze, sits opposite* **The Pilot** *as* **Leena** *tends to his wounds.*

Hani   Ten dead. Maybe twelve. Just in my trench.

Leena   And Dalia?

Hani   She's ok. Treating the wounded.

Leena   You're bleeding.

Beat.

Hani (*to himself and* **Leena**)   The tanks reached the other side of the sand barriers at nightfall. We could see right down their turrets. Every time we settled in, thinking the worst has passed, they'd hit us again.

Leena   Be still. I have to sew up that shoulder.

Hani   I'm alive. Bassam and Salim are not. Dalia says Omar el-Issa won't make it through the day. Mamma, you know Shadia, don't you? From Shatila? The blonde one.

Leena   Yes.

Hani   A shell. Ripped her in half. That's what I heard.

Leena   I'll visit her parents later.

A beat.

Hani (*to* **The Pilot**)   Hey, Eyad. You remember Omar?

He shakes his head.

Hani   Of course you don't. I'll help you recall. He was one of the fighters who protected the synagogue in Beirut. During the fighting in '76. Stood guard for nights on end to make sure it didn't come under fire. Hey! Don't you remember? You wrote a poem about it.

Leena   Hani.

Hani   Recite it.

Leena   Stop.

Hani Come on. I heard you read it a thousand times.

Leena Enough. Be still.

Hani Said you wanted it translated into Hebrew. So they could read it. So go ahead. Recite it.

Hani *moves towards* **The Pilot.** **Leena** *steps between them.* **The Pilot** *speaks.*

The Pilot
There are men armed
With conscience and Kalashnikovs
Who stand outside the temple doors,
Vigilant, as death explodes from all sides.

Your books are safe with them,
Just as you too would have been
Had you not insisted on devouring
The wheat of our world
And crushing our stones;
Had you not insisted on drinking our aquifers dry

And sacrificing our animals
At the altar of a God
Who chooses you
And only you.

Still, your prayers and candles will be safe;
Your star of six points too, which you fly upon
Your iron ramparts and machines of war.

All will stay under the protection
of those who were born lost in time
Because of you.

One day you will thank them.
One day you will love them
as I do.

Sofyan *has come out for the last lines. He is moved. After a moment of stillness,* **Hani** *calmly, quietly leaves the room.*

Shelling rises in the distance, followed by the electricity once again cutting to darkness.

Scene Nine

In the darkness there is rhythmic breathing and with the light of day we see **Hani** *alone, doing push-ups, listening to the radio.* **Leena** *enters.*

Leena Are you going back out there?

Hani Yes.

Leena Your arm?

Hani The stitches will hold.

He finishes, jumps up and switches off the radio.

Leena Will you speak to the others? About him?

Hani I don't know. (*Beat.*) The way he read. Eyad's words.

Leena Your father . . .

Hani He is happy. With his Eyad. I know.

Leena Had it been you . . . he would have mourned you, Hani.

Hani But he would have accepted it. That's the difference.

Leena He loves you.

Hani I will not be the one to break his heart. But God help us if . . .

He gathers his stuff, preparing to head to the front.

Leena My little lion. Been a fighter since you were in my belly. Always trying to kick your way out. Just like you would fight your way out of this camp.

Hani This prison.

Leena Don't be so angry with the world.

Hani Why not? Look around.

Leena A warrior must be full of love too.

Hani Just because I'm not a poet like Eyad, it doesn't mean I don't understand love.

Leena I know. I know that.

Hani God knows, I wish I could do something every morning besides pick up this rifle. I do.

He kisses his mother, picks up his gun and exits.

Scene Ten

The General *enters as* **The Pilot** *types.*

The General Since you are playing the part of the poet, I have a little something I jotted down for you.

He takes out a piece of paper and reads it.

The General
>A fiddle, a fiddle, an American fiddle
>I play it soft, I play it hard,
>making music like a bard.
>
>But I prefer the sounds of tanks,
>the sounds of bullets,
>the marching ranks.
>
>So I play my fiddle
>to the tune of war,
>and the Americans dance
>while my eagles soar.

He crumples the paper into a ball and tosses it to the floor by **The Pilot**.

The General   Peace is coming. Prepare for battle.

He disappears into he darkness. It is quiet. There is no shelling, no jets, no gunfire in the distance. **The Pilot** *looks up from his typewriter.*

Scene Eleven

Dalia *and* **Hani** *alone. They speak quietly.*

Dalia   We could have held out.

Hani   Enough. It's done.

Dalia   Hani, they would've been vulnerable. As soon as their tanks entered the city.

Hani   But this is a Lebanese city, Dalia! We owe it to those who fought with us, who sacrificed their city and their families, we owe it to them to leave now, before it's too late.

Dalia   We owe it to them to keep fighting!

Hani   Beirut is not ours.

Dalia   It's all we have.

Hani   Not to turn into Stalingrad. The Israelis will not stop. Not until they have wiped the city off the face of the earth. You know that. We can all see that now. They are mad.

Dalia   We could have gotten better terms. (*Beat.*) You sound like your father, you know.

Leena *enters the house with bags.*

Leena   Is it true?

Dalia   Yes. We just heard.

Leena (*calling off*) Sofyan!

Hani Our fighters will be evacuated. All of us. All the PLO units.

Leena Evacuated?

Hani Some by sea, others through Syria.

Leena And once they've gone? What about us?

Dalia The Americans will come, to uphold the truce. That's what they agreed.

Sofyan *and* **The Pilot** *enter.*

Leena Will you go? With the rest?

Hani If the fighters leave I leave with them.

Sofyan Where? Where will you go?

Hani Whichever countries will take us. Some will go to Yemen maybe. Or Tunis.

Dalia Others to Iraq. Maybe even to Sudan.

Hani But the city and the camps will be spared more fighting. And that is the price.

The Pilot Dalia. Go. With Hani and the others. Leave. You should all leave.

There is a silence; all look at **The Pilot**.

Sofyan Eyad is right. You should leave with the fighters.

Dalia And who will take care of you?

Sofyan We can manage. If they find you and say you are with the resistance, it will be dangerous.

Dalia I'll stay. With you. Hani will be back.

The Pilot They'll kill you.

Another beat.

Dalia Stay out of this.

Leena Hani. Stay. With us.

Hani I stay with the fedayeen. With my brothers.

He exits.

Sofyan He'll find his way back. Like his brother. It's best this way.

Dalia I'll help him get ready.

She exits.

Leena How can we let our little boy go?

Sofyan The script is written, Leena. Trust it. We have to trust it.

He exits.

Leena (*to* **The Pilot**)   Write. Don't say anything. Just type.

The Pilot *sits and begins to type.*

Scene Twelve

Hani *and* **Dalia** *sit alone as* **Hani** *packs. He places the last of his things in the bag and closes it.* **Hani** *hands her a pistol.*

Hani   Hide it well, but keep it near. The Americans guaranteed the safety of camps but I don't trust them. The Phalangist militias want to have at us and the Israelis won't stop 'em.

She nods.

And keep an eye on him. Keep an eye on The Pilot.

Dalia   I watch him. From across the house. I pretend he's him; imagine he was still here.

Hani   Don't let it fuck with your head, Dalia. He's not Eyad. However much everyone wants him to be. However much you miss him.

Dalia   Don't worry about me.

Hani   If anything happens, use him as you see fit. Or get rid of him.

Dalia   Yes.

Hani   You sure?

Dalia   I said yes.

Hani   You won't have to hurt him necessarily. Just trade him if you need to.

Dalia   I saw the way you look at him.

Hani   How's that?

Dalia   The same way you looked at Eyad. With a kind of love. And a kind of hate.

Hani   I loved Eyad.

Dalia   I know that. And I know it wasn't easy being his brother. He told me he wondered if he wouldn't be more use fighting than as a writer. Said he wasn't as brave as you, though. Used to tell me no one was as brave as his little brother. That he wanted to write a story about you.

Hani   He never told me that.

Dalia   Never got the chance, Hani. That's all.

She puts the pistol away and leaves. **Hani** *is still for a moment then takes one of Eyad's books from the stack left by* **Sofyan** *and* **The Pilot***. He looks at it and puts it in his bag.*

Scene Thirteen

Sofyan Son.

Hani Father.

Sofyan Well, you're off to sea, boy. An adventure. An epic.

Hani I hadn't thought of it that way.

Sofyan You should. It will help when it gets hard.

Leena Food. For you and the others.

She hands him a package of food.

Hani Thank you, Mamma.

Sofyan I'd like you to take this too.

He hands him his black beret.

A "radiovka." Got it in Prague. Let it get a nice view from the top of your head. Just remember, it only understands Czech. And a bit of English.

Hani *wears it. The two men shake hands.* **Sofyan** *pulls him in and kisses him.* **Hani** *hugs his mother.* **The Pilot** *enters.*

Hani *leaves, stepping out towards the audience.* **Dalia** *follows. As they walk, we hear ululations, gunshots in the air, car horns. The two of them are at the port now with hundreds of others.*

Hani *continues on and turns to* **Dalia**. *She raises her hand into a victory sign.* **Hani** *does too and then disappears through the audience.*

Silence. All stare out towards the sea They speak to themselves.

Sofyan At the mercy of the same seas as Odysseus now.

Leena I should have prepared more food.

She exits.

Dalia They look so small on that boat.

Sofyan "As flies to wanton boys are we to the gods . . ."

Dalia Like little specks . . .

Sofyan "They kill us for their sport."

Dalia Driven into the sea.

Sofyan Again.

Dalia And again we are disappeared.

Sofyan But there is another act yet to play out.

Dalia *exits. Only* **Sofyan**, **The Pilot**, *and the typewriter remain.*

Sofyan   I know it in my bones like rain coming over the mountains.

He exits as lights dim to black and the sound of a ship's fog horn gives way to the clacking of a typewriter in the darkness.

Act Two

Scene One

It is night. **The Pilot** *sleeps next to the typewriter.* **The General** *enters. He eats a piece of meat on the bone.*

The General Up. Get up. Uli's waiting and here you are writing some faggot play. Up. You need to shoot your way out of this nest, soldier. Before it's too late.

He sucks the marrow out of the bone and drops it. He sniffs the air.

I smell a weapon nearby. The smell of steel is unmistakable, even through the stink of these Arabs.

The Pilot What do you want?

The General A napkin, if you don't mind.

He takes a sheet of paper out of the typewriter and wipes his hands clean with it.

And for you to act like a man. For the nation. For Uli. You can see her, can't you? Clear as day. In her apartment on Herzl Street, above the little pastry shop.

Dalia *appears as* **Uli***, her hair down, in a miniskirt. She sits across from* **The Pilot** *and smiles, her legs creeping open playfully.*

Uli I'm here. Waiting, Eyal. Waiting.

The General Wondering when her man will return from the war and give her a good patriotic fuck. But she can't wait forever, soldier.

Uli *gets up, exits.*

The General And our country is full of men who are up for the job . . . if you aren't.

The Pilot What do you want me to do?

The General Find the gun. And be ready to use it. The time to move is near. We're getting closer. All you need to do is make your way to our lines and you're home. Wait for my signal. Look to the sky. When the light of midday explodes the night, the operation will have begun.

He disappears. **The Pilot** *lies down and goes back to sleep.* **Dalia** *enters on tiptoes. She carefully removes the gun from its hiding place, and then puts it back. She watches* **The Pilot** *for a beat.*

Dalia (*to herself, to* **The Pilot** *and to no one*) What kind of cruel trick is this, Eyad? What kind of fucked-up story are you writing from the grave. You always loved a practical joke but I swear, this isn't funny. (*Beat.*) How can one of them . . . look so much like you. If it weren't so sadistic I would say it was brilliant . . . Or is it really you in there? Is your father right after all? That you've somehow managed to evade death at their hands and find your way back to us from . . . I want to smell him. You.

Him. To see if he smells like you. I shut my nostrils, hold my breath when I'm close. Because I'm scared. That if it's the same . . . if he . . . what would I do then? How could I bare to smell my favorite dish, a taste I have been deprived of for years and not breathe it in, not taste it, not devour it and indulge in it?

She takes a step towards the sleeping pilot and stops.

Fuck! No. I won't. I won't let you trick me, Eyad. I wouldn't let you win an argument then and I sure as hell won't let you win now. I won't be made into one of your characters, your damsels in distress, your proud peasant woman pining over her man. . . . Or maybe one whiff . . . One whiff will resolve it all. Maybe he'll smell nothing like my Eyad and then I'll know for sure.

The Pilot *sits up.*

The Pilot   Is that you?

Dalia   Go back to sleep. You're dreaming.

He does. **Dalia** *exits.* **The Pilot** *tosses and turns. Then, a woman's voice is heard singing a song offstage.* **The Pilot** *sits up again to see* **Uli** *re-enter. She sings and then dances above him.*

Uli   Remember when we spent all night on the beach near Jaffa after training, Eyal. The bonfire and the stars, up all night, dancing above us, and the empty stone houses framing the sky behind us? And then this song came on and you grabbed me by my hips and pulled off my fatigues . . .

He grabs her and pulls her to the ground. They kiss and the passion builds. He starts to tear her clothes off and she does the same. **The General** *reappears from the shadows. He watches them as they become more intertwined.*

The General   Nothing hotter than a pair of horny Sabras if you ask me. Demographically speaking.

The Pilot (*to* **The General**)   Not now, sir, please.

Uli   You always talked about birds, about how you wanted to fly.

The General   And yet you couldn't keep from plummeting to the ground, could you?

Uli   You could name the birds migrating over the sea from the way they moved their wings, the way they spoke to each other over the waves.

The General *burps out the throaty call of a sea bird.*

The Pilot   Uli. I have to go. To Lebanon.

Uli   No.

The General   Get up, soldier!

Uli   Call me Habibti, Eyal. Speak to me in Arabic. We're alone. No one will hear. I promise.

The General   I hear everything.

Uli   Don't go. We'll leave. Travel. To Europe. We'll get away from here.

The General   Is that what you want, Sabra, to be a deserter?! A traitor?

The Pilot   No.

The General   You know where it is.

Uli *unbuckles* **The Pilot***'s pants.*

The Pilot   Yes.

Uli   Don't go. Don't fight.

The General   Get the weapon, soldier.

Pilot   Uli.

The General   That's an order!

The Pilot, *half-naked, jumps to his feet and to the pistol's hiding place.* **The General** *slides over to* **Uli** *and begins to pet her.* **The Pilot** *takes the gun.*

The General   Good.

Sofyan *enters the space. He sees* **The General** *and* **The General** *sees him.*

Sofyan (*to* **The Pilot**)   What's he doing here, Eyad?

The General (*also to* **The Pilot**)   Shoot him.

The Pilot *points the gun at* **Sofyan**. **The General** *continues to undress* **Uli**. *She is down to a slip, but has "become"* **Dalia** *again.* **The General** *restrains her from behind, petting her.*

Dalia   Eyad. Help me.

Sofyan   Help Dalia!

The General   Help your country. She's a terrorist too, pilot. Armed! You have the proof right there in your hand. Let's take her, you and me, soldier.

Sofyan (*to* **The General**)   "I know thee well; a serviceable villain."

The General   "I know thee not, old man."

Sofyan (*to* **The Pilot**)   Why is this beast in my house? Who let him in?

The Pilot   I don't know.

Sofyan   Leave us! Eyad!

The General   Take the shot. He's a terrorist, and the father of a terrorist.

Dalia   Give me the gun. Hani left it for me.

The General (*to* **Dalia**)   I'm going to destroy you, tear you up, make you cry.

Sofyan (*roars*)   Let her go!

The General *releases her.* **Dalia** *turns around and slaps* **The General**. *Hard.*

Sofyan (*to the* **General**)   Now walk downstage, three paces.

The General *follows all of his orders obediently and precisely now, almost marionette-like.*

Sofyan   Give me a pirouette . . . Good. Now cry, but gently. On your knees.

The General *does all of this and is crying gently on his knees.*

Sofyan   Now get down. On all fours. And bark like a dog. I want you to really feel your character . . . Nice . . . Now lick your crotch. Like a dog, lick your own balls.

The General *tries but cannot reach and gets tangled, rolling onto his back.*

Sofyan   Get up. That's enough for today. Leave.

The General *exits.*

Sofyan   Fucking actors.

He exits. **Dalia** *stares down* **The Pilot** *before exiting.* **The Pilot** *is alone. He notices the gun, still in his hand. He sticks it under his pillow and puts his head down on it. Lights fade.*

Scene Two

The same night, just before dawn. **Mira** *sits by the sleeping pilot.*

Mira   Your face has changed, Eyal. Maybe it's the Arabic that you speak with them, working the muscles of your jaw, around your mouth and neck and eyes. You look like my father with that mustache.

She sings:

> Oh my boy, my boy Who wanted to fly.
> My boy, my boy
> named the birds of the sky.

> My boy who passed
> Every one of their tests,
> Learned to fly hard
> And was taught to look West.

> Look away, look sharp, boy
> Be ready to kill!
> Be a master of war
> Out for his fill.

Look West, not East
Though once that was home.
Look West, for your health,
It's every man for himself!

Look up, look up
Where the night sun shown.
Look alive, look alive,
It's each boy on his own.

She leans over to kiss him as a jet overhead shakes the house and the electricity flickers off and then on. **Mira** *has disappeared.* **Sofyan** *now stands over the sleeping pilot.*

Sofyan   Time to wake up.

The Pilot *jolts up.*

Sofyan   I have a something for you.

He brings out a small slide projector. As he sets it up **The Pilot** *checks under his pillow. The gun is there. He hastily re-hides it.*

Sofyan   You used to look at these pictures all the time. Made up stories with each one.

He starts the slides. A picture of a group of men in the 1950s.

That's me at the university. I wasn't enrolled but I would attend classes anyway.

A picture of an old village in the 1930s.

Abu Shusha. Our house was right by the mosque. My mother always complained the muezzin's voice sounded like a tortured dog when he made the call to prayer.

A picture of three women wearing dresses in the 1950s, smiling.

Sofyan   That's your mother, with Selwa and Thulafa.

The Pilot   Wait. Go back. Back.

Sofyan *reverses to the picture of the village.*

The Pilot   I know that place. That's your village?

Sofyan   A long time ago. Yes.

The Pilot   I've seen that place. But it's different now. None of these buildings are left. Some stones in the valley. But I know it. It's full of new houses. And a parking lot. There's a supermarket. Right there, on the hill.

The General *enters.* **The Pilot** *is alarmed.* **Sofyan** *cannot see* **The General**.

The Pilot   I don't understand. But I remember it.

The General   Tell him.

The Pilot I must be mistaken.

The General Tell him.

Sofyan Or remembering.

The General Tell him you grew up on top of the ruins of his shitty little village, pilot.

The Pilot No.

The General That your mother would take you to that supermarket.

The Pilot No.

Sofyan What's the matter?

The General Tell him how when you and your friends chased out the old Arab couple who tried to come back to their house. How you threw garbage at them and called them names. Dirty, dirty . . .

The Pilot Arabs . . . Dogs. Roaches.

The General That's it. While you're at it, tell him I remember his village too.

The Pilot Your village.

The General On our way back from Latrun in '48, some of us joined up with boys from the Giv'ati brigade and paid a visit to Abu Shusha.

Sofyan I remember when they appeared in their jeeps. They shouted at us.

The General Fucking Araboosh!

The Pilot I don't want to know.

The General Those were the good ole days.

Sofyan First they singled out the men who had fought against the British.

The General You know what they say . . .

Sofyan One by one.

The General Once a terrorist . . .

Sofyan I saw it with my own eyes.

The General Always a terrorist . . .

Sofyan Then I saw two women. Taken aside.

The General I heard they were asking for it.

Sofyan They shouted and screamed. Kicked and pushed to get away but . . .

The General They were used.

Sofyan They came at dawn.

The General And then they were disposed of, like filthy rags.

Sofyan The men were shot on sight. I don't like to talk about it, boy.

The General I don't talk about it much.

Sofyan Not even after all these years.

The General At the occasional dinner party I suppose.

Sofyan We fled. And we lost everything.

The General I lost men at Latrun in the fighting. Took a shot to my groin. My foot too. So those shits in Abu Shusha deserved what they got.

Sofyan No one deserves to die like that, Eyad. Nobody.

The General I reckon we took out fifty of 'em that day. Give or take.

Sofyan Some were axed to death. At least that's what some of the women said.

The General No comment.

He starts clearing his throat of something.

Sofyan We ran and at night we slept in the groves, in the woods, in caves. After that day the sun didn't rise for a week it seemed. I couldn't sleep, couldn't even close my eyes. I can still hear the sound of my little cousin Selma rolling her green marble across the hard summer ground, over and over. No one could bear to tell her to stop.

The General *hacks and then retches up a green marble which rolls across the floor.* **The Pilot** *and* **The General** *watch it, but* **Sofyan** *does not see it.*

Sofyan Her family tried to return to their house afterwards. We walked north with the others.

The General Great bird watching in that part of the country, you know.

Sofyan I was barely eighteen.

The General I went a couple years back with my wife. She's the real expert. Lured me with a picnic in the ruins.

Sofyan I used to share a rifle with another boy named Rabea. An old gun. One shot at a time. To scare off the jackals at night, to protect the herds. Not a weapon meant for war.

The General Saw a Eurasian hoopoe fall right out of the sky! Just like that. It was hot as hell. A drought year.

Sofyan Rabea stayed and fought. He told me to go with the women and children that morning, so I did. I looked for Rabea when we got to the border, and then the camps. But I never found any trace. I don't know what happened to him.

The General It was quick. But unmemorable, really.

The Pilot I didn't know.

The General   You never wanted to know.

The Pilot   I'm sorry.

The General   My God, you're fond of the old man, aren't you?

Sofyan   It's not your doing, boy.

The Pilot *kisses* **Sofyan** *on the top of his head.*

The General   Just promise me that if you don't have the balls to use that gun on the trash in this camp, you'll be sure to use it on yourself.

He exits. The two men sit in silence for several beats. Time passes. Hours or days, with the two men next to each other but alone.

Dalia *enters. She is numb.*

Dalia   The Americans are gone. They've left Beirut. Pulled out. We're alone.

Sofyan   It's not the first time.

Dalia   I miss Hani.

Sofyan   And it won't be the last. (*Beat.*) You should've gone with them. Should have made you go.

Dalia   They'll come back.

Sofyan   Too many departures for me to keep track of. Too many returns that never were. Too many faces in and out of focus.

He rises. He looks older somehow.

Sofyan   Stay with him. Perhaps it's time he remembers. Everything.

He leaves with the projector. **Dalia** *and* **The Pilot** *are alone. She sits next to him. Between them on the floor is the marble. They both look at it.* **The Pilot** *picks it up and hands it to* **Dalia**. *She turns it between her fingers. After a beat the electricity cuts out, giving way to darkness.*

The Pilot   Dalia.

Dalia   Yes?

The Pilot   Help me . . .

Dalia   Why should I?

The Pilot   Eyad is dead. Isn't he?

Dalia   Yes.

The Pilot   He was shot.

Dalia   Yes.

The Pilot   I'm not like you. I'm not him.

She tilts her head. She smells him deeply. A beat.

Dalia No. And yes.

The Pilot Tell me then. I want to know.

The General *enters in the darkness.*

Dalia It starts with death, after the month of strawberries; the months when war comes to us, war and fruit and sticky red juice. They came in June, under the command of the fat general, crushing strawberries and villages under foot.

The General (*singing quietly*)
  War and fruit and sticky red juice
  Dripping down arms
  Dripping down chins
  Dripping down walls into everything.

Dalia And with endless columns of armor, with their 140,000 feet and their 700,000 toes on the ground they marched northwards, supported from the skies by the best fire Washington could provide. To disappear us.

The General It's in the west of the city and in the camps that the cancer of self-determination has grown unabated.

Dalia Because this is where our poets, our painters, and our warriors who wish to be free have assembled.

The General So we planned our operation and executed it.

Dalia Then he arrived. In the August heat.

The General My records say the 11th.

Dalia When the skies and the sea rumbled with the science of an invasion meant to put the affliction of being Palestinian into remission.

The General Bomb the affliction. Hunt the affliction. End the affliction.

Dalia And it was on one of those endless nights of endings, that it began; that he fell to us from the sky; from where he flew pressing buttons to heal us from afar.

She lights a match.

His wings were on fire, so he jumped. And he fell.

The Pilot I'm afraid, Dalia. I'm shaking.

Dalia He should have exploded too, like a ripe strawberry. From that height, he should have ended. But he didn't . . .

The General *blows out the match, casting all into darkness.*

Dalia You should have ended. But you are right here, pilot. You are right here. Do you understand?

Scene Three

The Pilot *stands over the typewriter. He wraps it carefully in the cloth it came in.* **The General** *is behind him.*

The General   Your mission is coming to a head.

The Pilot   Yes, sir.

The General   You seemed a bit turned around for a while. Mixed up. A touch of the Stockholm bug. Normal for a soldier behind enemy lines. Especially one who fell from 30,000 feet.

The Pilot   A lot's still not there, sir.

The General   Well, you know what they say; a soldier with a short memory has a long career.

The Pilot   And these people?

The General   Their time has come.

The Pilot   Sir . . .

The General   Focus on the mission. The camps must be cleansed. You still have access to the weapon?

The Pilot *nods.*

The General   Good. You'll neutralize all threats as you make your way South to our lines. Five hundred meters from here. Understood, soldier?

The Pilot   How will they know it's me?

The General   Who?

The Pilot   Your soldiers.

The General   A soldier of ours is easy to recognize. You just shout out in that Hebrew of yours, pilot.

The Pilot   But I look like . . . one of them.

The General   You do look like quite the camp-dweller, don't you. Not to worry. They'll know. That said, you should consider joining one of the undercover units when you're back.

The Pilot   Like the one that killed him? Eyad?

The General   You mean the terrorist? Akawi? Yes. And if you'd bothered to ask me, son, you'd know Akawi wasn't writing romance novels. He was publishing seditious books, books that would rile up the Arabs living amongst us. Books and articles and poems that got those faggot leftists in Europe feeling guilty and righteous. And this Eyad, he was a spokesperson for a group that attacked us on our soil. So he was eliminated. To protect us. To protect democracy. The unit that put bullets through his tongue did a sacred duty.

The Pilot   Yes sir.

The General   And relax.

The Pilot   I remember being up there. And feeling relieved. To be alone, you know. I could see the sea to one side usually, islands, mountains, the desert. I even saw Iraq once, on a run over Syria. I thought of her. My mother. And I imagine flying to Baghdad. Not to bomb it, but to visit. Or like a bird returning from afar. And I had this desire. To see the city, cross the rivers, pass under the date palms, to walk past where my grandfather lived. To know this place that was only 600 miles away but we would never go. And it would have been so easy, so fast from up there. Half an hour, like that. Tops.

But then the voice came over the radio. Orders. Some maneuver or another, a roll to the left, and Iraq was gone and it all looked barren and ugly below again, like I was taught at school, enemy territory for miles, to the horizon. And I realized I wasn't really alone. Or at least that I wasn't me. And I was no bird, I was just a machine, or a piece of it, doing whatever the voices told me. And I decided . . . that I was fine with that.

The General   Spoken like a true soldier. To your position, captain. Look to the sky.

The Pilot *salutes* **The General***.* **The General** *exits.* **The Pilot** *places the gun in its original hiding place and then sits on a stool directly below the hole in the ceiling and stares up.*

Scene Four

Leena   He's different. There's a darkness in his eyes.

Dalia   I know.

Leena   He's starting to remember.

Dalia   Yes.

Leena   Good.

Dalia   I'm going to turn him over. For terms.

Leena   Sofyan just sits and stares at the wall now.

Dalia   I know.

Leena   He would get like this after a show was finished.

Dalia   He is ready. To see things. As they are.

Leena   Always a bit of an odd one, that man. Either a happy man stuck in a world of sadness or a sad man floating through a happy room. But now . . . Now it's only sadness.

Gunfire, tanks moving in the distance. **Dalia** *goes off.* **Leena** *tries the radio but there is only static.*

Dalia (*offstage*)   I can see the tanks above on the ridge. They've pushed past the ceasefire lines.

Dalia *reappears, takes the gun from its hiding place, counts the bullets.*

Dalia   They're surrounding the camps. We have to trade him.

Leena   What if doesn't work?

Dalia   And what if it does? Maybe they'll pull back if we offer them a prisoner.

Leena   Let one of the men go, someone involved, someone official.

Dalia   Who? There are no fighters left in the camp. And if a man approaches their lines, they won't hesitate to shoot. I can get closer. If its me, there's a chance.

She reloads the gun and re-hides it.

Dalia   Pack some things. And watch the pilot until I'm back.

She slips out.

Leena   Dalia, wait!

She is gone.

Leena (*off*)   Sofyan! It's time. Up!

She exits. After a moment **The Pilot** *enters, removes the gun and tucks it in his pants then exits.*

Scene Five

Sofyan, *in pajamas, enters from the other side of the stage just after* **The Pilot** *has exited. The typewriter lies covered in its cloth. He carefully uncovers it as if trying not to damage a delicate creature. He runs his fingers over the keys.*

Leena *enters behind him with a bag.*

Leena   Sofyan . . .

Sofyan (*gently*)   "Cease; thou know'st he dies to me again when talked of."

A moment.

Leena   There is no time.

Sofyan   He would tease me. My God that kid was funny.

Leena   Yes. He was. Take these. Put them on.

She hands him pants and shoes. As he speaks he dresses. **Leena** *helps him as they talk, though they do not make eye contact.*

Sofyan Do you remember, Leena, how he would kiss me every time he saw me, just like when he was a little boy. He never stopped being tender the way most sons do when they become men.

Leena I know.

Sofyan You didn't want him to be like that with you, but I did, I cherished his attention.

Leena I was always harder than you. But he had his ways of melting me, you know that.

Sofyan How he would pound these keys when he was writing.

Leena Like a piano player.

Sofyan In a trance. Playing a hard jazz. My boy Thelonious. When he wrote he was complete.

Leena And loud. The more he wrote the less we slept.

Sofyan They would never have been able to get to him if he had stayed in the camps. With us.

Leena Oh please. He was busy. Writing for the paper, meetings at all hours. He outgrew this camp, just like everyone does. He just had a ticket out.

Sofyan But he was alone when they came for him. Alone when those bullets tore him apart.

Leena No.

Sofyan All I want is to feel him kiss my neck again, Leena. To call me Babba. To hear his laugh; that ridiculous laugh of his.

Leena You think Dalia and Hani don't miss him every day? He was stolen from them too. And from me. For you I ate my grief. But he was my boy too. My baby.

Her body is overcome with a tremendous sadness, but she doesn't cry.

The two look each other in the eyes for what seems like the first time in years.

You would spend your nights at the theater when he was little, and I'd be with him. I'd listen to him making up stories. The endless details he would come up with. "This boy won't shut up," I would say to myself.

Sofyan The cricket Sharif . . .

Leena . . and Rami the roach, who rode Mustafa the mouse to Beirut to meet the bird called Bilal.

Sofyan I thought he would be an actor. I tried. Maybe too hard. He never held it against me, though. I was grateful for that.

The sound of tanks is again heard.

Leena Sofyan.

Sofyan I know. It's time.

Leena *exits.* **Sofyan** *is dressed by now. He takes out the handkerchief with blood on it and puts it over the keys. He then re-wraps the typewriter in its cloth. He lifts it into his arms and exits.*

Scene Six

Dalia *stands facing out, towards the Israeli lines waving her arms. She shouts to be heard.*

Dalia You! In the tanks. Yeah you! I come on behalf of the people in the camps. To make a deal. There are no fighters left here. We are defenseless. But we have one of your pilots! You withdraw and you get him back, unharmed.

A shot rings out. She ducks and then stands again.

I'm unarmed, man! I said we have your soldier! Fell from his plane on the 11th. Look it up and let your commander hear my offer.

Another shot over her head. She flinches.

We could have shot him on the spot, but we didn't. If you'd prefer we can try him for the crimes of your generals and end him right here in these alleys running with shit and blood. And I'll do it too, if I have to, I will!

The sound of laughter in the distance.

I can see you laughing behind your tanks, assholes!. Hey you! Don't you want to go home? You drive us from our land and you're not even there! It wasn't enough to chase us out and build your parks over our villages? To erase the names and make them your own?!

Another shot in the air. This time she does not flinch.

I've heard how you take off those uniforms and travel the world after the army: India, New York, Thailand. While we're stuck here. Your freedom to walk on the beach smoking hash and strumming a guitar comes at my expense, soldier. So what more do you want from us?!

You've hunted us into the sea, blown us into the sky and driven us under the earth. Now there's nowhere for us to go! So take your pilot and leave us alone! Please! All I ask for is a swap. Your man for our camp.

She paces back and forth as night descends on the world.

So what's it gonna be?

The darkness is broken all at once by the explosion of flares in the sky above her. The night is illuminated with the crude light of day. **Dalia** *looks up and then all around her. The sound of shots and commotion rises in the distance. She runs offstage.*

Scene Seven

The Pilot *sits on his stool looking through the hole in the roof. At his feet a stack of paper and the typewriter, back in its case.*

Eyad *enters. He sits across from* **The Pilot**. *He too looks up and the two are, for a moment, reflections of each other.* **Eyad** *then picks up the pages and flips through them. After a moment or two,* **Eyad** *takes a pen and begins to write on the last page. He does this for several beats and then returns the stack of pages. He looks at* **The Pilot** *and then up through the hole in the roof before rising to his feet and exiting.*

The light of the flares above suddenly illuminate the room through the hole. **The Pilot** *jumps to his feet.* **Sofyan** *stands in the doorway.*

Sofyan Hello, son.

The Pilot Sir.

Sofyan Sofyan. Sofyan will do. Where are you off too?

The Pilot I must go. I have to leave.

Sofyan You can stay. If you want. You're a good kid.

The Pilot That's not possible.

Sofyan And your writing?

The Pilot *picks up the papers.*

The Pilot It's not very good. I got stuck. My mind. It's messy.

The General *appears and looks over* **The Pilot**'s *shoulder, reading what is written.*

The General Oh, that's clever, soldier . . . "The End" . . . Very fitting. I like it. I like it a lot.

The Pilot (*to* **Sofyan**) I wanted to be able to write. But I'm not who you think I am.

Sofyan I know who you are. And who you aren't.

The General Lord, I don't know who's more fucked-up, you or the old man.

Leena *enters with the uniform belonging to* **The Pilot**. *She hands it to him.*

Leena I almost lost my stomach washing and patching it for you. It represents only death to me. But it is yours. If you want it.

The General Ukh, I want to throw up listening to these people. The moment's come, soldier. End this.

Dalia *enters, winded.*

Dalia They've allowed the militias through. Lit their way. They're entering the camps.

She goes to the gun's hiding place.

The General (*to* **The Pilot**)   Where's / the gun?

Dalia   Where's my gun?

The Pilot *pulls out the pistol, nervously, defensively.*

Dalia   Give it to me, pilot. I won't hurt you. You can go. They won't shoot you.

The sound of shooting outside, approaching.

The General   Don't. They'll kill you if you give it to them. You know your mission, soldier.

Dalia   Let us defend ourselves. Or let us go.

The General   Tell them there's nowhere to run.

The Pilot   There's nowhere to run.

The General   Put them out of their misery.

Dalia   You may look like Eyad, pilot, but you are nothing like him. You're a coward. And a killer. Nothing more.

The Pilot   No.

The General, *standing behind* **The Pilot**, *lifts his arm for him so that the gun is pointed at them.*

The sound of screams in the distance, and more shooting.

Leena   They're here.

Sofyan   I won't run. I refuse to die with a bullet in my back.

Dalia *turns and calmly barricades the door with whatever she can.* **The General** *takes his hand away from* **The Pilot**'s.

The General   See you in Tel Aviv, kid. Break a leg.

He departs, singing quietly, **The Pilot** *whispering along.*

The General

>War and fruit and sticky red juice
>Dripping down arms
>Dripping down chins
>Dripping down walls into everything.

Voices outside, and shooting, closer now. **Sofyan** *picks up the stack of papers.*

Sofyan   If this were your story, Eyad, how would it end?

He reads the last page then looks up at **The Pilot** *as a banging on the door is heard.* **Sofyan** *lets out a kind of smile. Lights cut to black . . . All is silent. All is still.*

End of Play.

Further Reading

Anziska, Seth. "A Preventable Massacre." *New York Times*, September 16, 2012.

Clifton, Tony and Catherine Leroy. *God Cried*. London: Quartet Books, 1983.

Darwish, Mahmoud. *Memory for Forgetfulness: August, Beirut, 1982*. Berkeley, CA: University of California Press, 1995.

Hirst, David. *Beware of Small States: Lebanon, Battleground of the Middle East*. New York: Nation Books, 2011.

Al-Hout, Bayan Nuwayhed. *Sabra and Shatila: September 1982*. London: Pluto Press, 2004.

Khalidi, Rashid. *Under Siege: PLO Decisionmaking During the 1982 War*. New York: Columbia University Press, 1985.

Petran, Tabitha. *The Struggle Over Lebanon*. New York: Monthly Review Press, 1987.

Randal, Jonathan. *The Tragedy of Lebanon: Christian Warlords, Israeli Adventurers, and American Bunglers*. Charlottesville, VA: Just World Books, 1983/2012.

Pappe, Ilan. *The Ethnic Cleansing of Palestine*. Oxford: Oneworld Publications, 2006.

Said, Edward. *After The Last Sky: Palestinian Lives*. New York: Columbia University Press, 1998.

Sayigh, Rosemary. *The Palestinians: From Peasants to Revolutionaries*. London: Zed Books, 1979.

Sayigh, Rosemary. *Too Many Enemies: The Palestinian Experience in Lebanon*. London: Zed Books, 1994.

Schiff, Ze'ev and Ehud Ya'ari. *Israel's Lebanon War*. New York: Simon & Schuster, 1984.

Liban: L'ete '82. Beirut: Express International, n.d.

Historical Note

Starting in about 1970, Beirut became a hub for Palestinian nationalism, culture, and resistance. Already home to tens of thousands of Palestinian refugees from the 1948 and 1967 wars, the Lebanese capital—long a center of Arab culture—attracted Palestinian artists, poets, and intellectuals, as well as political and military cadres of the Palestine Liberation Organization (PLO). The PLO, after being expelled from Jordan by its Western-backed Hashemite rulers in 1970, made Beirut its base of operations. By the mid-1970s Lebanon had become a sort of Palestinian para-state, a fact that perturbed Israel as well as many sectors of Lebanese society, especially the right-wing Maronite Christian population. As a consequence, during the bloody Lebanese Civil War, which started in 1976, the Palestinians were major players, along with the Syrians, the plethora religious and political sects of Lebanon, and Israel. One of the main Lebanese Maronite militias, the pseudo-fascist Phalangists, became sworn enemies of the Palestinians and their left-wing Lebanese allies. This, combined with their opposition to Pan-Arab nationalism, made the Phalangists and the other right-wing Lebanese parties natural allies of Israel. The animosity lead to a series of massacres and instances of horrendous violence between Maronites and Palestinians during the civil war, most notably the massacre of Palestinian refugees in Tel-a-Zaatar camp in 1976.

During the period of Palestinian ascendancy in Lebanon (1970–82), Israel increasingly interfered in Lebanese affairs both directly (Israel briefly invaded Southern Lebanon in 1978 before the massive invasion of 1982) and indirectly via their right-wing Lebanese allies, whom Israel hoped to prop up as a proxy or vassal state in Southern Lebanon.

During this same period many Palestinian artists, intellectuals, and political leaders were assassinated by Israel and her allies. Among those killed was the novelist, playwright, painter, and Palestinian spokesman Ghassan Kanafani and the poet/activist Kamal Nasser. Kanafani was killed in a car bomb along with his young niece in July 1972 while Nasser was killed in his home in 1973.

In early June 1982, Israel launched a massive invasion of Lebanon. With well over 70,000 men and the support of armored divisions and a powerful air force and navy, Israel pushed across its northern border and swept through Southern Lebanon in a matter of days, decimating the Syrian air force along the way. After roughly a week the Israeli army stood at the gates of Beirut. Once there, however, they met formidable resistance from the 15,000 or so Palestinian fighters and their assorted left-wing and Muslim Lebanese allies. But the PLO and its supporters were pinned in their West Beirut stronghold, between the Israelis to the south and the Maronite militias to the north and east. For over two months Israel laid siege to West Beirut, subjecting the city to relentless bombing from air, land and sea. Despite being desperately outgunned the Palestinian irregulars and their Lebanese allies held the Israeli army at bay, staying in the field longer than any Arab regular army had managed to in over three decades of conflict with Israel.

On August 18, after some of the heaviest days of aerial bombardment (namely August 12), the PLO agreed to a ceasefire mediated by the US. Under the terms of the ceasefire, PLO forces would be evacuated from Lebanon and sent to different Arab countries in exchange for an Israeli withdrawal. US, French, and Italian soldiers would then enter the city as a peacekeeping force. One of the major tenets of the deal was the US guarantee of the safety of the tens of thousands of Palestinian civilians left in the city.

After the PLO withdrawal, however, the US Marines and their French and Italian counterparts quickly left Beirut, and after the September 14 assassination of Lebanese President and Israeli ally Bashir Gemayel, the Israeli army quickly re-occupied Beirut and surrounded the Palestinian refugee camps. On September 17, with the Israelis in control of West Beirut and with the help of Israeli flares, the Phalangist militias entered the Palestinian camps of Sabra and Shatila and over the course of forty-eight hours massacred over 1,300 men, women, and children.

This play, which takes place in the Sabra camp, begins in August of 1982, during the last days of heavy Israeli bombardment of Beirut.

Dead Are My People

Dead Are My People was commissioned by Noor Theatre.

Original music for *Dead Are My People* composed and performed by Hadi Eldebek on commission from Noor Theatre.

Song lyrics by Ismail Khalidi, Hadi Eldebek, Patrick Lazour, and Daniel Lazour.

Characters

Nicola Najour, *an Arab immigrant, mid- to late twenties.*
Weevil, *African American, thirties.*
Esau Perkins, *Sheriff of Lakewood, forties or fifties.*
Ellis Corey, *late thirties.*
Helene Corey, *Ellis' wife, thirty.*
Henry Aldridge, *alderman and stonemason of Lakewood, white, fifties.*
Passenger*, *a train passenger of any age or sex.*

The Hooded Ones / Chorus*, *a shape-shifting group that is faceless, with a kind of hood.*

Hood One *, *you know the type.*

The Musicians, *they are in the world of the play and not, both East and West, of the period and yet not totally.*

Setting

Time: circa 1918.

Place: Between Lebanon / Syria and Lakewood Township, a small town somewhere in the far Southern United States, and it's the nearest port.

Set: Minimal.

A Note on Language: Lines spoken in Arabic are *italicized*. English translations follow directly within brackets [   ].

---

* Double-cast.

"No one was white before he / she came to America. It took generations, and a vast amount of coercion, before this became a white country."
—James Baldwin

The wind brings your names
We will never dissever your names
nor your shadows beneath each branch and tree
—Elizabeth Alexander (from "Invocation")

Gone are my people, but I exist yet, Lamenting them in my solitude . . .
—Khalil Gibran (from "Dead Are My People")

Prologue

A rhythm. From the darkness it grows.

Lights come up slowly on **Nicola**, *who is searching for something or someone, humming to himself. He has a bag and a small drum slung over his shoulder.*

Elsewhere, a world apart. A dim light rises on **Weevil**, *who is also humming as he writes by lamp light, a barrel his makeshift desk.*

Nicola (*to himself, in Arabic*)   Shoof matshoof, ebkee mattibkee, lenjoom m3abye sama, bass ba3da meswaddi [See, don't see, cry, don't cry. The stars are out though the heavens are black.]

Weevil (*to himself*)   Seen, ain't seen . . . cryin', ain't cryin' . . . the stars are out though the heavens are black.

A sound. Both men look up, alert. **Weevil** *hides the letter in his hat and puts it on his head.*

A call in the distance, like an owl's. Both **Weevil** *and* **Nicola** *understand its meaning and respond in kind.*

Weevil / Nicola   Hoo-hoo-hoo.

Another hoot in the distance. A response. **Nicola** *crouches, as if expecting someone's arrival.*

Meanwhile **Weevil** *removes his hat to retrieve the letter but cannot find it. He turns the hat inside out and back (each side of the reversible hat is a different color) but the letter is not there!*

He sticks his hand into his hat again and finds it. A bow to a non-existent audience. We realize it was a magic routine. He puts the letter back in his hat and exits.

Behind **Nicola**, *a man in a fez appears, his face unseen.* **Nicola** *lightly taps a coded rhythm on his tabla. The man echoes the rhythm with his feet. They speak (in Arabic) without looking at each other, back to back.*

The Smuggler   Ent el sabi Lli nezel sarikh dodd el atrak? [You the kid who ranted against the Turks?]

Nicola *doesn't answer.*

The Smuggler   Shu hal habal. RaH tet3alla2 mashna2tak [That was stupid. You'll hang.]

Nicola *tuns and stares at him.*

The Smuggler   Shou, shou raH ta3mel ya walad? RaH ykounou hon b ayya d2i2a [Look, what's it gonna be, kid? They'll be here any minute.]

Nicola *nods. The man opens the barrel (the same* **Weevil** *had been writing on).*

The Smuggler   Mnih. Foot Yalla. W sedd 7al2ak [Good. Get in. Shut up.]

Nicola *squeezes in. The man nails it shut.*

The Smuggler (*off, in a half whisper*) H7amlouha shabeb. SH7abol mersett. Tol3et el shams. [Load it up boys and pull up anchor. The sun's coming up.]

He turns the barrel on its side and rolls it out of sight, then disappears. Lights shift. We see the band now, for the first time. They tune their instruments. As they pluck and tap and strum, the noise turns into the sound of a port.

Act One

Scene One

A bustling Mediterranean port. **Nicola** *emerges from the barrel. He is in a new place.*

Man (*calling out to all*)   On y va, yallah, andiamo. For America, Amreeka, Amerique! New York, Buenos Aires, Neworleen! On board to wherever you please!

The man hands **Nicola** *a ticket in return for a coin and then disappears.* **Nicola** *blends with other bodies and the band as a darkness falls.*

The sound of fog horns, the sea, a steamer, gulls and then coughing, whispers, and talking, overlapping, and little by little, instruments coming alive, and then together into a melody. It is night in steerage.

Migrants (*in Arabic, English, and Italian*)

> *Shoof matshoof, ebkee mattibkee, lenjoom m3abye sama, bass ba3da meswaddi*
> [See, don't see, cry, don't cry, The stars are out though the heavens are black]
>
> See, don't see, cry don't cry
> The stars are out though the heavens are black

Migrant Chorus

> The sea the sky
> From old to new
> From death to birth
> Poor to rich
> > We sway and spew
> > We sail the earth
> > In search of him / in search of her
>
> We hold our breath
> We hold our tongues
> We count the days
> We count the months
> > We count the faces we see at night
> > The ones we know
> > The ones who hide

Nicola (*in Arabic*)

> *Balladi L Habib* [My beloved home]
> *Ghali W 2Areeb* [Close to my heart]
>
> *3Alayya W 3A* [Cherished by]
> *Kullel 27bab* [My loved ones torn apart]
>
> *Mnetmanna Yseer* [Everyday, we hope]
> *Ta7rir el 2ard* [For liberation]

Men Kel Me7Tall [From the invader's rope]
Men Kel Saffa7 [From the butcher's occupation]

Baladi 3Amma [My land becomes]
Li Zikra Yseer [A memory]
Zikra B Bali [A memory]
Kel el 2aw2at [Of the time that fades]

Men Lama Trakt [Since I have left behind]
2Boor El 2A7bab [My brethren's grave]

Migrant Chorus

We sail and fight
We sell and buy
We starve, survive
In the blink of an eye

The music fades. The migrants disperse to sleep in shadow. **Nicola** *stands alone. He practices greeting people in English out loud.*

Nicola Hello, sir. I am Nicola, happy to meet. I am looking for-

Migrant One *Stai zitto / stronzo!* [Shut up, turd]

Migrant Two *Shoo malak ya ahbal, / Iskut!* [What's wrong with you, dumbass]

Migrant Three Shut it ya, feckin gobshite!

Nicola Sorry. *3afwan* [sorry]. Sorry.

Migrant Chorus Shhh!

Nicola *moves off to find rest with the others. Lights shift.*

Scene Two

Weevil *speaks to a public that is unseen but sometimes heard.*

Weevil Here it is. Done.

He holds up the letter, takes it carefully out of the envelope and reads to us / public.

"Dear Mr. Dubois."

He looks up.

Wasn't sure if he pronounced it "Do-bwoi" or "Do-boys." I like "Do-boys" best . . . "Dear Mr. Dubois. Greetings from the people of Lakewood, our fair and foul town located in the heart of Lakewood county in the state of"—

(*Again to his public.*) Y'all said make it sound more poetic, and Shakespeare poetic. Anyway . . . (*Back to letter.*) "By 'the people of Lakewood' I mean our people. For as you know, down here there's a distinction between citizens, leaving those of our race subject to every form of heinousness.

As your publication has shown, we're under constant threat. The Klan in our county is strong, and when the war ends their ranks will swell with the return of soldiers. We've therefore been raising funds through secret raffles, parties, and magic revues. In this way, we've supported twelve families in their migration up North. But our neighbors disapprove of the exodus of their cheapest and most valuable working hands. Eight people lynched in our county alone since 1912, including Ms. Nora Mosely, tied to a bridge . . . after being gutted and emptied of her unborn. (*Beat*)

We've managed, at great risk to life and limb, to collect a trove of documents which shed light on this and other crimes, and which we hope to send safely to you at the first opportunity. In the meantime, Mr. Dubois, we are writing with the following requests:

1. That your organization continues to expose the aforementioned violence.
2. The support of your organization in helping families make it North.
3. The sending, clandestinely, of more literature to educate and mobilize our people.

Sincerely, The besieged citizens of Lakewood.

(*To public.*) I'll leave this right here for anyone who wants to sign.

Gonna meet a contact down at the docks. Hope to send it to New York through her. Headin' there at dawn. With the letter in question invisible to prying eyes, of course. Cause y'all know how the Smoke King do.

He removes his hat, taps it, producing a pen. He places the letter and pen down for folks to sign. After a moment the band starts to play.

(*To band.*) Come on now. Stop with all that. It's late. And some of y'all got homes to get to.

He starts to leave but they goad him on.

Tell you what: the more I see y'all *signing,* the more you'll hear me *singing.* And those of you can, go ahead and put something in the hat for the less fortunate need help migrating.

He places his hat on ground in front of public. The tune picks up and **Weevil** *obliges.*

Weevil (*singing Dubois' poem*)

"I am the smoke king,
I am black.
I am darkening with song,
I am hearkening to wrong!
I will be black as blackness can—
    The blacker the mantle, the mightier the man!"

This top hat is magic
This letter is clear
Its message is tragic
A tale from Shakespeare
But i'm no Othello
I'm unmoored of my fear
'Cause we're destined for freedom
For freedom ya hear

For blackness was ancient,
'Ere whiteness began.
For blackness was ancient,
'Ere whiteness began.

I'm daubing God in night
I'm swabbing hell in white
I am the Smoke King

I am the Smoke King
And i am black.

The music picks up but **Weevil** *quiets them.*

Weevil Don't want to draw too much attention now, being a week night. And I got a long road to the docks. So I'll bid y'all adieu.

He collects the letter and leaves.

Scene Three

The next morning. At a port of entry. We see **Nicola** *with other migrants awaiting inspection.*

Elsewhere at the port, we see **Weevil**, *who makes a call, much like a seagull's.*

Weevil Kweoh . . . Kweoh . . . Kweoh.

Another person, barely visible, enters. **Weevil** *hands the letter off. The other figure disappears.* **Weevil** *lights a cigarette just as a sound in the distance is heard. A rumbling or humming.*

He looks around.

Elsewhere, **Nicola** *is inspected (by a figure in a white coat). He lifts his arms, then his shirt to reveal his bare chest. He turns, studied from every angle. His eyes are inspected. His lungs. He is then pushed out of sight with the others.*

As **Nicola** *disappears* **Weevil** *calls out again,*

Weevil Kreeaah . . . Kreeaah . . . Kreeeah!

He switches his hat inside out to the other color, as well as his jacket, so that his outfit is different from the one he arrived in. He produces a newspaper and reads it.

Nicola *enters. At the port now. He stands frozen, unsure where to go, letter in hand.*

Weevil *sees* **Nicola**. **Nicola** *stares back, still.* **Weevil** *begins to leave.*

Nicola   Hello.

Weevil *stops but doesn't turn around.*

Weevil (*an aside / to himself*)   Thought he might've been a statue. Or an apparition.

Nicola   Hello?

Weevil (*an aside / to himself*)   Reckon he's one of them Syrians. Looks more *serious* than anything.

Nicola   Happy morning to you.

Weevil (*to himself*)   Just pretend you didn't see him, Weevil.

He moves to leave again.

Nicola   You can help? Please . . . Nicola. My name, I am Nicola Najjour. You?

Weevil *turns towards* **Nicola**. *Takes him in but doesn't speak.*

Nicola   Nicola.

Weevil   Weevil's what they call me. At least most of the time.

Nicola   Weevil?

Weevil   Yeah. Like the bug. The boll weevil. Scourge of the kings of cotton.

Nicola   Weevil . . .

Weevil   That's right.

Nicola   Nicola.

Weevil   I got it. And Weevil better be on his way, / so—

Nicola   I look for my brother-father.

Weevil *laughs despite himself.*

Weevil   Your brother-father? That some crazy Turkish shit?

Nicola   Uhm, brother of father.

Weevil   That's an "uncle," then. Where he live at?

Nicola   He send letter from Lakewood, my uncle. You know / it?

Weevil   Probably better you move on, now, to New Orleans. Or New York. Ain't / nothing in—

Nicola No. I am need work to make money for to go find uncle Tanios. Lakewood. No other place. Alone. Lakewood. Look I show you.

He takes out the paper to show **Weevil**.

Weevil Best close up that sack, before some long fingers relieve you that weight.

Esau Perkins *enters.*

Perkins (*playfully*) What they call you? Weasel?

Weevil *now speaks with a very slight stutter.*

Weevil Nnnoo, sir.

Perkins Cockroach? Spider?

Weevil Weevil, Sheriff Perkins. That's what I g . . . go by.

Perkins Yeah. Seen you up in town. You bothering this man?

Weevil No sir, just—

Perkins (*to* **Nicola**) He botherin' you?

Weevil He . . . he don't speak much, sir.

Perkins (*to* **Weevil**) Wish I could sa-sa-say the same for you, boy. (*Beat.*) Just messin' with you. Now let 'im answer me his self. (*To* **Nicola**.) He botherin' you?

Nicola Lakewood.

Perkins Lakewood?

Weevil He was just asking me where—

Perkins And I bet you wouldn't've minded slipping your hands in the man's bags neither, huh?

Weevil No, sir. Yes, I mean, I would mind. Meanin' no, I had no such intentions, sir.

Perkins Weasel is as weasel does.

Weevil Weasel a gentle creature, sir. Ain't got no qu . . . qualms with that critter, smart as she be. But the name ain't weasel, sir.

Perkins *takes a step and is upon* **Weevil**.

Perkins I reckon you have work to do inland, so go on n' git . . . instead of hangin' around foolin' with mongrels on the docks. Go on now.

Weevil *leaves.* **Perkins** *studies* **Nicola**.

Perkins Let's get a look at them eyes, boy. To verify you ain't carrying trachoma. Not a doctor myself. But I am the law. Not here. Up in Lakewood. And I know Sheriff Beauregard—man in charge of this sinful array of docks and bordellos—would applaud my vigilance.

Nicola *is lost.* **Perkins** *examines his eyes from a distance. The faint sound of marching in the distance.* **Perkins** *takes note and continues.*

Perkins   All that's to say, there's no work in Lakewood, son. But I got a friend at the docks might know where a pair of hands like yours can be put to work. It's the Christian thing to do. And in this here square there's a gathering tonight. An event. Might be best you're elsewhere. For your own sake. Come on.

He exits with **Nicola** *behind him as the sound grows.*

Scene Four

The sound of a rally. We cannot see anyone clearly but can feel and hear them. They are the **Chorus of Hoods**. *The speeches and songs are met with alternating cheers, laughter, echoes, whoops, and stomping.*

Chorus of Hoods (*chanted*)

> We climb and hang
> We loop and slip
> We tie and knot
> And haul and lift
> We pop and pull
> And kick and watch
> We purify our land

Chorus Member One (*sung and spoken*)

> I know you've seen 'em come
> By boat, by foot and by hoof,
> Lyin' an' hidin' and bidin' their time
> All huddled then smuggled
> Behind our fair lines.
>
> But a cursory inspection
> Of the peculiar specimen
> Points directly
> To a semi-Negroid confection.
>
> Heathens that carry ocular contagions
> They'll try an' sell you their trinkets
> But best you don't go engagin'
>
> 'Cause first comes that itching
> Then a nasty inflammation
> And before you know it
> You'll have become half-Asian
>
> So take 'em for us, yankees
> With the Spick and the Jew

But first wait a tick
While i castrate 'em fer you.

Cheers, laughter, and stomping.

Chorus of Hoods (*chanted*)

Fear it shows
And fear it tells
So form your lines
And strike the bell

Chorus Member One   Form your lines, brothers, and strike the bell. Protect what's white, come high waters or hell!

A tremendous sound builds and then dissipates.

Scene Five

The port. Two weeks later. **Nicola** *enters moving a barrel on his shoulders and / or rolling it, from one side of the stage to the other, then repeats. It is hard work. He sings an improvised ditty as he does this.*

Nicola

See / don't see
Wala hada shayefnee [No one is seeing me / I am invisible]

Cry / don't cry
Wala hada ma3birnee [No one cares about me]

Wala 3am, wala khal [(I have) no uncle paternal, nor a maternal uncle]
Wala khay wala saaheb [and (I have) no brother and no friend]

2E3mel dinar ya walad [Make some dinars my boy]
Khallik rajel shater [Become a capable man]
Jamme3 2ershayn ya walad [Gather some coins, boy]
Dallel kel el makhater [Overcome that aching heart]

Khallik rajel rajel [Steady yourself man and maybe then]
Nicola sheikh el marajel [Nicola will be the sheikh of good men]

Weevil *passes by, his head down. He hears singing and stops. He sees* **Nicola***, who spots him before* **Weevil** *can turn around and bolt.*

Nicola   Hello. Mr. Weevil. Hello there. Remember? Nicola.

Weevil   Oh hey. I see they made you downright American with all that liftin' and heavin' and crackin yo back.

Nicola   Yes. Back. Heavy. Two week carry like this.

Weevil   Song ain't American, though, Nico. Not yet at least. You take care now.

He begins to leave.

Nicola (*pointing to barrel*) You know I live inside one of these? On boat.

Weevil *turns back to* **Nicola**.

Nicola So that I am not capture by soldiers.

Weevil Outlaw, huh.

Nicola Hurt more to be inside than to carry on back.

He lifts the barrel onto his shoulder again.

Weevil You found any of your kind round here?

Nicola One. But he go to New York. I work with ones from Italia. Can't speak Arab with them.

Weevil Tongue of yours sound like sandpaper on plywood, man choking on his own throat if you ask me, / but . . .

Nicola I am contract, boss say. Only Sunday off. But when I try to go Lakewood they will not see me on road, go past. Like I am ghost.

Weevil They see you. But they don't see you.

Nicola Yes. But then I pay to go to Lakewood, in truck with the fish. But when I'm there, I see it's Lake City. Not Lakewood. Man laugh with no tooth. So I come back.

Weevil Docks more fun anyhow.

Nicola Yes. At night. Sad singin' with sad guitara. (*Beat.*) So how far this damn Lakewood?

Weevil 'Bout an hour an' a half's trip upland. They woods there, but no lake come think of it.

Nicola You know it?

Weevil Don't live too far from Lakewood, no.

Nicola So we are deal?

Weevil What you mean?

Nicola Weevil takin' Nicola. If you say no I walk alone with myself.

Beat.

Weevil Wish I could. But I already got a heavy load to bear. And like I said, ain't nothing there for you. Better off headin' North. /

Nicola No. I go there. No Lake City. No Lakeville or Lake / town—

Weevil or Lakeopolis. Just Lakewood. Yeah. I got it. Listen, you make it, you ask for Elias Corey. Goes by Ellis. One of yours.

Nicola Mine?

Weevil Your people, I mean, from back home. Best stick to your / own.

Nicola Mine are dead. At home . . . From war. From hungriness. Dead. Many run. Come here. Instead of die for Sultan. But I am alone there and alone here.

Weevil Talk to Corey. Reckon he can help you. Least he should.

A work bell or whistle. **Nicola** *leaves.* **Weevil** *traces his cigarette smoke, checks the time, and then moves off.*

Scene Six

The **Corey** *home.* **Helene** *knits as* **Ellis** *speaks.*

Ellis Helene, dear. I know you aren't always so keen on it. Here, I mean. But church—

A look.

I know, they made Jesus into a tax collector. And their singing reminds you of seagulls. I know, Helene, by God I know. But you must talk.

Helene Elias?

Ellis Ellis.

Helene Here I call you by your name, Elias. And don't call me "dear." This is an animal's name.

Ellis No. Yes, but it's also a nice thing to call someone . . . We can go to the Syrian church sometime. If you'd / like.

Helene It's two hours away. And I don't care about church.

Ellis So what's the problem? (*Beat.*) . . . You have to talk to / me.

She says nothing.

Ellis (*to himself*) So, how's the store, Ellis? Fine. Thanks for asking. Produce is moving. I tell you about the new sign? Gotta keep with the times. Lakewood is up and coming up! Sign says, "Corey Bros." Even though I don't have a / brother.

Helene It's "up and coming."

Ellis How's the wife, Ellis? Oh, she's smart as a whip. A beauty, my Helene.

Helene (*in Arabic*) Baddi erja3 3al balad. Lal ziara bass [I want to go back. Home, I mean. To visit.]

Ellis We are not going back there. Even to visit. Since when do / you—

Helene Min Zamen [For a while]

Ellis America is home now. You've been in this country nearly ten years.

Helene   Eleven. It's a long time.

Ellis   But you just got here. To Lakewood. Barely a year. You've got to . . . give it / time.

Helene   Just to see it. Together. Then we can come back. If you / want to.

Ellis   What is there to see there? The people starving? The fighting? The empty looms. The Ottoman officers asking for bribes.

Helene   The war's ending, they say. The Turks will be gone.

Ellis   Well, I'll believe it when I see it.

Helene   So let's go see it!

Ellis   Our life is good here. No?

Helene   We have a lot. More. Than before. / Yes. But—

Ellis   Which is what I promised you. Helene, back there, home . . . The mountains, I mean. It's not . . . There's *nothing*.

Helene   I miss being . . . around people. Other people. That's / all.

Ellis   Arabs?

Helene   People. Like us. Arabs. Sure. *Lesh La2?* [Why not?]

Ellis   Why not go back to New York, then, to Washington Street?! Plenty of Arabs / there!

Helene   That's not / what I—

Ellis   Or back to peddling. Going, coming, re-stocking, / lifting.

Helene   I was good at that at least. /

Ellis   Is that what this is about? Is that what you want? To go back to being that / kind of—?

Helene   That kind of what? Woman? Or that kind of / Arab?

Ellis   Back to the fleas?

Helene   There are fleas every / where.

Ellis   Not here. /

Helene   There are fleas everywhere! And here it's humid. /

Ellis   The diseases. The shouting and the / filth.

Helene   I never got a disease. /

Ellis   You were lucky. You left. /

Helene   And you don't even know New York, Elias. I lived there. Not you.

Ellis   I've been plenty. Too many times to count. I was there for over a month last time.

Beat.

Helene You mean when you came to kidnap me?

With this, he softens.

Ellis To save you. I left a peddler and came back a businessman. With a store and a house, ready to receive you.

Helene There *were* some rather unsavory suitors after me in New York . . .

Ellis And I fought them off tooth and nail.

Helene *Battal wallah* [What a hero!]

Ellis And you were happy to be saved! The way the others looked at you when we left for the train. *Ya Allah!* [My God!] (*Beat.*) And up north is humid, too. And it snows! Wet and cold, and up to your waist.

Helene In the mountains, the winter before I left, it snowed for days. *Bitzakkar Shajar ez Zaytoun wil mishmush, mghattayeen bet-talej* [I remember seeing the olive and apricot trees covered in snow]. I played with the other kids. Our hands went blue.

Ellis I said I'd give you a good life.

Helene And you didn't lie. Even though you always spend too much. When you want to impress people.

Ellis Helene, the people here, in town, they know me now. Know what kind of a man I am. Honest. Hardworking. They wave and say, "Hello there, Ellis Corey" and I wave back, "Good afternoon, Mr. Hardy, Mr. Darcy." I like that.

Helene Do you know what it was that made me come here with you, Elias? What finally won me over? *Lamma sme3tak betghanne.* [When I heard you singing]

Ellis (*caught off guard*) You never heard me sing. Where/?

Helene Amin Sadallah's coffee house. The night before you proposed.

Ellis How did / you—

Helene It's under my uncle's apartment, *dear*. And those New York walls are as thin as paper.

Ellis (*shyly*) I didn't know that / you . . .

Helene Go on. For / me.

Ellis That was / there.

Helene *sings the intro to an Arabic song to lead him in . . . He obliges but sings Henry Burr's ballad "I'm Sorry I Made You Cry." She turns away, softly singing* **Migrant Chorus** *reprise.*

Helene (*Arabic intro*)

Ellis

> Roses entrapture my thoughts with love,
> You are in ev'ry rose
> And like the golden sun above,
> Your smile with heaven glows!

Helene

> (*Arabic in between the following*)

Ellis

> I'm sorry, dear
> So sorry, dear,
> I'm sorry I made you cry!
> Won't you forget?
> Won't you forgive?
>
> Don't let us say goodbye!
> One little word
> One little smile
> One little kiss
> Won't you try?
>
> It breaks my heart
> To hear you sigh
> I'm sorry i made you cry!

She claps politely.

Helene   Ellis?

Ellis   Yes?

Helene   I'm not going to church.

Ellis   I'll think of an excuse. I'm late.

Helene   Tell them I . . . was not feeling well.

Elllis   I will.

He leaves.

Helene (*to herself*)   If they ask.

Scene Seven

Nicola, *with his piece of paper in hand, asks unseen passersby for help.*

Nicola   Do you know where to find Tanios Najour? Please, sir. Mr. Elias Khoury?

Nothing . . . He turns to try again

Hello, miss. I am looking for Elias Khoury. Yes. Mr. Ellis. There? Ok, thank you, miss.

Sheriff **Perkins** *appears in a white suit. Near him is* **Aldridge**.

Perkins   Well, hello there. Mister . . . ?

Nicola   Nicola.

Perkins   Mister Nicola.

Nicola   Nicola.

Perkins   I'll call you Cola. I see you made your way to Lakewood after all? What about the job? At the docks?

Nicola   Back, forth, up, down, carry, drop . . .

Perkins   Hope you haven't walked away from good work, Cola. Lots of good men looking for an honest day's labor.

Nicola   The work is fine, Mister Perkins.

Perkins   Mister Sheriff Perkins to you. (*Beat.*) Not to worry. Mister Perkins'll do. Or Sheriff Perkins. Even better. Sheriff Perkins.

Nicola   Sheriff Perkins.

Perkins   And this is Henry Aldridge. Alderman Aldridge. But that's a mouthful.

Nicola *gives* **Aldridge** *a little bow.* **Aldridge** *nods and looks away, disinterested, hanging back.*

Perkins   Now, I put in a word for you, Cola. Man's word is a man's reputation. His everything. And what else? Told you work is thin up here in Lakewood. Right? Henry over here can attest to that seeing as he has access to the inner workings of town government.

Aldridge   Work's real thin.

Nicola   Am working, thank you. Hard work. Am learnin' more English. Bit bit bit.

Perkins   Bit by bit. Good. Well, since I'm the Sheriff, I spose I'll offer another helping hand. Though it *is* Sunday. This is my church suit, see. Not my work suit. Wife sewed it. Got the material from one of your people matter of fact, down to see her parents in Jacksonville last fall. I told her better to get it from the Wilson's shop. Or the Abbot's. But she insisted the quality was good for the price. Here, feel that.

Nicola *touches it, looks at stitching.*

Nicola   Good. Very good. Very fine, sir.

Perkins   Well, I'll tell her that. At church. Heading there now. My wife, she likes to get there early.

Nicola   Church?

Aldridge   Ding dong, God, Lord Jesus, thank you, Amen, hallelujah.

Nicola   Yes, church. *Amin.*

He crosses himself.

Perkins   That's right. The place where we do all that's called "church" in English. Well you're a Christian, of a kind, so that's a start.

Nicola   When I am boy I go to with mother. Now, no church for Mr. Cola.

Perkins   Well, we all have our shortcomings, son. How about I get my deputy to escort you back down to the coast. Assume you oughta be at the docks bright and early Monday. Most everyone in Lakewood'll be at worship now. At church. Town's dead.

Nicola   I come to find a man. His name Tanios.

Perkins *lights a cigarette and is about to speak.*

Aldridge   No one goes by the name Tanios lives round here. (*to* **Aldridge**.) Or am I mistaken, Esau?

Perkins *shakes his head.*

Perkins (*to* **Nicola**)   Sorry son.

Nicola   And Elias Khoury? The woman telling me this way.

Perkins   Ellis? Ellis Corey?

Nicola   You know him?!

Perkins   Grocer. Joined the congregation last year . . . Well, I suppose it's good to know Ellis will keep an eye on you. Get you back safe. He'll be at church now, but that right there's his house, end of this road. Better you wait for him there.

Nicola   Thank you, Sheriff.

He walks off, then **Aldridge***, then* **Perkins***.*

Scene Eight

The **Corey** *home.* **Helene** *practices the role of the Southern housewife, a tea cozy on her head.*

Helene   Geowrgia, Flowida, Missusssssiippi, Alubama, up in Vuginia, gon buy some strawberries fo you. Hank . . . Oh Hank. .

A knock on the door

Helene   Why do you even knock, Ellis? Come in.

Nicola *enters. They stare at each other.*

Helene   Get out.

Nicola *steps out.*

Helene (*calling out*)   Who are you?

Nicola   Nicola. Najour. I am looking for Elias. *BteHki 3arabi?* [Do you speak Arabic?]

She opens the door. She studies him.

Helene   *Ana Helene.* [I'm Helene]

He looks at her strange "hat." She removes it.

Helene   I was just . . . Come in. Just come in.

She signals for him to enter. He does.

Nicola (*in Arabic*)   *Marhaba. Tsharrafna. ktir Helou baityk. Allah ykheleekee ya Helene.* [Peace be upon you. A pleasure to meet. You have a fine house. God keep you, Helene.]

Helene   *Ahlan wa sahlan. Ahlan wa sahlan.* [Welcome. You are welcome.]

Nicola   *Ahlan feeki.* [And to you.]

Helene   It feels good.   **Nicola**   It feels good.

Nicola   *Afwan?* [What?]

Helene   *La2 ma shi, bas . . . el Haki . . . El aswat* [No. To speak. The sounds, I mean.]

Nicola   *Metel sherbel mai.* [Like drinking water.]

Helene   Yes.

Nicola   *Temmeh malen may-yet nab3a.* [Like my mouth is full of spring water.]

Helene   *Ba3d sneen bes saHra.* [After months in the desert.]

Nicola   *SaHra. Shu b7ebba hal kelmeh. Ma 3am eHkeh. Heik, bSot 3aleh. Ma 3am eHkeh heik ma3 Hadan teneh. Ekher marra men Shahrein. B Hal bekhra sharmoota.* [Desert. I love that word. I haven't spoken. I haven't spoken out loud. I mean I haven't spoken like this. To anyone else. In two months. The boat was the last time. That fucking boat.]

Helene   *Shaiy?* [Tea?]

Nicola   *Khai.* [A relief.]

Helene   *Khai maheyk?* [It is a relief isn't it?]

Beat

Nicola   *BurtaQalee.* [Orange.]

Helene   *Baddak? Burtuqal?* [Would you like one? An orange?]

Nicola   *La2. Bass BHeba la hal kelmeh.* [No, I just like the word.]

Helene *subdues a laugh and takes the baton.*

Helene   . . . *Khiyar.* [Stuffed vegetables. Cucumber.]

Nicola   *Khyoul. HSaan.* [Horse.]

Helene   *Areeb.* [Near.]

Nicola   *3amee'2.* [Deep.]

Helene   *Qarnabeet.* [Cauliflower.]

Nicola   *Ghareeb.* [Strange.]

Helene   *Gharb.* [West.]

Nicola   *Ightiraab. Muhajir.* [Exile. Immigrant.]

Helene   *Muhajira.* [Immigrant (f).]

She sings now. **Nicola** *jumps in and accompanies lightly on his drum.*

Helene

Muhajira. Wahidi [A lone immigrant girl]
3Ala 2arden jadidi [Landed in a cold new world]
Ba3idi mesh 2aribi [So far from close]
3An kullel ahbab [To the love of kinfolk]

Sa3eedi mesh sa3eedi [An unhappy happiness]
Ya albi shul jawab [Oh which one my dear heart]
2Aribi mesh ba3idi [For I'm closer than I'd like]
Men kul el ashwa2 [To the pain of being apart]

She gives him a word. It's his turn to improvise.

Mahjour. [Desolate / Abandoned.]

Nicola

mahjour ya albi mahjour [My desolate heart is abandoned]
2Ta3na sawas sab3 bhour [After the seven seas we crossed]
Gharrabna ktir [We're west of the west]
Weshta2na ktir [Longing for loves lost]
W 3am 2es2al hali [I'm asking myself]
Shu houweel maseer [What is this fate]

Wahdi ana, metlik ana [Alone, like you]
Dayer ana 3ala hana 3ala ghina [For joy I will wait]
Mahjour ya albi, mahjoor [Abandoned my poor heart]
Mahjour ya albi, mahjoor [Abandoned and far apart]

Helene   *MaSeer.* [Fate.]

Nicola   *Ah. MaSeer.*

There is a stillness between them. **Ellis** *enters the house.*

Helene   Elias. *Ta3a.* [Come.] This is Nicola. He came looking for you.

Nicola   *Marhaba.* [Hello.]

Ellis   *Marhabteyn* [And to you.]

Ellis   How can I help you? What do you—Sorry. Please, sit. Helene, bring tea. Nicola what? . . . *Min Beiyt Meen?* [What family?]

Nicola   *Najour.* [The Najour family]

He hands **Ellis** *the letter. He scans it.*

Ellis   He sent for you. You're . . .

Helene   Who? Who sent for / him?

Ellis   His uncle.

Nicola   The young brother of / my father.

Helene   *Ba3at warak? La hown.* [He sent for you. Here?]

Ellis *continues to scour the letter.*

Nicola (*to both of them*)   Tanios. Uncle. Yes. You know / him?

Ellis   Nearly two years for this to get there. This was sent . . . /

Helene (*to* **Nicola**)   I just came / here

Ellis   Two years / ago.

Helene (*to* **Nicola**)   To Lakewood I mean. I got here less than a year / ago.

Nicola   Sherrif Perkins, he say . . . He say . . .

Helene   In Arabic. *EHkeelou bil A3rabi.* / [Say it in Arabic.]

Ellis (*calmly*)   Let him speak. (*To* **Nicola**.) Go on.

Nicola   I understand maybe Tanios not living here.

Ellis   Yes. Well . . . He's not . . . Sit. Please sit.

Helene   He's already sitting / Ellis.

Ellis   Your uncle . . . I'm sorry, he's . . . I'm sorry.

He is having trouble continuing. **Nicola** *realizes the meaning. A buzzing or humming sound overtakes the space, as if inside* **Nicola**'s *head.* **Ellis** *is talking but he cannot be heard.*

Nicola *is there but not there. Lights shift.*

Scene Nine

Weevil *stands in a cape and hat. He breathes rhythmically, almost in a trance, and utters a string of words in an unknown tongue. He hurls a small object to the ground which explodes and releases smoke. He is enveloped in the grey blue smoke. As it dissipates, he is still there.*

Weevil (*to the banjo player / band*) Shit. . . . Still workin' on it. This is when the master of ceremonies'll say: "Another round of applause for the one and only, 'Smoke King'!"

He spins back into a bow, then gestures towards an imaginary audience (us).

And I pass the hat to the public, they'll be there and there more or less.

To banjo player / band:

Now I go into my soliloquy. Y'all can give me a little somethin' here underneath. Keep it soft for now. Never know who's lurkin' in these woods.

A banjo and a beat, plus the occasional snare or bell quietly underscores **Weevil**, *who speaks, sings and rhymes with cigarette in hand.*

Weevil (*to "audience" / us*) Thought you had yourselves a magical Negro just now, didn't you? Well, I ain't. Just a plain ole magician. I can't fly or read your mind. All I know is ain't one of us here wouldn't trade a day pickin' cash crops, or an evening swingin' from a pecan tree for the simple miseries and complex freedoms of the northern factory floor. And that's why I do this, folks. To disappear y'all, to the promised land. Call it "black liberation magic."

A flourish from the band.

The magic of it is making white folk *think* you somethin' you ain't. 'Cause they the sun in their universe, and we revolve around them. So you gotta play the role they wrote for you in *their* story, turn it to your advantage by the time the curtain falls. That's why I got some of them thinkin' Weevil a bit s . . . s . . . slow. Nothing much between the ears.

He pulls each side of a string in and out of his ears, as if he's flossing an empty brain cavity.

> To them i'm just a fool
> A sharecroppin' clown
> But when they ain't lookin'
> I wear this smoky crown

Spoken:

> Yeah they see you but they don't see you,
> Let tongues get loose with information
> But unbeknownst to them
> The Smoke King's makin' observations.

With a flick of his wrist he produces a small accordion-like ream of notes which cascades across the stage. He reads one.

Taking notes! And I quote: "Nathan and the Alderman said they'd be there Saturday when we round up the boys for a ride." January 10, 1918, outside Steven's General Store. Broad daylight. They wasn't talking about no equestrian club neither.

> Them fools are hoods,
> Riders through and through
> One day they'll be haunted
> By all they say and do.

He pulls a flower out of his sleeve.

And maybe some of 'em even suspect that I might be just a little magical? So they keep a distance. But none of it exactly the truth, is it? Sleight of hand. Yeah, it's serious business being a *real* illusionist.

The sound of horses in the distance as a darkness descends.

Setting sun bodes well for a night ride. Time to dissipate. Let y'all know where to meet for rehearsal tomorrow.

He produces a puff of smoke as he and the band retreat out of sight. The **Hooded Ones** *descend, barely visible.*

Hood One *enters the space, silences his unseen riders. He picks up the flower left by* **Weevil***. He smells it, as if tracking an animal.*

Hood One (*spoken quietly*)   Keep your eyes open, boys. Somethin' like voodoo in these woods.

He rejoins the others in the shadows and they melt away.

Scene Ten

Ellis *and* **Nicola**. *They sit far apart.*

Nicola   Flu?

Ellis   Influenza. / Yes.

Nicola   Influenza?

Ellis   Yes. Flu.

Nicola   Tanios . . .

Ellis   I wasn't here. When / he . . .

Nicola   Dead . . .

Ellis   And when I heard, it was too late. Nothing could be done.

Nicola *Lezim ektob risele la 3ayelteh.* [I have to write a letter to my family.]

Ellis Of course. We can write to them. Or a telegram.

Nicola *Bess fish Hada.* [But there's no one to write to.]

Ellis He was here and then he wasn't. (*Beat.*) Yes. Who would we write to now that / everyone is . . .

Nicola Where? /

Ellis I should have but I didn't / know who to—

Nicola Where is he / buried?

Ellis It all happened so fast. Oh. There is a / spot.

Nicola *W aghrado?* [And his stuff?]

Ellis In the cemetery. But there's no . . . What? I don't know, where his things are, I . . . We knew each other for a long time, your uncle and me. I'm so sorry. That you came all this way—

Nicola Drink.

Ellis The circumstances / . . .

Nicola Drink.

Ellis *Allah yerHamo.* [May God rest his soul.] What? /

Nicola I need drink.

Ellis Of course.

He gets up, pours **Nicola** *a shot. He throws it back in one motion. Lights shift.*

Scene Eleven

Weevil *at home at his "desk" that night. He sips from a bottle as he writes something down and adds it to a large stack of official-looking documents. He takes a small pile of pictures and starts looking through them one by one, then placing them with the appropriate file.*

Weevil You all won't stop looking at me, will you? Even when I ain't looking at you.

He holds one picture apart.

You know I never liked you much, George. But that doesn't mean I ain't mad they took you. Shoulda never done you like that. Not never.

He looks at another.

Evenin' Miss Nora . . .

He kisses the picture and speaks to it.

Tell me, baby: How in the hell I'm supposed to get this stack of papers to Mr. Dubois in New York? Call too much attention send 'em by mail. Contact down at the docks can't help with somethin' this size. And you know I' ain't about to send it with one of the families heading North. Dangerous enough as it is. Can't afford to lose these papers, Nora. Price paid to get 'em was a man's life. I'll be damned if I let some two-bit, night-riding station clerk make it all in vain.

A moment with the picture and a swig of his drink. A banjo riff being played nearby.

Weevil (*calling off*)   Oooh I like that, man.

Weevil *takes a moment then sings, quietly, almost to himself.*

> Oh I survived
> When I thought I would drown
> Yes I survived
> But oh, I wanted to drown
> It was the Devil that took my baby down
>
> [*Instrumental*]
>
> They tell me flee
> Yeah they want me to run
> But oh I know
> I know what's gotta be done
>
> Since the night they
> Stole my Nora away
>
> [*Instrumental*]
>
> Gonna make the Devil pray
> Gonna make 'em rue the day
> Make the motherfuckers pay
> Make 'em kneel and say
>
> "Sorry!
> We took your baby away."
>
> Make 'em sorry
> They took my Nora away.

He lights a cigarette, relaxes. After some beats, a dog barks. An eerie silence. More barking. **Weevil** *disappears the stack of documents into a compartment in his "desk."*

The thunder of horses, the light of torches. He takes a deep breath, walks towards the "door."

G . . . Good evening. Is there a problem, sir?

Scene Twelve

Nicola *walks to a spot and looks down. He takes off his hat. Says a silent prayer. Elsewhere we see* **Weevil** *dressing wounds.* **Nicola** *starts a simple beat (on his tabla) and a simple, melancholic humming / singing and / or prayer.*

Weevil *looks up, as if hearing the beat in the distance.*

Nicola *leaves.* **Weevil** *hums as he finishes tending his wounds.*

Scene Thirteen

Late that night, **Nicola** *is at the table alone with a drink.* **Helene** *enters.*

Helene Ba3dak feye2? [Still awake?]

Nicola Eh. [Yes.] I'm up. I found *'arak* to drink. Will Ellis be mad?

Helene Only bourbon now for Ellis. When he drinks.

She takes a glass and helps herself.

He will be up soon.

Nicola I don't sleep well here anyway. *Mish 2edir* [can't]. Too hot. And hoomid. *Hoomid*?

Helene Humid. He-oomid. /

Nicola (*in his best American accent*)   Heeoomid . . .

Helene *Moomtaz*. [Excellent.] You'll be American in no time.

Nicola I come here only with Tanios to see. But now he is just face in my head. A song I remember. Now he just a small tree. I do not have even picture of him.

Helene What do you mean he is a small tree?

Nicola I go to cemetery today. But there is no stone. No name. *Ma fi Hata ismoo maktoub.* [His name's not even written here.] Just a tree Ellis plant near fence. To remember Tanios.

Keif bitoule arz bil engleezi? [How do you say Cedar in English?]

Helene Oh. Cedar. I think. Yes. Cedar . . . *Allah yerHamo.* [May God have mercy on him.] I wish I had met him. Your / uncle.

Nicola I like to hear you.

Nicola Hear me?

Helene Speaking Arab. I like it.

Helene *Arabic.* You are Arab. But you speak Ara*bic*.

Nicola I remember this. From American missionary. He was teacher in village. Reverend Johnson.

He drinks.

Maybe I go back now. Home.

Helene They say there is nothing left. There.

Nicola Maybe. But what I have here? And if there is nothing there, why do French and British want it for themself?

Helene Sometimes I think about going back, but . . .

Nicola Ellis, he likes America?

Helene Oh, he is American. We all are. It's what he believes. We're here, so we're Americans. (*Beat.*) . . . Why did you leave?

Nicola My sister and little brother. And my mother. I bury all in grave. Many others. *Kenet la Haleh.* [I was alone.] *Kenet za3alan.* [I was upset.] So I do things. Against Sultan.

Helene Like what?

Nicola First, I don't fight for his army. He hate this. Then I sing about him in the square. Many people come and they shout against Sultan, too. Shout to be free. Then his men come for me. Only place to run is America. To Tanios.

Helene What did you sing?

Nicola You want to hear?

Helene But quiet.

He gets his tabla and plays a riff as he sings / chants in Arabic.

Nicola

> *Oumou ya shabab* [Get up / let's go, guys]
> *Thourou 3alal 3usmani* [Revolt against the Ottoman]
> *Oumou ya gedaan* [Get up / let's go brave men]
>
> *Dekkoul babel 3aali* [Bring down his highness]
> *Nehna badna 3eeshi karimi* [We want a decent / generous life]
> *La saffah la sultan* [No butcher, no sultan]
>
> *3Arfeen shu badkoun? . . . Ehhhh* [Do you know what you want? . . . Yes]
> *Arfeen shu hamkoun? . . . Ehhhh* [Do you know what you're concerned with? . . . Yes]
>
> *Tab yalla oumou kheffouha* [Ok so get up let's go]
> *Oumou yalla 3ala sultan* [Let's go get up against the Sultan]

She claps, quietly. He bows.

Helene So then you ran?

Nicola Better than to hang?

Helene And you found your way . . . to Lakewood. To us.

Nicola *Jeet, la a3lum min eyn, wa lakinee eteytoo w la2ed ebsartoo 2udami tareeqa femasheyto*
[I came, I know not, yet came this way: I saw a path and along it made my way.]

Nicola *Keef jeetoo? keef ebsarto tareeqee? lesto edree* [How have I come? How did I find my way? I do not know!]

Helene *Keef jeetoo? keef ebsarto tareeqee? lesto edree* [How have I come? How did I find my way? I do not know!]

Helene You know I once heard Abu Madi read his poetry. In New York.

Nicola Ah, in your Little Syria?

Helene Yes. In *my* Little Syria.

Nicola Helene? *2ilili, kell es-souryyeh hawnik kteer zghar?* [Tell me, are all the Syrians very little there?]

Helene *laughs then covers her mouth.*

Helene No. Not all the Syrians are very little in Little Syria. But we have our own newspapers in Arabic, in English. And books. And you can get anything from back home.

Nicola Like 'arak?

She nods, they throw back their drinks.

Nicola New York. You miss it.

Helene Sometimes. Yes. But it is also dirty. Crowded. With horses and cars and people. Shouting and fights in the streets. *FawDa!* [Chaos!]

Beat.

Nicola Wait, I sing for you now. Quiet. And you dance.

Helene I only dance for my husband.

Nicola Like we dance in mountains? Or you can dance only to funny American song he play on record?

She takes his drum.

Helene Why don't you dance. For me.

She drums and sings and he dances. It is playful. **Ellis** *enters. Silence.* **Nicola** *urges him on, drumming.* **Helene** *claps.* **Ellis** *gives in, singing to Helene and dancing in traditional Arabic style, "We're Here, We're Here."*

Ellis (*in Arabic*)

  Jeena u jeena u jeena [We've come, we're here, we're here]
  Jeena el 'aroos wa jeena [We've brought the bride]
  Kirmal 'ayoonha el kahl [To honor her dark black dusted eyes]

Sevan Greene (Ellis Corey) and Nadine Malouf (Helene Corey) in Noor Theatre's production of Ismail Khalidi's *Dead Are My People*, directed by Leah C. Gardiner, produced by Noor Theatre at New York Theatre Workshop, 2018.
Photo by Tess Mayer. Photo courtesy of Noor Theatre.

Wa khadoodha ehloo el ehl [Her trusting eyes]
Badr al samaa yndahlha [The full moon calls out to her beguiled]
Wa yiqoolha janintina [Tells her you are driving me wild]

It is ecstatic, a release. A rooster crows. **Ellis** *looks at his watch. He gets ready to go.*

Helene   It's barely light out, Ellis.

Ellis   But it's Monday.

Helene   Don't you want to eat?

Ellis   Shipments coming in early. Nicola, as long as you're here, you need a job. Tanios . . . He'd want me to look after you. Until you are on your feet. Come by at eight thirty. Sharp. Helene, lend him something to wear. Respectable. (*Beat.*) I was thinking you could go by "Nick." Shorter.

Ellis *kisses* **Helene**'s *hand and exits.*

Helene   We'll get you ready. You wanna make a good impression in town. "Nick." Come.

She exits. He follows. Somewhere else we see **Ellis** *moving and arranging goods.*

Helene *re-enters,* **Nicola** *behind her, and sets down a trunk. She goes through it.*

Helene The suit is here, I'm sure. Just buried under all this . . .

She tosses out trinkets, which **Nicola** *collects.*

Nicola *Shu hayda*? [What's all this?]

Helene For peddling. Selling. This is Ellis' stuff. From the road. I was much more organized than he was I can tell you that. *Kell Shi bi maHallou* [Everything in its place.]

Nicola You peddle too?

Helene *Min Zamen.* [Long time back.] But not anymore. What? I wasn't always in the house. I'm strong. Look.

She flexes. He touches with his index finger. She goes back to searching in the trunk.

Nicola Tanios, my uncle. He was peddle, with Ellis, yes?

Helene I believe so, yes.

She finds what she is looking for.

Here! Take off what you are wearing.

She hands him an outfit, turns away as he strips.

They're small for Ellis now. Too much sitting.

Nicola It is nice.

Helene I told him, "Go to the Bandalis in Jackson. They're good tailors. From Beirut. *Ktir shatreen* [Very skilled]." But he insisted on this Wilson. Or Winston.

She takes him in.

MniH [Ok], it will do. For now.

Nicola Thank you.

She leaves. **Nicola** *feels the fabric of his suit, looks at his new "skin." Feels it, walks in it. He then puts on the hat and leaves quietly.*

Scene Fourteen

That morning. In the store. **Perkins** *and* **Aldridge** *enter.*

Aldridge Mornin', Ellis.

Ellis Mr. Aldridge. You're up early. Sheriff Perkins, how do you do?

Perkins Just fine, Ellis. Thanks for / asking.

Aldridge I don't sleep much, tell you the truth.

Perkins Heat doesn't / help.

Aldridge Alderman's a full-time / job.

Perkins In term of sleepin' I / mean.

Aldridge Also, working on a statue these days.

Ellis You're a sculptor, Mr. Aldridge? I knew you worked at the quarry. Before you were / alderman.

Aldridge Well, I am. A sculptor. And like to get an early start. Like you.

Ellis Yes. A busy morning. I'll be restocked by noon I hope.

Aldridge You been up for a while, Corey?

Ellis Yes. I suppose.

Perkins Couple things I wanted to talk to you about, Ellis.

Ellis Of course, Sheriff. You know, I was gonna head over to Scott's Diner for a bite. Would you care to join?

Perkins Afraid I can't, Ellis.

Aldridge Me neither.

Perkins But thanks.

Aldridge Already ate. Couldn't sleep.

Perkins Henry, we'll get to that, let us talk / here.

Ellis I thought you don't sleep much, Mr. Aldridge?

Perkins Ellis, we've received some complaints. Over at the station, / you know.

Aldridge When I ain't woken up I sleep some.

Perkins Henry.

Aldridge Go on, Esau.

Ellis Sir, I'm a little unclear.

Perkins It's about your, well, you know I'm happy you joined the church, got baptized. And I think you run a good business here, respectable and all.

Aldridge Your stands are too far onto the sidewalk.

Perkins shoots **Aldridge** *a glance.*

Perkins Well, Ellis, it's a matter of order. You know? I think there was a feelin' your products were gettin' a bit chaotic.

Aldridge (*under his breath*) Like a souq in Baghdad or Timbuktu. /

Perkins So I wanted to come over and let you know, first / thing.

Aldridge Istanbul.

Ellis Thank you Sheriff. I'm glad you told me.

Perkins It's my job, nothin' personal.

Ellis When I rented the store, Mr and Mrs. Stokes, they showed me where the produce could extend to. It's just I thought I was respecting the . . . But I'll be sure to move them today.

Perkins That'd be great.

Ellis Could you show me? Exactly? I have chalk. To mark it, so I won't forget.

Perkins *measures and puts his foot on a spot.*

Perkins There.

Ellis *draws a careful line where* **Perkins**' *foot is.*

Ellis I'll move everything right after I get my shipments in.

Perkins Thanks, Ellis. How's that boy by the way? Cola? One I sent your way.

Ellis Fine. I'm putting him to work. Here. Until he's more accustomed to the way things work.

Perkins Good. Good. You know, we *will* get some breakfast over at Scott's. Care to join?

Aldridge Or do you have work to get to?

A beat.

Ellis I think I'll stay. Thank you.

They start to leave but **Aldridge** *nudges* **Perkins**.

Perkins Oh, and last little thing, Corey. There was some concern about . . . music. Quite early in the morning. Coming from your house perhaps. Music of a peculiar kind of . . .

Perkins Genre. **Aldridge** Provenance.

Aldridge Oriental.

Perkins No reason why it should amount to anything, though, Ellis. If it's . . .

Aldridge Contained.   **Perkins** Quiet.

Perkins Best to just use common sense is what I'm getting at. Keep it down. / Private.

Ellis It won't happen again.

Perkins *and* **Aldridge** *leave.* **Ellis** *is frozen in thought just as* **Nicola** *enters.* **Ellis** *sees him.*

Ellis You look good. But maybe the mustache can go. Yes, shave it. Better. Come. Help me with these.

He moves a crate off. **Nicola** *looks at the chalk line, then picks up a crate. Lights shift.*

Scene Fifteen

The cemetery. **Weevil** *enters with a flower. He is about to step over the line but stops. Looks around. He hears a sound and retreats as* **Nicola** *enters.*

Nicola Hello. Mr. Weevil. Is that you? Come.

Weevil *looks around. He inches closer but maintains a bit of distance throughout, as if respecting an invisible line.*

Weevil Not allowed to be in certain parts of the cemetery is all.

Nicola Why?

Weevil Two sections. One for us, one for them. My mamma down that way. My daddy too. And over there is . . . Well, anyway, what I mean to say is the lines can be a bit murky.

Nicola Murky?

Weevil Muddy. Tenebrous. Shadowy. Unclear. Not clear . . . I'm not quite sure which section we in right now. Neither here no there, ya know. Kinda no-man's land. You follow?

Nicola A land with no man in it, not a good place for any man?

Weevil *rolls a cigarette as he speaks.*

Weevil Let's just say it can be hard to know exactly where one stands all the time. What with all the lines drawn by certain men. In the sand, in the air, the seas, and rivers, even in the blood. I call those types "delineators."

Nicola Delina-yators.

Weevil That's right. Read in Mr. Dubois' newspaper they carved up where *you* came from, too, French and English, up and delineated Syria, Lebanon, Palestine, too. The Holy Land. Whole new map full of their lines. Two of 'em, Pikes and Psycho.

Nicola Ah, yes, Sykes and Picot.

Weevil That's right! Sykes and Picot.

Beat.

Nicola Mr. Weevil. You know, I find my uncle. Is dead. This tree for him.

Weevil Look more like a bush to me. I suppose it'll grow with time, though.

He removes a flask and pours a splash on the ground and then closes his eyes as if in prayer. He hands it to **Nicola** *who follows suit.*

Nicola   Very nice of you. To pray for a man you don't ever know.

Weevil   Least I could do.

They stand in silence for some moments.

Nicola   You know person to make stone, to put for Tanios?

Weevil   Gravestone. I know a guy. You think you can give me some of them loopy dips, dots, and scratches? Your language I mean. To have chiseled on the stone?

Nicola   Arabic. That would be good.

Weevil *hands him a piece of paper and pencil.* **Nicola** *writes something and gives it back.*

Weevil   Yeah, I figure my guy Vernon can do that.

They pass the flask again.

Nicola   *Allahyirhamou.*

Weevil   Amen. You take care of yourself now.

He begins to leave.

Nicola   You know, I think I leave sickness behind when I come to America. But I come and Tanios dead, from influenza. Dangerous here. Like any other place.

Beat.

Weevil   Well every place got the flu . . . Every place got its own sicknesses.

Nicola   I never want come to America like others. Why I need a street made of gold? But I have nowhere to run. So I hide in little boat, then in very big boat over the big sea. To America.

Weevil (*half to himself*)   Funny, ain't it? How much depends on the kind a boat you arrive in. And where you was sittin' on it.

Nicola *has been handling the letter.* **Weevil** *notices.*

Weevil   What he tell you? In that letter.

Nicola   Askin' about my family. Tellin' me to bring him things. If I come. Soap from Nablus. Strings for the 'oud.

Weevil   Turtle-back guitar you mean? . . . Guitar. Shaped like a turtle?

Nicola   Tortle, yes. *'Oud.*

Weevil   Oood?

He tries to pronounce 'Oud repeatedly, **Nicola** *tries to help with the guttural first letter.*

Nicola   Tanios play this and tell stories. Kids always love Tanios. He sing and do funny thing.

Weevil Like magic, you mean?

He pulls a coin from **Nicola**'s *ear.* **Nicola** *claps.*

Weevil Shh. No applause.

Nicola I like this. You teach me.

Weevil Gotta have a reason to do magic. Gotta have a meaning. Deep down. Or else it just . . . tricks. (*Beat*.) Now you find out your kin is gone, might want to hit the road, peddle your way up North. I could take you as far as the station in Salem.

Nicola I wish you meet my uncle when he is alive. He would like you.

Weevil And I'm sure I'd like him.

A shot in the distance. **Weevil** *is alert.*

Weevil I better move on now. Take this here flower. For your uncle.

He hands **Nicola** *the flower.*

Nicola I seein' you soon?

Weevil Best you don't. See me.

Nicola We are not friends?

Weevil Don't think so, Nico.

Nicola Because you are Negro . . . Or you say / nigger?

Weevil I say Black. Black.

Nicola At shipyard, the boss and the other men, they this other word. Soon, the Italian . . . One of them, Paolo, he start saying this word, like boss, then another and another say it too.

Weevil Don't have to do what others do.

Nicola I know. This what Tanios always tell me, too.

Weevil *tips his cap and starts walking off.*

Nicola Other night, Weevil, there is men. Ride through town on horse, shouting. With fire. Who they are?

Weevil What Ellis tell you?

Nicola He say they just making show, not gonna do nothing to us. Because we not Negro. Black.

Weevil Well you listen to Ellis, then.

Nicola What they do in their show?

After a moment **Weevil** *lifts up his hat / shirt to reveal marks of torture.*

Nicola Why?

Weevil I guess they scared, Nico. Scared half to death . . . of magicians.

Another shot in the distance. **Nicola** *looks off, but when he turns back,* **Weevil** *has left.*

Lights cut to black.

Act Two

Scene One

All in their space, alone with themselves, the men shaving, **Helene** *preparing for the day. They sing a round of sorts, growing and growing . . .*

Nicola
Shoof matshoof, ebkee mattibkee

Weevil
Seen ain't seen, cryin' ain't cryin

Helene
Lenjoom m'abye sama, bass b'ada meswaddi

Ellis
The stars are out, though the / heavens black

Aldridge
We tie and knot and haul and lift
We pop and pull and kick and watch

Perkins
Fear it shows, fear it tells
Form your lines and strike the bell

A church bell in the distance. All stop look out then tap their razors on their shaving cup and continue shaving. Out of this prayers.

Helene   *Quddusun allah, quddusun il-qawwi, quddusun elathi la yamut, ir7amna.* [Holy God, Holy Mighty, Holy Immortal, have mercy on us.]

Perkins   May the Lord steady my hand, for weakness is strength and my strength my weakness. I am a sinner, / Jesus. Save me.

Ellis   Holy God almighty have / mercy on us.

Nicola
2eshya ktiri ya ammi ana meshta2la
L ba7r l ghaymi el day3a w teebet ahla

Aldridge   And he said, Cursed be Canaan; a servant of servants shall he be unto his brethren

Weevil
Away with all your superstitions
Servile masses arise, arise
We'll change the old traditions
And spurn the dust to win the prize.

Aldridge   Servants, be obedient to them that are your masters according to the flesh, with fear and trembling, / in singleness of heart, as unto Christ.

Perkins   With fear and trembling in singleness of heart, as unto Christ.

All   Amen / Amin.

All wipe faces clean and turn into the world. It's a month or so later. **Nicola** *prepares for work as a phonograph plays. He is well grroomed. Near him* **Ellis** *reads the papers.*

Somewhere else **Aldridge** *with* **Perkins**, *who also reads the paper.*

Elsewhere **Weevil** *discreetly opens up a floorboard and takes out a wad of money, counts it.*

Helene *stands with a basket, in the midst of running an errand.*

Aldridge   I'll be / damned.

Perkins   I'll / be damned

Weevil   I'll / be damned.

Ellis   I'll be / damned.

Helene   I'll take two please. And I'll sign for the parcel.

Ellis   Things are looking up for us, / Nick.

Perkins   World's going to hell, Henry, I'm tellin' / you.

Ellis   Another court case in our favor.

Aldridge   Let me guess . . . A nigger's gonna be president?

Nicola   I don't understand these court cases you always / talk about.

Perkins   Not yet. Though I ain't sure it won't happen, way things look sometimes.

Helene *opens her package. In it is a newspaper in Arabic . . .* **Weevil** *re-hides the box and leaves.* **Helene** *closes her package and exits.*

Ellis   It's simple. We want to be citizens and have the rights and freedoms that come with it. These court cases help us prove we are citizens.

Nicola   How?

Perkins   Another one, Esau. White.

Ellis   By proving we're, you know, white.

Aldridge   Says right here that another Arab won in court. Imagine. American as you and me. White as any white man.

Perkins   What the judge said. White.

Nicola   What is white?

Ellis   What do you mean?

Nicola   You are white? And Helene?

Ellis Sure. Well the law says. The judges. Think about it; was Jesus white?

Nicola What?

Ellis We are Christians. The original Christians, right?

Aldridge Jesus Christ almighty /

Nicola Jesus was Jewish, no?

Ellis Jesus, Nick, we're allowed to be citizens, so we're white.

Nicola Why?

Ellis 'Cause you have to be a free white man to be a allowed citizenship. That's all that matters.

Nicola Ellis? You ever think about going back? Home? To the / mountains?

Ellis No. Why?

Nicola What about Helene?

Ellis Did she say something to you? About that?

Nicola No. No.

Beat. **Ellis** *goes back to his paper.*

Nicola (*genuinely*) So we're *allowed* to be white?

Ellis We just are. We just are.

Aldridge You're the one let Ellis join church, Esau.

Nicola As white as Perkins? Or Aldridge? /

Perkins Corey's a special case, I / guess.

Nicola What about Jeremiah White? The postman. You white as him? Even his name is white.

Nicola *laughs,* **Ellis** *does not.*

Perkins Hard worker. Clean. Speaks proper English.

Nicola What about men who ride on horses in white. Hitting people. We are white like them?

Beat.

Ellis Nick. I'm American. Would have fought, too. In the war. If it weren't for my knee.

Nicola Ellis. You didn't tell me the truth about you?

Ellis What do you mean?

Nicola You are coward . . . And traitor. You would have fought against the Sultan's army?

Ellis   Of course!

Nicola   Shhh. He hears everything.

Ellis   Stop. Anyway, the Ottomans are losing. All of Syria will soon be free. Thanks to the French and the British. Here look.

He hands **Nicola** *the paper.*

Nicola   Ah, yes. Psycho and Pie-co.

Ellis   What? /

Perkins   One reason I suggested that Pastor Davis baptize Ellis and all was I saw him, Ellis, over in Valdosta. End of last year. He was trying to join up with the army, fight overseas against the Kaiser and the Sultan. I guess that made an impression.

Aldridge   I suppose it did. He also didn't say nothin' / about-

Perkins (*interrupting loudly*)   Looks like the Red Sox went ahead and made Babe Ruth from a pitcher to an outfielder. And a slugger at that. The big oaf is knockin' the cover off the damn ball.

Nicola   Ellis? Is the Sultan white?

Ellis   No. I don't know. Stop asking questions.

Nicola   What about Tanios?

Ellis   Tanios was . . . Tanios.

Nicola   Yes. There was no other like him.

The two men smile, as if both remembering Tanios. **Ellis** *crosses himself.*

Ellis   Enough. We've got work to do.

They rise and leave. **Perkins** *and* **Aldridge** *too.*

Scene Two

That same morning. **Helene** *enters the house. She makes sure she is alone. She removes a record from her package, places it on the Victrola. Arabic music fills the space. After a moment with the music, she takes out a piece of paper and begins to write, humming along to the music.*

After some moments, **Nicola** *enters.* **Helene** *hides the paper on which she has been writing.*

They look at each other a moment.

Nicola	Sorry, I . . .	**Helene**	Sorry, you . . .
Helene	Startled / me.	**Nicola**	I forget my hat.

He points to his hat on the table. He grabs it and then starts to leave but stops, turns to **Helene**.

Nicola You are spy. For Sultan?

Helene What?

Nicola You write secret notes.

Helene No. No! To my cousin. She's in New York.

He laughs. She relaxes.

Nicola Just a joke. I can take it to her. The letter.

Helene You're leaving?

Nicola Maybe it is best, no? My uncle is not here. I am a bother to Ellis and you, and Lakewood, / it is—

Helene No. You aren't. A bother.

Nicola I cannot go back to Beirut. *Mish adir*. [I can't] Dangerous. And maybe in your Little Syria there are more like me. Who are worry about big Syria. About home.

Helene I am worried, too.

Nicola I know you are. I just / mean . . .

Helene Yes. I think it is the right thing to do. You will be happier there. (*Beat.*) I should go. And finish up my chores.

She walks by **Nicola** *but he gently grabs her hand. She stops but does not look at him. After a beat, she pulls her hand away, then touches the side of his head, still without looking at him.*

After a beat they move away from each other and stand in place, in silence.

Ellis *enters.*

Ellis Nick. Helene. Afternoon.

He senses something off, but ignores it.

I don't know about the two of you, but I'm starving. I closed up early. With this / heat . . .

Helene Ellis. Nicola is thinking of leaving us. To New York.

Ellis Already? But I just . . . Are you / sure?

Nicola No. I stay.

Ellis What do you mean? Then why did / she say—

Nicola I stay.

Ellis Oh. /

Nicola In Lakewood.

Helene I'm hungry too, / Ellis.

Nicola For now. I'm learning. In the store. And I am not ready. To say goodbye.

Ellis Ok. Good. / Fine.

Nicola Ok. Good.

Ellis Shall we eat then?

The three look at each other, frozen, as if time passes. Gradually the two men peel away, leaving **Helene** *alone.*

Helene
Traknaki baladna trakna [We left our home]
W jeena 3a baled mesh baladna [And came to a place not ours]

El layl hawn mesh nafsu layl [The air here is strange in the late night hours]
2ashba7, 2aswat, 3a door el khayl [Ghosts, voices, and the horse's breath]
Amreeka 7ayat w mawt [America is life and America is death]
Amreeka mawt w 7ayat [America is death and America is life]
Men el bar7a kan 2albi bard [Yesterday my heart was ice]

Wel yawm, albi defyan [And today, my heart is warm]
B3ezz el we7di, shaw2i w dajari [amid the longing, and boredom]

Da22 babi zalami [On my door a man knocked]
B sawtol qarawi, w 7akyoul 3arabi [With his village twang and his Arab talk]
Rajja3 nil baladi [He took me back home]

Samma'ni sawtak ya ghali [Let me hear your voice oh precious one]
Samma'ni baladi [Let me hear my country]
Daffili 2albi ya ghali [Warm my heart]
Walla3li hobbi [Fire up my love]

Me7tara ... bein shaghafi w adari [Torn, between a passion and destiny]
Meshta2a, l loughati w ahli [Longing for my tongue and my family]

B3ezz el we7di, shaw2i w dajari [In the midst of loneliness, longing, and boredom]
Da22 babi zalami [On my door a man knocked]
B sawtol qarawi, w 7akyoul 3arabi [With his village twang, his Arab talk]
Rajja3 nil baladi [He took me back home]
Rajja3 nil baladi rajja3 nil baladi

On the final few lines, **Ellis** *enters. He is still. He takes* **Helene** *in. She moves off, unaware. He stands alone for a beat. Lights shift.*

Scene Three

Ellis *is in the store.* **Nicola** *enters, waving to an unseen person.*

Nicola (*off*) Yes, Mrs Jenkins, we will have the flour brought to your house. Take very good care. Watch your step. And stay fresh, it's damn hot summer days.

Ellis (*through his teeth, smiling and waving*) Don't say "damn." And it's "stay cool," not fresh. "Stay cool, summer's heating up."

Nicola Do I have to say it with my mouth smiling and not moving my lips?

Ellis As long as you say it right I don't care.

Nicola (*Southern accent*) Stay cool, Mrs. Jenkins. Summer's heatin' up.

He feigns spitting just as **Aldridge** *enters.*

Aldridge Shouldn't spit in your own store, Nicola . . . Nicola Nijer. That your family name?

Nicola Najour.

Ellis Nick. He goes by Nick. Now, what can I get for you, Henry.

Aldridge The Stevens' place is closed.

Ellis I know.

Aldridge But I needed a half dozen eggs. Some grits. Plus a bag of that sugar you got back there.

Ellis Coming right up. Nick? Could you get all that while I add it up for Mr. Aldridge?

Nicola *fills and ties bags.*

Ellis How is your statue coming?

Aldridge Oh. Fine. Goin' just fine. Takes time. To sculpt. It's delicate work. At the end of the day, it's the art of removing. Cutting away. Knowing what has to go and how. Piece by piece.

Ellis Fascinating. /

Nicola Grits is here. Sugar's here—

Aldridge You know, America—this country—it's like a sculpture, too. A work of art. Needs to be worked at. Like stone. Pared down. Shaped into its finest form.

Nicola And here. Your eggs. All wrapped up. Safe and surround.

Aldridge *laughs at this and leaves.*

Ellis "Safe and sound." *Sound.* Not "surround."

Nicola This makes no sense.

Ellis Trust me, ok. It only gets easier, Nick. It gets easier. Just follow the rules.

Scene Four

Helene *drags on a peddling box. She opens it, makes some calculations. She adjusts her skirt or pants and heaves the box onto her back in one motion. It is heavy. She* *looks at the door. At that moment we hear, from elsewhere, a phonograph. It is "I'm Sorry I Made You Cry."*

She removes the box, slides it back from where it came and exits.

Scene Five

Weevil *is alone with his box rehearsing.* **Nicola** *enters, watches, and claps as the trick ends.*

Nicola   I like your performance. It's swell.

Weevil *looks around to make sure they are alone.*

Weevil   Just practicing. Your English growing fast, for a couple a months ain't half bad.

Nicola   I am employed in Ellis store now. I like your side of Lakewood. I see donkey. Goats. Smell of fire and meat. This makes me feel like the mountains at home.

Weevil *starts putting his things away.*

Nicola   You do magic alone always, Weevil?

Weevil   Getting ready for a kind of show—

Nicola   You tell me when and where show happen and I / come!

Weevil   No. For myself I mean. I do it alone. Magic alone. Always. What business you got over here anyway?

Nicola   To say hello. To talk. And to pay Vernon. For stone. For Tanios.

Nicola *takes out a wad of money.*

Weevil   Put that away, man. I don't know how it goes over in Lebanon Mountain / but—

Nicola   In English it's Mount Lebanon. Helene teach me that.

Weevil   Well, here you best keep your money tight-like, to your hip. Hidden.

Nicola *hides it.*

Nicola (*whispers*)   Vernon live close? He is around?

Weevil   Not too far. But he ain't home at the moment.

Nicola   I can give to you? To give him?

Weevil   Best you don't. Prefer not to have a misunderstanding.

Nicola   Ah, you mean with one of the delineators you tell me about?

Weevil   Something like that.

Nicola   You know, at Ellis store, many week ago, I see a line in this thing, "chuck."

Weevil Chalk?

Nicola Chaawk. Yes. Helene tell me Perkins make Ellis draw it. And in my head it make sense, what you say about lines. So I tell Ellis, but he don't understand and then he get funny face when I speak Arabic, face like he is making shit.

He makes a face. **Weevil** *laughs.*

Nicola Weevil, when I'm with you, it's a ball. Right? A ball.

Weevil A ball, sure, yeah, why not.

He produces a ball from **Nicola***'s clothes.*

Nicola Ha! Magic!

Weevil You take care, Nico, you hear.

He lights a cigarette, gets back to his gear. **Nicola** *watches him intently.*

Nicola Not so fast, Weevil. We have other business. I know who you are.

A beat.

Weevil What you talkin' about?

Nicola I bring all letters Tanios write with me. To America. And I go back and read them. Because I remember he write something about a magic-maker he meet here. A man he call *Malek il Doukhaan.*

Weevil You talkin' nonsense.

Nicola It mean the "King of Smoke". I think *you* are him. You are *Malek il doukhan*!?

Weevil You got the wrong fella.

Nicola And thinkin' you know uncle Tanios.

Weevil No, sir. Never / met him.

Nicola Yes. You are bad liar, Weevil. Lying don't suit you.

Weevil *gets in* **Nicola***'s face.*

Weevil You callin' me a liar?

Nicola I callin' you the King of the Smoke.

Beat.

Weevil You tell anybody?

Nicola No.

A tense beat.

Weevil Good. You keep it that way. To your damn self. You understand?

Nicola   Yes. I understand. So you trust me now, like you trust Tanios?

Weevil   Why should I?

Nicola   Because Tanios friend is my friend. Like family.

Weevil   I prefer to keep to myself.

Nicola   Why everything in secret? What you hide?

Weevil   You ask too many questions, Nico. Just like Tanios.

He goes back to packing his things up.

Weevil (*imitating Tanios, almost to himself*)   Why don't American speak when they eat? Why don't they kiss on cheek when they meet? Why Lakewood divided in two? Weevil, why you don't never wear new shoe?

Nicola *looks at* **Weevil**'s *shoe.*

Nicola   True.

Weevil   What is white and what is black? What is difference between pile and stack?

Nicola   And what it mean "pull up bootstrap"?

Weevil   If Black is not slave, why they don't get paid?

Why a Black woman work but can only be maid?
If this land of free, why we still pay dues?
If America so great why poor people lose?
Weevil, can i teach you to strum on my oud?

Nicola   Weevil, you can teach me to hum to your blues?

Weevil

Who is the king of the Klan of the Klu?

Nicola

Do the horses they ride hate Black people too?

Weevil   That's good.

Nicola

Why must i call white man a mister?
By the way, Weevil, you have a sister?

Nicola   Tanios ask this? Weevil, I apologize to your family for this / question.

Weevil

Weevil, why you speak funny on that side of town?
Why English written down not like it sound?

Nicola   Yes! And when they do baptism, how they not / drown?

Weevil You are socialist, Weevil, so why no friends? These letters you write, to whom do you send?

Nicola Why people talk always about fire and hell? And why they think Arab only like to buy and sell?

A silence. **Weevil** *stares at* **Nicola**.

Weevil Can't answer that. See. You just like him.

Nicola And what about stone? For Tanios? When it ready?

Weevil Already done. Vernon been hard at work. Just dropped it off in fact. We was gonna put it up later this evening. When the townsfolk watchin' their picture show downtown.

Nicola I can see it?

Weevil *takes a sheet away to reveal a "stone."*

Weevil All the letters look right? Nothin' missin'?

Nicola No. Nothing missing.

Weevil Vernon knew Tanios, so the work is a gift. No money. Least he could do, he said.

Nicola I love him for this. Yes. It is perfect.

Weevil Vernon the best there is with a chisel.

Nicola Better than Mr. Aldridge?

Weevil Shit, no contest. Just that Henry Aldridge don't appreciate competition. Everyone know Vernon superior to Aldridge or anyone else comes to chippin' stone.

Nicola I will thank Vernon. At your show.

Weevil I'll thank him for you. Vernon stay home most nights takin' care of his mamma. Anyway, probably better you don't come to the show. I'm still working on my / act.

Nicola No. I go. But don't worry. I can cross invisible lines. I am white, like Jesus Christ. (*Beat.*)
So, where I go? And when? To see Mr. Smoke King make magic?

Weevil Tonight. Down Jefferson, past town limits. Poplar grove by a farm house, dressed up as a church.

They shake hands. **Nicola** *turns to leave.*

Weevil Just don't tell nobody. About the show. Or me. Not Ellis, not nobody. Just you.

Nicola What show?

He exits. **Weevil** *gathers his things and exits.*

Scene Six

Helene *and* **Ellis** *wait at home.* **Nicola** *enters.*

Ellis Nick! We've been waiting. Come in. Thirsty? Helene, get him some lemonade.

Helene I made it. You get it.

He pours a glass for **Nicola**.

Ellis Sit. I got you a birthday present.

Nicola What?

Ellis When's your birthday? The date you were born.

Nicola I don't know.

Nicola Exactly!

Ellis I don't understand.

Ellis That's it! No one from back there . . . from the mountains. Home, I mean. No one knows when they were born. No clue. So I picked today for you. Happy birthday.

Helene Ellis does this to everyone. From home. No one finds it funny. Except him.

Ellis Oh lighten up. Here. Your present.

He hands **Nicola** *a package which he opens.*

Nicola Decla-ration . . .

Ellis Of Independence. It was mine. Went everywhere with me. Fits in your pocket.

Nicola Thank you, Ellis.

Ellis Ah, it's nothing. Stick with it and the words will all make sense soon enough.

Nicola And I have to keep this birthday now?

Ellis Well. I thought. It's as good a day as any.

Helene I made pie. With peaches. I think it is not good.

As she passes **Ellis** *he takes her hand.*

Ellis Thank you, dear—sorry. Thank you, my *lovely* Helene.

She leaves.

Nicola I say to them that I am twenty-five when I come. But I don't know / really.

Ellis Here you can start from scratch. Become whoever you want to be. Age, name, birthday. Even religion. I was baptized.

Nicola You put on the funny white dress and go under water? Like I see them do under bridge?

Ellis I certainly did.

The hammering is heard again. **Helene** *enters with pie, clearly bothered by the sound.*

Ellis (*speaking over the sound*)   Good news, Nicola. I took the liberty of writing a friend. Up North. In New York. He said he has a position for you.

Nicola   Where?

Ellis   In a store. Like mine. Bigger! A good job. Not peddling. I wouldn't want you to do that.
It's the old way. And you're a good worker. You deserve a challenge.

Nicola   That's very kind of / you.

Ellis   You don't have to go, of course . . . I mean, I appreciate you here . . . I just thought maybe you were ready to move on, see the big city.

Helene   You hate the big city, / Ellis.

Ellis   No. Well, it's not for me. But he's young, Helene. And New York is exciting. Fortunes to be made. Wives to be claimed.

Helene   Like meat at the butcher?

Ellis   I only meant that perhaps Nicola wanted to find . . . to settle down . . .

Helene   He could read her the Declaration of Independence.

The hammering stops just as she has said this.

Ellis   I suppose he could.

The hammering starts. She leaves the room. **Ellis** *pours two drinks.*

Ellis   New York is much louder than Lakewood. Most places are. And I've been everywhere in America. Sixteen years peddling. Even went as far as Mexico. *Hola Senorita, como esta, tenemos todos las cosas que necesitara. Tenemos cruces de madera de la tierra santa.*

Nicola   What this means?

Ellis   We have *everything*, even crosses from the Holy Land!

Nicola   You have this? *Min beytlehem?* [From Bethlehem.]

Ellis   Yes. Crosses. From Bethlehem, Pennsylvania. In fact, believe it or not, the crosses I sold were made in a workshop belonging to a Jew. From Russia. In New York.

Nicola   *Ghareeb.* [Strange.]

Ellis   It's not strange. It's America, Nick.

Nicola   And Tanios? /

Ellis   America is /

Nicola   He go everywhere too?

The banging stops.

Ellis   It just is. (*Beat.*) We traveled the same roads. Then we'd split up. Meet up again in some place or another.

Nicola   Why you come to Lakewood?

Ellis   Hurt my knee. About four years back. Winter of 1914. Those carts and *Kashis* are heavy. A hundred fifty pounds easy. Have a callous on my shoulder. I had to stay in one place. For the knee to heal. Tanios kept me company until spring. My knee got better. Decided to stay. Good a place as any. Roads, train . . . port's not too far. I wanted to settle down.
Start a real business. Tanios, he . . . he stayed on the road. He would come back every month or two, stay a while and then . . . well, then . . . Well, you know. That was that. And here we are. I miss him, Nicola. Every day.

The banging picks up again. **Helene** *enters.*

Helene   *Khaleena nimshi?* [Shall we walk?] To escape this noise, and the heat?

Ellis   There's a picture show in town tonight. Fancy going?

Helene   Yes.

Ellis   Your wish is my / command—

Helene (*to* **Nicola**)   You can come. But you don't / have to.

Nicola   I can stay. You two go.

Ellis   Shall we, / Helene?

Helene (*to* **Nicola**)   Unless you want to come / along.

Ellis   Of course. You should come, Nick.

A moment. **Nicola** *rises, and as they prepare to leave we see somewhere else the preparation of a projector, which somehow seems to echo the preparation of a noose. The three Arabs set off.*

Scene Seven

The three Arabs stroll. They come across **Aldridge**. *He eats popcorn.*

Nicola   Evening, Henry.

Aldridge   Takin' a stroll?

Ellis   We are. That popcorn's a good idea.

Aldridge   I love the stuff.

Nicola   Mr. Aldridge. You are taking a break? From your statue?

Aldridge   Yeah. Well, we got a city to run. Anyway, what's it to you?

Nicola I don't understand, sir.

Aldridge You do. And I see you, *Nick.*

Nicola Well, I see you too.

Aldridge I mean I'm on to you. See, my sugar was where my grits s'posed to be, and my grits where my sugar should a been. Bags mixed up.

Ellis *is caught off guard but adjusts.*

Ellis I'm sorry about that, Henry. A simple mistake, I assure you.

Nicola *(feigning idiocy)* Yes. Word on bag in English make eye hurt. From thinkin' too much. No understand.

Helene *suppresses a laugh.*

Aldridge Well, maybe you oughta learn to read better then. And if your eyes hurt, you should get 'em checked. Make sure you don't got that disease y'all got over there.

Ellis Of course he doesn't, Henry. Please. Listen, you come on by tomorrow, and I'll get you some grits and sugar. On me. Courtesy of Corey Bros.

Aldridge Oh. Well. Ok. That's a start.

Perkins *arrives, also eating popcorn.*

Perkins Evenin'. Everything ok over here?

Aldridge Yeah. Sure. No problem, Esau. Just talking about popcorn. How good it is.

Ellis Fine, Sheriff. How are you?

Aldridge (*to* **Ellis**) I'll come by tomorrow.

Aldridge *steps away.*

Perkins You folks come to see the picture? Nice it's outdoors, seeing as how the heat's so stifling.

Perkins *scratches his eye.*

Helene Are you alright, Mr. Perkins?

Perkins All that dander and pollen in the air. Also went an' saw Henry's masterpiece in progress today. Think I got a tiny piece of stone in there. A little fleck or speck, you know.

A bell.

Oh, that's the signal. Movie's gonna start. Not every night that we got a picture show under the stars, is it? Grab some popcorn and find a seat.

They do. DeMille's The Arab *plays.* **Aldridge** *hisses at the screen, imitating Arabic, etc.*

Aldridge   Anybody smell camel shit? Sultan's a goddamn sonofabitch! Our boys on the battlefield'll stick em good, like a pig!

Perkins *turns back to the three Arabs without taking his eyes off the screen.*

Perkins   I apologize for Henry. He always talks over the movies. Natural exuberance, you know.

Helene *leaves.* **Nicola** *follows.* **Aldridge** *and* **Perkins** *remain in the flickering light of the projector,* **Ellis** *behind them.*

Elsewhere, **Nicola** *and* **Helene** *now stand together but apart. They make eye contact.* **Ellis** *enters as* **Nicola** *leaves.*

Ellis

> *3al rozana 3al rozana*
> *Kell el 7ala fiha*
> *Shu 3emlet el rozana*
> *Allah yijaziha*
> *3al rozana 3al rozana*

Helene

> I'm sorry, dear

Ellis

> *Kell el 7ala fiha*

Helene

> So sorry, dear

Ellis

> *Shu 3emlet el rozana*

Helene

I'm sorry I made you cry

Ellis

> *Allah yijaziha*

Helene *exits.* **Ellis** *is still for a beat then pours a drink for himself.*

Scene Eight

That evening. **Perkins** *and* **Aldridge** *walk outside, through the cemetery.*

Perkins   Nice night to take the long way home.

Aldridge   Be nicer with a bit of a breeze.

Aldridge *stops in his tracks. Looking down in front of him.*

Aldridge   What in the hell?

Perkins   Your work?

Aldridge *shoots him a glance.*

Perkins   No. I suppose it ain't.

Aldridge   Vernon Brown. Thought I heard his chisel in the wind.

Perkins   Pretty good.

Aldridge   This Ellis' doin'?

Perkins   No. Not Ellis.

Aldridge   The young 'un?

Perkins   I reckon.

Aldridge   Son of a bitch.

Perkins   Let it go, Henry. Just a grave.

Perkins *walks off.*

Aldridge   You stay out of this, Esau.

He leaves in the opposite direction.

Scene Nine

In the house. **Ellis** *sits with his drink in the dim light.* **Nicola** *enters.*

Ellis   Don't do that again.

Nicola   I didn't—

Ellis   No. You didn't think. And you don't know . . . what I've had to sacrifice, Nicola. *Ma'andaksh fikra* [you have no idea]! If you pull a stunt like that again, I might not be there to help. It's no way to treat customers, especially fellows like Aldridge / and—

Nicola   It was a / joke.

Ellis   It's wasn't funny.

Nicola   *Haadir.* I apologize.

Ellis   Fine. Fine. I didn't want to . . . I was just disappointed. And I worry sometimes. I want to make sure things run smoothly is all. I made my name that way. From nothing. I built trust. I did it for Helene's sake, too. For my Helene.

Nicola   I understand.

Ellis   Do you? Good. (*Beat.*) Think about New York, Nicola. About that job. In the meantime, you're welcome to stay, of course. *Ehlan wa sahlan.* [You are welcome here.]

Nicola *nods and leaves.*

Scene Ten

The noise of a party grows. Music and then smoke. Bam! **Weevil** *bows to us, cape and all.*

Weevil   Thank you kindly, ladies and gents. Now thank me kindly, donate generously to the refugees headin' up up and away outta this swamp.

He passes the hat into the crowd then turns to the musicians.

Let 'er rip, fellas!

As the music plays **Weevil** *sees* **Nicola**.

Nicola (*over the music*)   Very good trick, Weevil.

Weevil   I been workin' on that. You came?

Nicola   Yes. But secret.

Weevil   How about a drink?

The band comes forward and music rises. **Weevil** *and* **Nicola** *blend into / behind the band. The party grows. The two re-emerge with bottles which they drink from and pass around.*

Weevil   We throw a *mean* party don't we?

Nicola   No, it's nice.

Weevil   "Mean," when it's said like that, it mean good. Nice. Swell.

Nicola   Ah. Then you are a mean magician, Weevil.

Weevil   Thank you, sir. Very kind.

Nicola   And the moon is red.

Weevil   It sure is.

They both look up as the band moves to a more bluesy set . . . **Weevil** *and* **Nico** *sway.* **Weevil** *sings, to himself at first and then out to the rest of the party.*

Weevil
   There is no road/
   On this long heavy night/
   I feel my way left / I feel my way right/
   I see a tall man / or is it a ghost/
   He's all dressed in white/
   From his head to his toes /

So should I stay put / should I get up an' go
Stand and fight or run my ass home

These the things
Keep a man up at night
Make 'im break a hard sweat /
Give his sweetie a fright /

That's why we move
To that sound on the tracks /
To catch that last train
To them grey northern stacks.

Boom clackity clack clack
Doom snap to the bap, bap.

Nicola *echoes the boom clackity clack on the drum. It builds and builds, then* he *gives a try at something like blues.*

Weevil
Onward, brave men
Onward we ride
Fasten your boots
To the tyrant's backside

Nicola *turns and directs the band and they add Arab touch.* **Nicola** *sings his rebel song.*

Oumou ya shabab [Get up, men, as fast as you can]
Thourou 3alal 3usmani [Revolt against the Ottoman]
Oumou ya gedaan [Get up, brave men, as fast as you can]
Dekkoul babel 3aali [Destroy his highness and his caravan]

Nehna badna 3eeshi karimi [We want a decent life]
La saffah la sultan [Not the Sultan's butcher knife]

3Arfeen shu badkoun? . . . Ehhhh [Do you know what you want? . . . Yes]
Arfeen shu hamkoun? . . . Ehhhh [Do you know what you're concerned with? . . . Yes]
Tab yalla oumou kheffouha [Get up as fast as you can]
Oumou yalla 3ala sultan [Let's set out against the Sultan]

Weevil *and* **Nicola** *and the band jam in a call and response, spontaneous fusion at its best.*

Then, the sound of riders approaching.

Weevil   Leave, leave, move, run! (*To* **Nico**.) Get yo ass home, Nico! Move! Through the woods.

Nicola *runs off in one direction,* **Weevil** *in the other, as riders descend.*

Scene Eleven

Morning. **Ellis** *and* **Nicola** *at the store. Stocking and taking inventory.* **Perkins** *enters.*

Perkins Mornin', Corey.

Ellis Sheriff.

Perkins Come on over here, look out this window with me, Ellis.

They look out.

See that man, in my car? Not my deputy. That's Frank.

Ellis I know Frank.

Perkins I mean the nigger. In the back seat. With the bloody lip.

Ellis I see him.

Perkins Well, you remember when you said you might a had some of your cereals stolen from out back, couple months ago, Ellis?

Ellis Yes. A bag of rice. And some cornmeal.

Perkins Well, you think it could have been him? He did have access after all.

Nicola *hovers as close as he can to get a view.* **Perkins** *rubs his eyes.*

Ellis No. Not that I recall. No.

Perkins We arrested this man and when we did, we found stolen goods in his possession. At his mamma's house.

Nicola What was he arrested for?

Perkins Caught. Snooping on Mrs. Abbot, looking into her bathroom . Had it not been for Henry Aldridge passin' by that very moment, who knows what vile deeds he might've performed on his prey.

Ellis My God.

Perkins Yeah, it's a horrible thing ain't it? To think that while you are at work, something like that could happen to your own wife.

Ellis Poor Mrs. Abbot.

Perkins Well, she's fine, and we caught him. But when we got to his house I found those goods in his pantry. Struck me as curious. Remembered you'd reported some stock missing. So I figured I'd double check. See if maybe we can solve two crimes at the same time.

Ellis *and* **Nicola** *look carefully.*

Nicola I have never seen him here, Sheriff.

Perkins Askin' Ellis. This is his store. Take a good look, Corey, and think real hard.

Ellis Maybe. Maybe. I've seen him once or twice. Didn't see him do anything. But I suppose I might've seen him around.

Perkins Well, I'll let you know if we need you to come down to the station and give a statement to that effect.

Ellis Sure. Sure. Thanks.

Perkins Thank you, Ellis.

He exits. **Nicola** *and* **Ellis** *are still for a moment. Then* **Ellis** *goes back to work.* **Nicola** *stares at* **Ellis** *in silence.*

Ellis Stop looking at me like that.

Nicola You never seen him here have you?

Ellis I don't know.

Nicola Ellis.

Ellis *is silent.*

Nicola *Redd 3layyeh, Elias!* [Answer me, Elias!]

Ellis Don't talk like that to me! Not in my store.

Helene *enters from outside.*

Helene *Shu 3am biseer?* [What's happening?]

Ellis Nothing, Helene.

Helene Nicola?

Ellis Don't get involved, Helene. And don't ask *him*.

Helene Well, *you* won't tell me. I saw people outside the court building walking here. What is happening?

Ellis A man was arrested. Perkins thought he was the same one who stole from the store before.

Helene Was he?

Ellis Maybe. Who knows.

Nicola No.

Helene Elias?

Ellis He was guilty! Of worse things. It didn't matter what I said. Ok! It didn't matter.

Helene So you said what Perkins wanted you to say?

Ellis Yes. I said . . . I said I wasn't sure. I tried / to—

Helene Well, go there now. Go to the jail.

Ellis It's too late.

A shot in the distance.

Nicola   I'll go.

Ellis   No. You won't.

Helene *stands above* **Ellis**.

Helene   Go.

Ellis *is frozen.*

Helene   Now!

Ellis *gets up and leaves.*

Helene (*to* **Nicola**)   *Rouh ma'ou*. [Go with him.]

Nicola *follows.*

Scene Twelve

Unseen, the **Chorus of Hoods** *begins.*

Chorus of Hoods
  We climb and hang
  We loop and slip
  We tie and knot
  And haul and lift
  We pop and pull
  And kick and watch

Hoods *enter and stand around an large object, their backs to the audience.*

Nicola *and* **Ellis** *enter. As they do, a fire roars up from behind the wall of hoods. With it a tremendous, defiant yell which becomes a bloodcurdling scream. After several moments of the screaming and the crackling of fire, the* **Hooded Ones** *raise their arms in unison and fire several rounds each into the fire. The screaming stops.*

Ellis *backs away and offstage, followed by* **Nicola**.

Scene Thirteen

At the **Corey** *house.* **Ellis** *stands at his phonograph. A song plays. Something American. He's there but not there. Empty.*

Nicola *enters.*

Elllis *turns, but without looking at him.*

Ellis   She's out. Walking. (*Beat*.) What happened, Nicola, / it was –

Nicola   Very bad. We have to do / something.

Ellis You don't get it, do you?

Nicola *Shu raH na3mel?* [What are you going to do?]

Ellis What are *we* gonna do? Enough, damn it! Who do you think you are . . . I've been here a long time. You can't just come here like you've figured it all out.

Nicola No. You are right. You told me to read. It say all men made equal / here.

Ellis If you want to live here you follow the rules. Written and unwritten.

Nicola You sound like the Sultan.

Ellis You sound like a child. An innocent, naive / child.

Nicola How you call someone who lose family, Ellis? Alone. Who has no parents, no home?

Ellis An orphan, I / suppose.

Nicola Yes. That. Then maybe I am a kind of orphan. But I am not kid. I have seen death, you know. So what we see there, not so new for me. But . . . It don't make it ok. Or normal.

Ellis You're right. It's not ok. But it is normal. So normal that it can happen to you or someone you love before you know why or how. So you pretend. Or you leave. Go back to the old country and take your chances with what's normal there.

Nicola I am leaving then. Leavin' Lakewood. Tomorrow.

Ellis What could I have done?

Nicola Thank you. For having me. As a guest. In your house.

Ellis I've left you the name of my friend in New York. There on the table. And some money. Your pay. Nicola / I –

Nicola *folds the paper and puts it in his pocket.*

Nicola Go visit him some time. Tanios. Check on the tree. And see the stone I put. Have a drink with him.

He exits silently. **Ellis** *turns to say something but* **Nicola** *is gone. The record ends, skips.*

Scene Fourteen

Weevil *is alone.* **Nicola** *enters.*

Nicola Come with me. Leave. From here. We go to New York.

Weevil I'd like that.

Nicola I am ready.

Weevil I can't, Nico. Not yet.

Nicola Why?

Weevil Got a responsibility. To stay. Helpin' others make it out first.

Nicola It's dangerous. In Lakewood.

Weevil Yes it is. Not just in Lakewood. But that ain't nothin' new for me. For us.

Beat.

Nicola I never ask . . . About your family?

Weevil Dead. Gone. Just like yours, Nico.

Nicola How?

Weevil Taken. By fright. Flight. Hunger. Hounds.

Nicola I am sorry.

Weevil I know you are.

Nicola You will take care of the grave?

Weevil Yeah. I will. I got you something. To take along.

He produces a wooden peddling pack.

Belonged to Tanios. Figure you can use it. Re-stock it, make a little something for yourself. I was holding on to it. All I had that belonged to him but . . . Well, should have given it to you before.

Nicola *takes it.*

Nicola Heavy.

A beat.

Helene. / She –

Weevil She's a good woman. Got that look about her.

Nicola But not my woman.

Weevil No. No she ain't.

Nicola You will find me?

Weevil Every man gotta see New York once in his life. That's what they say. We'll see. But you go there. And then, if you wanna move, you just move, man. (*Beat.*) Man they took out the jail and burned last night. It was the stone cutter. Vernon.

Nicola I saw. What they did to / him.

Weevil Make a man sick.

Nicola Every place has a sickness. You tell me that.

Weevil There's something you ought to know. About Tanios . . . I owe that man my life, Nico.

Nicola What do you mean?

Weevil I mean he didn't die from no flu.

Nicola I don't understand.

Weevil We took some things. Me and a couple other fellas. Things that wasn't supposed to be taken. Papers, pictures, letters. From the courthouse. And a couple homes, too.

Nicola Why you steal paper?

Weevil To send up North. To a wise man. To Mr. Dubois. To show how we got Klansmen in every position, from the judge to the postman. So that they can publish the information, try to change the laws.

Nicola So what this have to do with Tanios? He steal too?

Weevil No. All I know is one second they closing in on us and the next, Tanios being hemmed up for the crime. He turned himself in. Said it was him who did it. And they was happy to believe him. Never much liked him that side of town. Way he looked, talked. Music he played. Tanios sacrificed himself. For me. For us. That ain't no small thing.

Nicola Why he is not in jail, then?

Weevil Down here, them cells magically open, crowd comes through and *poof*. Next thing, find the prisoner curled up in a ditch. And don't nobody remember who took 'em out the jail, neither. Guards, deputies, all got amnesia when it suits them. And when they wanna pin a crime on a Black man, well shit, they suddenly got the best memory and eyesight you ever seen, extra special hearin', too.

Nicola How . . .?

Weevil You really wanna know?

Nicola Yes.

Weevil Shot 'em up like a pin cushion. Left him on the side of the road. We didn't find 'im until two days after.

Nicola Who did this?

Weevil Everyone. And no one. (*Beat.*) But you can guess. Same ones did it to Vernon.

Nicola Ellis. He know?

Weevil He knows . . .

Nicola But he say nothing / to me.

Weevil Listen here, Nico. Ellis ain't do nothin' a hundred other folk do every day, which is put their heads down, say okeedokee, yessir and try to get by. Look out for themselves. Their loved ones. Might be easier for him to do that than for me. But who says I wouldn't do the same thing if I had the choice.

Nicola You wouldn't.

Weevil You believe that?

Nicola Yes.

Nicola
Ya hadi 3ees [Oh caravan driver, oh spreader of news]
Ketret a7zani [My sorrows mount]
3Ammi gataloo [My uncle is murdered]
W swadet a7lami [My dreams are deep blue]
Ya hadi 3ees [Oh caravan driver, oh spreader of news]

Weevil
Gonna make the devil pray

Nicola
Ketret a7zani [My sorrows mount]

Weevil
Gonna make 'im rue the day

Nicola
3Ammi gataloo [My uncle is murdered]

Weevil
Make the motehrfuckers pay

Nicola
W swadet a7lami [And my dreams are deep blue]

Weevil
Make 'em kneel and make 'em say
Sorry we took your friends away

Weevil *has his eyes closed by now. When he opens them,* **Nicola** *has left and night has fallen.*

Weevil   Nico? Nico?!

(*Almost to himself.*) Don't do nothin' stupid.

Scene Fifteen

Nicola *walks across the darkened stage and stops. A large object. A statue. Covered in cloth.*

He looks around then approaches the statue. He grabs a large hammer from among the tools on the ground and reaches his hand toward the sheet covering the statue. Lights shift.

Scene Sixteen

Nicola *enters, gets his things ready by the door.* **Helene** *enters.*

Helene   You are leaving? To New York?

Nicola Helene.

Helene Ellis went to the store. To get some things for you. To take.

Nicola Come.

Helene What?

Nicola With me. If you don't want to see me there, that's fine. But leave here.

Helene Why wouldn't I want to see you? There?

Nicola Something is wrong. Here. *Fi shi ghalat.* [Something off].

Helene There is something wrong everywhere./

Nicola I would think about it every day.

Helene About what?/

Nicola Why I didn't ask you. To come.

She looks at him for a long beat.

Helene There is a store. On Washington Street. You'll know the one when you see it. The spices are stacked to the ceiling. In crates and in bags, every color. And when you walk in, it hits you, first through your nostrils, then your eyes and your ears, when you hear the conversations. And then your fingers.

Nicola Come.

Helene Go. Just watch, listen, smell. Then close your eyes and let your fingers taste. Every crate. Don't let the shopkeeper see you though. Do that for me.

Nicola Every day.

Helene No. You have to space your trips. Or else they'll catch on to you.

He approaches her. They are almost touching, though without eye contact. He turns away.

When he turns back she has left. After a moment **Ellis** *enters.*

Ellis I thought maybe you had left. Without saying goodbye.

Nicola I am ready.

Ellis I'll drive you.

Nicola I can walk.

Ellis You will walk plenty. Trust me. Take a ride when you can get it.

Nicola Ellis.

Ellis I never. Told you everything. I . . . I was . . .

Nicola I know.

Ellis No.

Nicola About Tanios.

Ellis You don't. I have seen things. And heard things. Things that make you . . . Sick. That rob your sleep. I've been this close to being . . .

Nicola Why didn't you help him? Or stop them?

Ellis How?! You think that's how this works?! . . . (*Beat.*) . . . You think it was easy to walk away when they had him!? He brought it upon himself, Nico. If I hadn't?! turned away . . . then I would have been . . . And what sense does that / make?!

Nicola You lied. To me.

Ellis Because I've also seen that people can be good.

Nicola What are you / saying?

Ellis If they get to know you. If you get to know them. It doesn't make it go away. But it gets easier. You adapt. You move forward, you . . .

Beat.

Did you say anything? To / Helene? About . . . ?

Nicola No.

Ellis Thank you.

A knock on the door.

Who is it?

Aldridge *enters on his own.*

Aldridge Just spoke with Sheriff Perkins. He's on his way, so you just sit tight. You especially.

He points at **Nicola**.

Ellis What's this about, Henry?

Aldridge My statue. It's been violated. Ruined. And it was him. Neighbors said they saw someone just like this one.

Ellis Impossible.

Aldridge (*calmly to* **Nicola**) You broke my statue, now I'm a break you, boy.

Ellis He was here. All night. With / me.

Aldridge Well, I heard he was on the colored side earlier on. Probably *them* gave him the idea.

Nicola No one gave me any ideas.

Ellis	**Aldridge**
Shut up.	Shut up.

Aldridge We'll let Esau handle this.

A knock. It is **Perkins**.

Perkins Mornin'. Barely. Damn near still dark. But when Henry Aldridge calls you out of bed, you get up.

Aldridge Arrest him, Sheriff.

Perkins *approaches* **Nicola** *and looks him over.*

Perkins Won't be necessary.

Aldridge And why not?

Perkins 'Cause the man did it turned himself in. Confessed. Sittin' in my car as we speak.

Aldridge What you mean?

Perkins Weevil's his name. You remember Weevil? Said he did it. You can even wave to 'im. Go on. Look.

Perkins *waves off to* **Weevil**.

Nicola It wasn't him. I—

Ellis *shuts him up.*

Perkins What's that?

Ellis I was just taking him to the station, Sheriff. He's going up North. For good.

Perkins Leavin' us already, Mr. Cola?

Aldridge *and* **Perkins** *rub their eyes.*

Ellis He is, Sheriff. Thank you.

Perkins *tips his hat and he and* **Aldridge** *leave.*

Ellis Now! We go now! I'm putting you on that train.

Nicola I can't. He is a friend.

He tries to leave. **Ellis** *physically restrains him.*

Ellis Well, in that case you have a good friend. And when someone gives you your life back, you take it. You don't look back.

Nicola I don't want to become like you.

Ellis He's as good as dead, your friend. He made his choice. So do this for him. And for me. Because . . . this is my chance to . . . With Tanios I couldn't . . . If I let you go, then . . . This is the only choice for both of us . . . *Fhemet 3layye?!* [You understand?!] (*Beat.*) You can't miss that train.

Ellis *straps the box onto* **Nicola**'s *back and they leave,* **Ellis** *forcing him out the door.*

Scene Seventeen

The sound of keys, of heavy metal doors.

Weevil *on one side, pacing in a "cell." On the other,* **Nicola**, *sitting with his box and a bundle, as if on a train. In between them somewhere, a noose is meticulously prepared.*

Then the sound of a train. Day to night to day. A mourning song emerges, **Weevil**'s *voice overlapping, repeating lines like "There is no road" and then "I am the Smoke King."*

Nicola
    Ya hadil 3ees [Oh caravan driver, oh spreader of news]
    Ketret 2ahzani [My tragedies mount]
    3Ammi gatalouh [My uncle, they killed him]
    Rfi2i be zenzani [And my friend is behind bars of steel]
    La hobb w men ye'sha2 la [There's no one left to love]
    La amn w men yeslam la [And no safe harbour here]
    Kellou raye7 men 2eddami [everything is falling away]
    2Erbit el nihayee [And the bitter end is near]

Nicola *fades into sleep, but is startled awake with the scream of the train whistle.* **Weevil** *is no longer there but another passenger is now visible next to* **Nicola**, *reading the paper.*

Passenger   Good mornin'. Slept through the last four stops. Hope you weren't getting off.

Nicola   New York.

Passenger   Well you're fine then. Still not there.

The passenger turns to her / his paper. **Nicola** *opens the box. He finds a piece of paper.*

Nicola (*reading out loud*)   "Pull the string."

From the box he takes out a string. He pulls it. A click. A compartment on the bottom of box opens and a large parcel falls out, wrapped in paper and twine. **Nicola** *picks it up, studies it.*

Passenger   Hefty parcel you got there.

Nicola *considers the package for another beat.*

Nicola   Yes. I am delivering it. For a friend.

Passenger   Nice of you.

Nicola   No. Only the least I can do.

He hides the stack of papers back in the compartment, and holds the box to his chest.

Passenger (*reading the paper*)   I'll be damned. See this? Apparently a sheriff, down in a place called Lakewood, had a man in custody. A vandal. But he just disappeared. Vanished. Look at it yerself.

Nicola I know. The prisoner gone. Disappear. It always like / this.

Passenger Yeah. But not only him, see. The Sheriff too. And an alderman. "Witnesses say they entered the cell to get the prisoner, and all of a sudden there was smoke," and then right in front of everyone's eyes. POOF! Gone. They all were. Just like that. Into thin air.

Lights cut to black.

End of Play.

Further Reading

Baraka, Amiri. *Blues People; Negro Music in White America*. New York: W. Morrow, 1963.
Browne, Simone. *Dark Matters: On the Surveillance of Blackness*. Durham, NC: Duke University Press, 2015. Print.
Cone, James H. *The Cross and the Lynching Tree*. Maryknoll, NY: Orbis, 2011.
Davis, Francis. *The History of the Blues*. New York: Hyperion, 1995.
Dray, Philip. *At the Hands of Persons Unknown: The Lynching of Black America*. New York: Random House, 2002.
Du Bois W. E. B. *The Souls of Black Folk*. New York: Bantam, 1989.
Foner, Eric, and Joshua Brown. *Forever Free: The Story of Emancipation and Reconstruction*. New York: Knopf, 2005.
Gualtieri, Sarah M. A. *Between Arab and White: Race and Ethnicity in the Early Syrian American Diaspora*. Berkeley, CA: University of California, 2009.
Hahn, Steven. *A Nation Under Our Feet: Black Political Struggles in the Rural South, from Slavery to the Great Migration*. Cambridge, MA: Belknap of Harvard University Press, 2003.
Hooglund, Eric J. *Crossing the Waters: Arabic-speaking Immigrants to the United States before 1940*. Washington, DC: Smithsonian Institution, 1987.
Jacobs, Linda K. *Strangers in the West: The Syrian Colony of New York City, 1880–1900*. New York: Kalimah, 2015.
Kelley, Robin D. G. *Freedom Dreams: The Black Radical Imagination*. Boston: Beacon, 2002.
Kelley, Robin D. G. *Race Rebels: Culture, Politics, and the Black Working Class*. New York: Free, 1994.
MacLean, Nancy. *Behind the Mask of Chivalry: The Making of the Second Ku Klux Klan*. New York: Oxford University Press, 1994.
Naff, Alixa. *Becoming American: The Early Arab Immigrant Experience*. Carbondale, IL: Southern Illinois University Press, 1985.
Rodney, Walter, A. M. Babu, and Vincent Harding. *How Europe Underdeveloped Africa*. Washington, DC: Howard University Press, 1981.
Roediger, David R. *Working toward Whiteness: How America's Immigrants Became White: The Strange Journey from Ellis Island to the Suburbs*. New York: Basic, 2005.
Shakir, Evelyn. *Bint Arab: Arab and Arab American Women in the United States*. Westport, CT: Praeger, 1997.
Wilkerson, Isabel. *The Warmth of Other Suns: The Epic Story of America's Great Migration*. New York: Random House, 2010.
Wright, Michelle M. *Physics of Blackness: Beyond the Middle Passage Epistemology*. Minneapolis, MN: University of Minnesota Press, 2015.

Critical Essay: Arab, Palestinian, American—The Theatre of Ismail Khalidi

by Edward Blaise Ziter

Professor of Theatre History
Department of Drama
New York University

What are the contents and histories of the Palestinian identity? What are the contents and histories of Arab identity? The six plays in this anthology return to these questions, while covering ninety years of history in locations ranging from Palestine to the American South and depicting very different forms of resistance and accommodation. These two questions anchor Ismail Khalidi's examinations of the nature and persistence of racist violence, the mechanism of imperial oppression and settler colonialism across decades, and possible intersections between different liberation movements. These are plays about big historical processes, but that examine these processes through finely delineated characters who love and struggle, mourn the loss of culture, work to maintain a connection to their ancestral lands, contend with migration and dispossession, succumb to self-loathing, and triumph over (not through) violence.

To get a sense of the ambitions of Khalidi's project, it is useful to examine the plays in this anthology according to the periods depicted rather than their order of composition. The story begins circa 1918 with *Dead Are My People*. That play, set in the American South, examines shifts in the racialization of Arabs in the context of US racial terror against Black Americans. The play imagines the possibility of African American/Arab American alliances at the very moment that the US judicial system was awarding Whiteness to Arabs. Nicola Najour has emigrated from the Mount Lebanon region, fleeing both famine and authorities who would hang him for his resistance to Ottoman rule. He has smuggled himself into the South at roughly the start of the Great Migration, when Southern Blacks smuggled themselves to the North in order to escape racial violence and the oppression of Jim Crow laws. The play is set in the closing years of the third wave of US immigration when growing numbers of migrants came from Mediterranean countries and Eastern Europe. This migration prompted new questions about racial categories and the play references the court cases what would determine if Arabs were whites, and consequently eligible for citizenship. The process prompts the question: What will Arabs need to give up in order to enter fully into whiteness? The play posits different answers, but clearly whiteness may require the sacrifice of a great many personal qualities, ranging from one's native language and culture to one's ethics and morality.

Nicola serves as a connecting link between two narratives that engage the role of race and racial hierarchies in American identity. The first narrative centers on his friendship with Weevil, an African American magician who helps smuggle Southern Blacks into the North while he amasses documentation on lynching that he intends to send to W. E. B. Dubois. Weevil hopes that Dubois, through his paper, can publicize this violence and generate support for Northern migration. The second narrative centers on

Nicola's search for his uncle. He has come to the South looking for his sole remaining relative, only to discover that he has died (though in unclear circumstances). Instead, Nicola finds work in the grocery store of Elias Corey who is also from the Mount Lebanon region. Elias has changed his name to Ellis in his effort to Americanize and proclaims the benefits of acculturation. However, he and Nicola ultimately learn that one cannot benefit from an economy grounded in racial violence without becoming complicit in that violence.

The production, commissioned by Noor Theatre in New York and premiering in November 2018, featured original music composed and performed by Hadi Eldebek. Music runs through the play, serving to underscore a longing for Arab culture experienced by Nicola and Ellis's wife, Helene, who resists her husband's insistence on acculturation. Nicola brings Arab song back into their lives; before his arrival when Helene pesters her husband for a song, Ellis eventually obliges her with Henry Burr's "I'm Sorry I Made you Cry." Nicola no sooner arrives than he is reciting Arab poetry and improvising songs in Arabic. Music also connects Arab and African American cultures. Weevil transforms Dubois's poetry into a song of Black pride during a meeting of African Americans. Nicola similarly sings songs protesting oppression, specifically the oppression of Arabs by the Ottomans. When Nicola learns of his uncle's death he sings a mourning song in Arabic; in a separate space, Weevil tends wounds inflicted on him by the KKK and begins to hum Nicola's tune. Song connects the two in loss and resistance.

Song in *Dead Are My People* serves as a metaphorical (or perhaps magical) manifestation of shared experiences and possible alliances suggested throughout the play. When Weevil explains to Nicola how segregation practices in the US divide space in order to control it, the conversation segues into a discussion of the Sykes and Picot agreement, the Allied Powers' plan to divide Ottoman Syria (Arab territories from the Mediterranean Sea to the Euphrates River) between Britain and France. The juxtaposition of US white supremacy and international power politics suggest the need for alliances between those who face racial oppression and colonial domination. Over the course of the play, Weevil and Nicola support each other at considerable personal risk. For Nicola, this entails choosing humanity over the potential benefits of complying with a white supremacist regime. Nicola sees first-hand how his fellow Mediterranean immigrants quickly adopt racial slurs as they are schooled in an evolving racial hierarchy. He also sees how dehumanizing language can lead to physical violence.

The play is set at an inflection point for American constructions of whiteness, when federal courts were determining the racial category of Arabs. Ellis celebrates that Arabs are securing citizenship by proving that they are white and so not subject to racial exclusions in US naturalization law. At one point, he echoes an actual 1909 court case in which a Syrian man defended his naturalization with the argument that if he were Mongolian then so was Jesus since they came from the same land (see Gualtieri 52–80). If this keeps up, one white character complains, the country will end with a Black president. That line must have had particular significance at the play's 2018 premiere, coming one year after the end of Obama's presidency and one year into Trump's. The timing of the premiere underscores one of the play's more important points: fighting for one's whiteness, rather than making common cause with the racially subjugated, might be a losing strategy in the long term.

By referencing the Sykes Picot Agreement, *Dead Are My People* alludes to the division of Arab territories into European mandates that will follow World War I. Khalidi's *Tennis in Nablus* is set during the Arab Revolt against Britain's control of Mandatory Palestine. After the First World War, the charter of the newly created League of Nations entrusted the Allied Powers with the governance of colonies and territories previously controlled by Germany and the Ottoman Empire, so as to provide "tutelage" to "peoples not yet able to stand by themselves under the strenuous conditions of the modern world" (quoted in Sluglett 418). In fact, colonial administration in the mandates resembled colonial administrations elsewhere, the stated goal of tutelage notwithstanding (Pedersen 113). The Arab Revolt in Palestine began in 1936, and called for Arab independence and the end of open-ended Jewish immigration. By 1939, the British had crushed the uprising with the help of Zionist militias. The war left between 14 and 17 percent of the adult Arab population of Palestine killed, wounded, imprisoned, or exiled (R. Khalidi 44). *Tennis in Nablus* is set in the final year of the uprising, and centers on two Palestinians—Yusef and his nephew Tariq—with vastly different responses to British rule. Yusuf leads the resistance. Tariq, a successful businessman who profits from the sale of Palestinian lands to European Jews, asserts that the only pragmatic response is to accept British rule and rely on business connections to ensure one's own safety. Meanwhile, Yusuf's wife, Anbara, publishes nationalist editorials under a male pen-name rallying Palestinians to resist British rule.

Much as *Dead Are My People* imagines alliances between Arab Americans and African Americans, *Tennis in Nablus* presents Palestinian nationalism as part of a global liberation movement. Yusuf carries a photo of Emiliano Zapata with him for inspiration and a vision of the Mexican revolutionary visits Yusuf as he and his nephew languish in prison. The British see the suppression of Palestinian resistance as no different from the challenges arising throughout the Empire. A British Lieutenant notes the effectiveness of "the anti-terror experts from the Irish and Indian campaigns" and a General reminisces about the violence inflicted on prisoners in Rhodesia (now Zimbabwe) and Tanganika (in East Africa). Meanwhile, under her pen name, Anbara calls on Palestinians to take as an example "the brave Irish strikers" and "the mass movement of non-violent resistance led by Mr. Gandhi and Badshah Khan in India." While in prison, Yusuf tells an Irish soldier of his respect for the man's uncle, known for having fought the partition of Ireland (a line that foreshadows Arab's similarly failed resistance to the United Nations' planned partition of Palestine). The soldier notes that his uncle would give him "a hiding" for donning a British uniform, but it was that or "rot in a Belfast prison for five years." He serves alongside an Indian soldier, and the two undermine their superiors at every opportunity. The two provide comic relief in what is an otherwise dark and moving play. It is quite a feat when a play about the suppression of Palestinian nationalism is the 2009 co-recipient of The Mark Twain Award for Comic Playwriting (among other awards). Khalidi submitted the play while still a student in the MFA program in playwriting at New York University. It premiered a year later at the Alliance Theatre in Atlanta, GA.

Khalidi's other plays address more recent history. While *Dead Are My People* and *Tennis in Nablus* examine the political structures that inform our present—namely the reformation of racial categories in the US during the third-wave immigration period and the systemization of colonial violence prior to the Second World War—the other plays in this anthology examine ongoing conflicts. *Sabra Falling*, *Foot*, and *Final Status* examine Palestinian resistance to Israeli oppression. *Truth Serum Blues* examines the impact of the US War on Terror on Arab Americans.

Sabra Falling is set during the 1982 Lebanon War and concludes at the start of the Sabra and Shatila massacre of Palestinians and Lebanese Shias. The play begins when two siblings in the Sabra camp discover that an Israeli pilot, forced to eject after taking enemy fire, has fallen through the ceiling of their home. The pilot bears a striking resemblance to their elder brother, a writer who was assassinated by Israeli commandos because of his political writings and his role as spokesperson for a militant Palestinian organization. The pilot, born in Israel to a Jewish-Iraqi mother, spoke Arabic before learning Hebrew. He suffers temporary memory loss and reverts to the Arabic of his early childhood. With his fluent Arabic and physical resemblance, the pilot is the doppelganger of the dead Palestinian writer mourned by the family.

The Palestinian father of this household makes use of these magical coincidences to convince himself that his son had not died but was instead abducted by the Israelis. He rejoices in his son's escape and safe return and the family chooses not to disabuse him. The pilot enters into the man's delusion, taking on the role of loved son and liberation writer. However, as the Israeli army broaches Palestinian defenses, the pilot's Israeli identity enters his consciousness. He repeatedly hallucinates an Israeli general who informs him of his true past and urges him to complete his mission by killing this household of "terrorists."

The title of the play is a double entendre that speaks to the play's mounting tension. *Sabra* is a modern Hebrew word denoting any Jew born in Israel. It is also the name of the Palestinian camp in which the play transpires. "Sabra falling" could refer to either the Israeli pilot's plummet through the roof of a Palestinian home, or the massacre of Palestinians that came at the end of the Lebanese war. The PLO was based in Beirut after the organization was expelled from Jordan in 1970. In 1982, Israel invaded Lebanon with a force of 76,000 men and 1,250 tanks, supported by the air force and navy. Israel's *casus belli* was the June 1982 wounding of Israeli ambassador Shlomo Argov by Palestinian gunmen. However, Patrick Seale ascribes three objectives to the invasion: the annihilation of the PLO in Lebanon, the expulsion of Syrian forces and Syrian influence from Lebanon, and the installation of pro-Israeli government in Lebanon under Phalange party leader Bashir Jumayil (374). Under US pressure, Israel accepted a ceasefire allowing the PLO to evacuate its fighters to Tunis and the Lebanese parliament elected Bashir Jumayil to the presidency by a simple majority. Less than two months later, on September 14, a bomb planted by a member of the Syrian Social Nationalist party killed Jumayil and thirty associates—ending Israel's hopes for a partner in the Lebanese presidency. The next day, Israeli Minister of Defense Ariel Sharon ordered the IDF into West Beirut. On the 16th, Sharon invited Phalangist militia fighters to enter Sabra and Shatila after falsely asserting that the PLO had assassinated Jumayil (Fisk 489). The IDF cordoned off the camps and fired flares above to aid the militias and in the ensuing forty hours about a thousand men, women, and children were slaughtered (Seale 392). The play begins and ends with Sabra's fall.

The play masterfully marries the rising tension of the historical moment—the brutality of the Israeli invasion and the ensuing Phalangist massacre—with the growing tension within the family. The father loves the pilot as his son but the other family members know they are sheltering an enemy combatant, and the audience knows his subconscious urges him to kill his hosts. The first act ends with the withdrawal of the PLO (and with them the younger son in the family, a PLO fighter) and the second act begins a short while before the Sabra and Shatila massacre; there will be violence whether at the pilot's hand or Phalangist fighters. The text references historical figures such as Ariel Sharon and Moshe Dayan, and the dead son is presumably modeled on Ghassan Kanafani, the Palestinian author and journalist assassinated by Israeli agents in 1972.

For all of the play's historical references, its power lies in a magical bond between combatants. Not only do the pilot and the dead writer resemble each other, they have nearly identical names. At one point, the pilot would seem to recite from memory poetry composed by the dead writer. They are bound by ancestral ties to the same land and by a deadly struggle. Naomi Klein, following Caroline Rooney, has described Israel as a "doppelganger nation" based in a fantasy of symmetrical power between two people sutured like "conjoined twins in a state of unending struggle" (299). The idea that another people might have legitimate claims to one's land fosters the "lie of Indigenous absence" and Israeli projects of replacing Arabic place names with Hebrew ones, planting pine trees on former Palestinian villages, and a campaign of uprooting olive trees (300). This fear of the doppelganger requires a rigorous "unseeing of the other" and a doubling of everything from schools, roads, laws, and courts (302). Khalidi manifests this complex in a powerful stage image: the Israeli pilot who fully inhabits the Palestinian writer's vacated space. Even the play's title suggests this doubling, "Sabra" denoting both an Israeli beginning and a Palestinian end. *Sabra Falling* was commissioned by the Pangea World Theater of Minneapolis and premiered there in September 2017.

Tennis in Nablus and *Sabra Falling* both describe Palestinian national aspirations through armed struggle. The one-act monologue *Foot* takes up the wish to play soccer for Palestine as part of a struggle for national legitimacy. Like *Sabra Falling*, it makes reference to historical figures and events such as Jabra al Zarqa (a soccer star from the Mandate period), the Palestinian team's participation in the 1999 Arab Cup, and the 2006 travel ban on players from Gaza that prevented the team's participation in the World Cup, as well as the daily struggle of trying to practice when checkpoints and closures prevent players from accessing nearby playing fields. Most poignantly, the monologue focuses on Tareq Al-Quto, a Palestinian midfielder killed by the IDF in 2004. It is a death that has a new relevance at the time of writing; in March 2024, Palestinian footballer Mohammed Barakat was killed when Israeli forces bombed his family house in Khan Younis in the Gaza Strip. *Foot* premiered in a Spanish-language production at Teatro Amal in Chile in April 2016.

Khalidi's plays all engage Palestinian and Arab American history but *Final Status* is unique in his body of work as a fictional dramatization of specific historical events. The play largely focuses on the failed peace talks between Israeli and Palestinian delegations, which began in Madrid in 1991 and continued in Washington, DC in 1993. The title refers to the fact that Israel insisted that the issues of greatest concern to Palestinians—such as the return of refugees, the future of Jewish settlements, and the status of Jerusalem—be postponed for future "final status" talks. Khalidi's four-person Palestinian delegation substitutes for the fourteen-member Palestinian delegation and seven-member

Palestinian steering committee that attended the talks. Some of Khalidi's characters seem intended to bring to mind the better-known participants, such as Palestinian spokesperson Hanan Ashrawi, delegation head Dr. Haydar Abd al-Shafi, and the American diplomat Dennis Ross. As in reality, Khalidi's Palestinian delegation is unaware of the back-channel negotiations in Oslo that will establish the Palestinian National Authority. In Oslo, the PLO accepted a deal that the Palestinian delegation at talks in Madrid and Washington had rejected for over a year.

The play's second act departs from the historical record, imagining a debate between the head of the Palestinian delegation and the PLO official who participated in drafting the Oslo Accords. Khalidi's most cutting choice is to place this debate in Gaza in the midst of the 2008 war. That dramatic context is clearly intended to lend weight to the argument that the PLO—lacking adequate maps and overwhelmed in English-language negotiations—agreed to a bad deal. Much of the world was shocked by the suffering inflicted on civilian populations during the 2008 war, though the more than 1,400 Palestinian deaths in that war pales in comparison to the tens of thousands of Palestinians who have died in Gaza at the time of this writing. *Final Status* was Khalidi's MFA thesis project and it received a public reading at New York's Public Theater in 2009, some seven years before the premiere of J. T. Rogers' well-known dramatization of the back-channel talks in Oslo.

With *Truth Serum Blues*, Khalidi again examines the Arab American experience, this time in the post-9/11 era. The play shows how a surveillance regime can foster self-hatred in the surveilled. The play, set in the Guantanamo Bay detention camp, depicts the interrogation of Kareem, a US-born Palestinian-American in his twenties. After Kareem is forcibly administered a drug, the truth serum of the title, the play grows increasingly dream-like. Kareem hallucinates a chorus of experts and pundits who represent media views of Arabs. Under the influence of the drug, Kareem also conjures a Palestinian friend who counters the arguments of the interrogator and the pundits. The friend returned to Palestine after the American in him "started hating the Arab" in him. Kareem is questioned by a military interrogator for sending money to his Palestinian friend, though in Kareem's mind his greater crime is staying put and paying his taxes, even as US tax dollars support the Israeli military. While *Dead Are My People* imagines alliance between Arab Americans and African Americans and *Tennis in Nablus* depicts Palestinian liberation as part of a global anti-colonial struggle, *Truth Serum Blues* depicts the isolation many Arab Americans felt after 9/11. Kareem recalls an earlier sense of solidarity when he worked in a painting crew with African Americans and Latinos in wealthy suburbs where homeowners viewed Black and Brown laborers with equal suspicion. However, that feels ages ago; since 9/11, Kareem has seen the effectiveness of the US government's strategy of "divide and conquer." The play premiered at the Pangea World Theater in 2005. As the earliest play in this collection, it is interesting to see that Khalidi responded to this sense of isolation with a series of historical explorations of intersectionality.

These plays vibrate with the energy of lived experience. Khalidi traces his roots to Jerusalem on his father's side and Jaffa on his mother's (Handal). In depicting elements of Palestinian history, he is often covering terrain that directly intersects his family's history. In dramatizing the Palestinian–Israeli talks in *Final Status*, he is describing a moment in history experienced first-hand by his father. The historian Rashid Khalidi was a member of the Palestinian Steering Committee invited to the Madrid–Washington Peace talks—events that are detailed in his recent survey *The Hundred Years' War on Palestine* (185–200). Ismail Khalidi was born in West Beirut some two months after the massacre alluded to in *Sabra Falling*. He had lived through Israel's aerial bombardment of Beirut in vitro and, according to his father's account, "remained extremely sensitive to loud sounds" for a long time after (R. Khalidi 141). The main character in *Truth Serum Blues* explains that his grandfather came to the US from Palestine to study, but before his planned return "the Palestine he knew would disappear forever" (R. Khalidi 46). Khalidi's own grandfather had come to the United States for graduate study intending to return to Palestine, never to see his homeland again (R. Khalidi 82). The main character in *Truth Serum Blues* spends his youth in Chicago, as did the play's author, because of their families' common dispossession. Reading these plays, not only does one encounter a playwright grappling with history, but a playwright grappling with a history integral to his personal and family identity.

Works Cited

Fisk, R. (2005), *The Great War for Civilization: The Conquest of the Middle East*. New York: Alfred A. Knopf.

Gualtieri, S. (2009), *Between Arab and White: Race and Ethnicity in the Early Syrian American Diaspora*. Berkeley, CA: University of California Press.

Handal, N. (2016), "The City and the Writer: In Jerusalem and Jaffa with Ismail Khalidi," June 14. Available online: https://palestine.mei.columbia.edu/central/2016/6/14/ismail-khalidi (accessed April 6, 2024).

Khalidi, R. (2020), *The Hundred Years' War on Palestine: A History of Settler Colonialism and Resistance, 1917–2017*. New York: Henry Holt and Company.

Klein, N. (2023), *Doppelganger: A Trip into the Mirror World*. New York: Farrar, Straus and Giroux.

Pedersen, S. (2005), "Settler Colonialism at the Bar of the League of Nations," in C. Elkins and S. Pedersen (eds.), *Settler Colonialism in the Twentieth Century: Projects, Practices, Legacies,* 113–34, London: Routledge.

Seale, P. (1989), *Asad: The Struggle for the Middle East*. Berkeley, CA: University of California Press.

Sluglett, P. (2014), "An Improvement on Colonialism? The 'A' Mandates and Their Legacy in the Middle East," *International Affairs* 90.2: 413–29.

Interview: "The reason Palestine matters ... is because it is about everything"

An interview with Ismail Khalidi

with editors Hala Baki and Michael Malek Najjar

You were born in 1982 in Beirut, Lebanon, the same year as Israel's catastrophic invasion of that country. Your family left Lebanon for the United States in 1983. Your father said once that you were very much affected by the 1982 war in your mother's womb, as your mother had to flee from bombing while pregnant with you in June 1982. He said, "It's a testament to the fact that you can, not having lived through something, you can write a play like [Sabra Falling]*." As you look back now, how did those events influence your life as a person and as a writer?*

IK: I was born in Beirut, just after the massacres of 1982 and in the wake of the Israeli invasion of Lebanon and siege of Beirut, which my parents lived through, along with my sisters. I do not have memories of Beirut. We left Lebanon and came to the US when I was less than a year old. I know that my mother, five months pregnant, had to run from where she was working, at WAFA, alone, through some of the heaviest bombardments of the summer of 1982, to get back home to her two young daughters. She apparently did not want to be pinned in the bomb shelters. I of course have heard many other stories about what it was like to live through the Civil War and the siege of Beirut and I have seen the impact it had on my sisters and my parents and other family members. War is traumatic and trauma swirls around and between generations and communities, politically, energetically, even biologically we now know. There is no question that the war affected my family, although we were of course lucky enough to not be in the camps, and lucky enough to be able to leave to the States. I can definitely tell you that the way that the war broke up our extended family and re-dispersed us definitely had an effect on our family, especially my mother. But even my older sister, who was seven when we left Beirut, I think she suffered because of that rupture, not to mention memories of the war itself.

In terms of writing the play, surely my distance allowed me to approach that moment differently than someone who lived it. I will say, though, that Beirut and 1982 were a constant presence in my life, in my imagination, for as long as I can remember, whether in New York or Chicago. A presence of an absence. And also anger. We must remember that for Palestinians, before the genocide we are witnessing today in Gaza, the siege and bombardment of Beirut in 1982 was a watershed moment in exposing to the world the brutality of Israel, and the dehumanization of Palestinians. We are talking about tens of thousands of casualties over the course of several months. It was also this heroic stand by the PLO, and also their exile, their departure and really the end of the PLO in many ways, so there is a lot of meaning, a lot of loss packed into that moment for Palestinians. It was the loss of another home, a kind of mini-Nakba, collectively and for us as a family. So it was inevitable that I would write a play about it, really. And in fact,

Beirut is also present in other plays of mine. *Final Status*, written before *Sabra Falling*, is actually connected to the story of Sabra by a tendril: the presence of an assassinated writer, the father of Ibrahim. And that is because both are based in their own ways on actual occurrences and people that were important in our history, that were part of my world growing up, or were talked about and remembered around the dinner table.

You once called yourself a "historical playwright . . . a son of a historian." Given that you come from a family of journalists and scholars, how does your own family's history writing about Palestine inform your own work as an artist? Also, do you also consider yourself a political playwright?

IK: I don't buy into the "political" artist label. I think it is problematic and often dismissive. Sometimes one has to use it. But in truth, as you well know, to write about frivolous things, to turn away from the pain of the world, the crimes of one's own country or class, to ignore the dark times as Brecht referred to them, and to write pure entertainment or even liberal identity politics schlock, that is a political act in itself. It is the politics of privilege, the politics of the status quo, the politics of imperial obliviousness. And for me, that very overlooking of the bones and ashes underneath our feet is a kind of imperial disdain for the other, for the wretched of the earth. So yeah, everything is political, even or maybe especially the "apolitical" or "neutral." That is not to say that everything has to be gloom and doom and that we have to take ourselves seriously. There is space for humor and joy in so-called "political" art. That is often the best kind.

To get back to the other part of the question, my family on both sides and my chosen families too provided me with a lot of the tools I need to excavate the past and understand the present with a certain degree of political and class awareness. Of course, it is a constant process, to keep removing the film from one's eyes, to be aware of one's privileges, and to be alert to the way we are all conditioned and lied to and propagandized and hypnotized to look away. And the ways in which we also fall short in our values and actions sometimes. So it is all relative. But I am thankful to have had the family I have and the people from which I come. And the traveling I was able to do or had to do growing up. In addition to my parents, I also was raised in an environment where there was a constant stream of folks coming in and out of our house: activists, artists, intellectuals, journalists, exiles, and outcasts. I have many memories of Edward Said growing up. His sister was like an auntie to me. I still remember my mother and Edward speaking on the phone many mornings and the two of them laughing together on those calls. They were both good shit talkers, gossipers, and also both Palestinians who grew up in Egypt. So they had this very particular background in common. They both appreciated Egyptian humor but from the perspective of having lived in Egypt. They both came from a sort of cosmopolitan diasporic milieu in Egypt, but also overlapped in Beirut and then in New York.

I would be remiss if I didn't mention that my godparents (for lack of a better term) during my formative years in Chicago (1987–2001) were Bill Ayers and Bernardine Dohrn. They were in the Weather Underground in the 1960s and 1970s. Radical, compassionate, engaged people. My parents and Bill and Bernardine created a kind of mini-tribe on the south side in Hyde Park where we lived, and we would eat together at one house or the other two or three nights a week for nearly fifteen years. And so Bill and Bernardine had a huge impact on me. I really soaked in their radical politics from early on, their humor and cadence too, and was exposed to a whole different substratum of people and movements and ways of being and thinking. I think I would be a different person and a different writer if I didn't grow up with them. I think my parents would have been different parents too. So I cannot say enough how lucky I was to have that.

You wrote and acted in your one-person play Truth Serum Blues. *You've also acted in other important Arab American dramas such as* With Love from Ramallah. *What impact has acting as an Arab in Arab American dramas had on your ethos and technique as a playwright?*

IK: I think most of all, I realized how hard it is to act and to act well, but also how good writing can do a lot of the lifting for actors if they let it. But it is delicate of course, because bad or mediocre acting or directing (and I have certainly been guilty of mediocre acting) can really kill even the best writing. But I think in general I am thankful to have been involved in theater from so many sides of the table as it were, as an actor/performer, as a writer, as a dramaturg and now as a director. I think you really begin to understand things about writing as an actor and you understand things about acting as a writer/director.

What, in your opinion, are the greatest differences between plays written by Palestinians in Palestine and plays written by Palestinians living in the diaspora?

IK: That is a great question. First of all, I am by no means an expert on either, but most of all that which is coming out of Palestine. But language is the biggest difference obviously, although there are a handful of writers from inside Palestine that write in English (Dalia Taha and Amir Nizar Zoabi, for example, but there are others). It is hard to say, though, because neither group is a monolith. A writer from '48 (that is Palestinian citizens of the Israeli state) has different experiences than those in the West Bank and those in Gaza. And of course each region and village has its own accent. Also in the diaspora itself, I think I am a very different writer than someone writing from the camps in Lebanon or from Yarmouk in Syria, for example, who is different from one writing from Germany or Chile, just as I think I am even different in my writing than other Palestinian American writers. I think my politics and language has been quite different, in fact, from other Palestinian American writers. I would say I was writing with an internationalist and intersectional perspective twenty years ago, something that is now, thankfully, more prevalent.

Another difference worth mentioning is that there is a lot of devised, collaboratively created work in Palestine. Also, generally in the diaspora there is a need to explain certain things and sometimes to explain them in certain ways for a general audience that, in the West, is at worst hostile and at the best well-meaning but under-informed about Palestine. So the issue of exposition is big. As is the issue of censorship. One can write differently for a Palestinian or Arab audience who get the jokes and the references and the vibes and even the unspoken without an explanation or an asterisk or a disclaimer. And of course there are also good things that come out of having to think carefully about exposition. One of the challenges, I think, about writing in the diaspora would be in terms of production and staging. That is if you are lucky enough to get through the censors and the other obstacles and onto the stage. There is this orientalist aesthetic that very often, even in the most well-meaning of institutions, is present. And so even if you write the perfectly calibrated play, the journey from page to stage can really leave it deformed. This is true with any play, of course, but the dangers are many when staging a piece about Palestine or the Arab world or Middle East. Really a play about anywhere but the US is a tricky endeavor to be fair. But the layers of orientalist and racist tropes about the Arab world are pretty astounding. The level of ignorance can be mind-blowing. Of course, there are probably things that we writers in the diaspora create that don't feel totally authentic to folks in Palestine or living in the region. And perhaps we too, in the diaspora, can at times be guilty of simplifying or orientalizing or exoticizing or idealizing in our own ways.

In a preface to Tennis in Nablus *you wrote that the play conveyed an important truth about Palestine, "namely, that Palestinians did exist and were in fact struggling to achieve their freedom from a colonial power in the early part of the last century." Given that Palestinians have been occupied by colonial powers from the Ottomans to the British to the Israelis, do you believe that the theme of occupation is one that is central to your work?*

IK: I think occupation and colonialism and empire more generally are absolutely part of my work, just as they have shaped my life and the world around us. If we live in any of the settler colonies (the US being one) then whether we choose to see it or not, occupation and colonialism and empire have shaped our lives and our environments profoundly. Even Europeans in the heart of Europe are implicated. For example, do the beautiful buildings and the efficient metro systems and the monuments and wealth in Paris and Madrid and Brussels, in Rome and London arise out of thin air? Are they the results of a superior more advanced or "developed" strain of humans? No, they are the direct result of racial capitalism, of empire and colonialism, of brutal subjugation and exploitation and wealth extraction that went on for centuries. All of the cities of the so-called developed world are built on the bones and the suffering and the gold and labor of Indigenous Americans and/or enslaved people from West Africa, from resources plundered from the Middle East and Asia, upon the bodies of the Congolese tortured and exterminated by their millions in Belgian rubber plantations and through the schemes of the East India Company and the engineered famines in Bengal and on and on.

So as a Palestinian and as an American I cannot help but to deal with occupation as a theme of my work. I have yet to write my Ottoman Empire play or movie (I will) but I think that is a different creature when it comes to the idea of occupation. I think for me it really is important to understand the degree to which Palestine, as well as Syria and Lebanon and Egypt and Algeria and Iraq in different ways, have been profoundly shaped by encounters with European imperial and colonial projects over the past several centuries (more if we go back to the Crusades). And of course I would include Zionism in that category. It is an extension of European colonial subjugation. It is a European settler colonial project. It has its peculiarities of course, but it is a product of and a recreation or amalgamation of many other European settler colonial projects. We can see it from its inception over a century ago in the heart of Europe to the present moment as a genocide is enacted with the same racist dehumanizing brutality and accompanying language as in Ireland or India or Algeria or South Africa or the Americas before. And, of course, look who this genocide is being aided and abetted by? Not the global south. Not the formerly colonized of the world, but exclusively by the former colonizers and imperial powers and the most notoriously genocidal nations of the past centuries, namely the US, France, Britain, Germany.

In your play Sabra Falling, *Dalia shouts at Israeli soldiers, "So what more do you want from us?! You've hunted us into the sea, blown us into the sky, and driven us under the earth. Now there's nowhere for us to go!" Given the horrific Israeli siege of Gaza after October 7, 2023, those lines seem even more prescient today than ever. What does it mean for a playwright like yourself to have written such plays, only to see this carnage repeat itself generation after generation in Palestine?*

IK: This is not unique to the Palestinian experience. The colonized, the Indigenous, the subjugated the world over understand these lines. This could have been uttered by a character from any number of countries or cultures. But in the case of Palestine I think it speaks to the consistency of the Zionist project. It was always what it is today. The Palestinians have known this for a century and certainly for seventy-five years and we have been trying to tell anyone who would listen. Now the Zionist colonial project has, I think, gone into a kind of narcissistic injury and rage this past year, and is showing the most fascistic and racist elements of its character without any restraints or pretense. The mask is fully off in other words. But that vindictive supremacy and brutality has always been there, just more effectively hidden or held in check, either by the US, as in 1982, or by some counterbalance within Israel that for strategic rather than ethical reasons would say, "Hey now, let's pull it back, this doesn't look good." The Zionist project, though, from its very beginnings has always telegraphed its intention and its character, in word and/or deed, as a settler colonial supremacist project that will necessarily need to employ ethnic cleansing and/or apartheid for it to exist. Herzl, Jabotinsky, Ben Gurion, Rabin, and Shamir, all of them, said it, just as Bibi and Ben Gvir and Smotrich say it. Now the execution of the thing is being live-streamed in a way it never was before. And perhaps more important than the extremist nature of the current Israeli government (which we will be told is the problem) is the degree to which this American administration is proving itself to be the most craven enablers of Israeli criminality in the history of American administrations, and that is saying quite a lot. The United States is an active and willing participant and sponsor of this genocidal war. This, of course, would not shock any Native American or any Vietnamese person or any survivors of the US-sponsored death squads of Latin America. This is what the US has, in effect, always done. We are just witnessing it in real time, and the weapons being used are incredibly advanced and destructive.

In your play Foot, *you write about the March 30, 2006 Israeli bombing of the Palestinian football stadium in Gaza. Now, in 2024, we have what some are calling "cultural genocide" with the deaths of creative professionals, destruction of mosques and cultural sites, and the damage and destruction of cultural centers and libraries. How do you see your work contributing to the cultural/historical memory of Palestine?*

IK: Part of settler colonialism has always been to erase not only the native but her culture, and ways of knowing and of being, and to alter the relationship with the land, with space and time and language, etc. Again, nothing new there. Brian Friel writes brilliantly about it in the Irish context in *Translations*, for example. And so, yes, I consider my work and the work of so many others in the arts and academia and journalism and architecture and archaeology, etc. to be critical in the re-membering and the documenting of Palestine in the face of this ongoing process of erasure. It is cultural resistance. Documenting our stories, our villages or agricultural practices, our historical figures, our embroidery, it is all part of that, as is our imagination and our generative creativity, our imagining of new stories and new futures. Because part of the process of erasure and subjugation is trying to sever the present not only from the past but from any viable future. It is the erasure of hope. By systematically killing young people and slaughtering mothers and destroying schools and universities in Gaza, for example, the Israelis are trying to amputate the Palestinian from his future. And by making the present so unlivable, so burdened by the daily task of survival, or the weight of constantly trying to prove that you exist, that your past is real, you lose the capacity to think of and move freely into a future of your own choosing. This is an engineered dismantling or deforming of the future. So I see both those things, cultivating memory and imagination, as going hand in hand. I think, my work, so far, focuses more on the historical side of things, on the reclamation of memory, but it is also a reimagining, and in so doing it seems to me that we are better equipped to also imagine a future different from the one that the masters of war would have us relegated to.

Your play Dead Are My People *examines the horrific history of lynching in the United States. As a playwright, how did you reconcile the lynchings of African Americans and the lynchings of Arab Americans during the early twentieth-century Jim Crow South?*

IK: This is the only play in this collection not about Palestine. But I think it is relevant and connected. Of course, my grandmother Selwa was originally from Lebanon and emigrated to the US in 1920, which is the time period the play takes place. So there is a personal connection to that story. My intention in writing this play was by no means to equate the few lynchings of Arab Americans with the extended and widespread racial terror visited upon African Americans in the United States. There is of course no comparison, and in fact the play is very much an exploration of the Arab relation to whiteness, and the negotiation of race and place in the US. Of course these things are not unique to Arabs, except in that Arabs in the US have had a particularly interesting trajectory relative to, say, Italians or Jews or Irish immigrants and the "achievement" of whiteness. In many ways Arabs kind of made it into the country club as it were but then got kicked out. Not all, not across the board, I am not speaking literally of course, but there is no denying that Arabness is today very much an identity of otherness. We could go into this, and its connection to Islamophobia and to US imperial policies in the Middle East with the War on Terror, and also the degree to which Zionism's hold on the American imagination for much of the second half of the twentieth century and even until today (though it is cracking and becoming more polarizing now) had an impact on how Arabs and Palestinians and Muslims were seen. It is not to be underestimated the degree to which Zionism's alliance and overlap with elements of white supremacy and Islamophobic currents in the American political and cultural arena has contributed to the othering of Arabs, some of whom were well on their way to becoming "white" four or five generations back. Being pro-Israel was successfully equated in the imaginary with being pro-American, pro-"Judeo-Christian." Today of course, on the census, and in part due to the insistence of Arab Americans themselves, there is a category for us separate from "white" which was not the case. This is very telling. And of course, too, we can see today a much stronger affinity between Arabs and Black folks, especially around Palestine. But also with other folks of color. So yes, this play was always meant to be an exploration of assimilation, of white supremacy, with an Arab perspective. The work of Sarah M. A. Gaultieri is very instrumental to our understanding, so I want to shout out to her. And again, I think because race is a construct, and it is tied to imperial designs and to capitalism's whims and objectives of the day it is a constantly shifting thing, as is our relation to it. *Dead Are My People* is a kind of snapshot of one moment. But I think it is an interesting and instructive moment nonetheless.

In your play Dead Are My People, *Helene sings, "Amreeka is life and Amreeka is death." When writing this play, what struck you about the idea of "Amreeka" as both a land that offered Arab immigrants sanctuary away from Ottoman and European tyranny in the Levant, with the simultaneous notion of how they were discriminated against as "the Phonecian curse" here in the United States?*

IK: I mean, I think that line could be uttered by many immigrants to any metropole from the "periphery" or the colonies over time. I think that applies to Haitians or Salvadorans or Eritreans or Afghanis or Senegalese or Vietnamese or Moroccans or Palestinians or Syrians trying to make a go of it in the US or in Europe today. That contradiction, that dichotomy is part and parcel of the immigrant experience, of the refugee experience. To leave one's home is usually the only way to survive at that moment, and yet there is a dying in that departure, and there is often the specter of death or destitution awaiting the immigrant or the exile or the refugee once they arrive at their destination. So it is both metaphorical and literal. I mean, look at the way migrants and refugees and folks seeking asylum from the global south are penned and deported or left to die, or the way Palestinians, even those here to attend university, have been gunned down or stabbed here in the US just in the last six months. Those are lynchings in a sense. Look at the folks being left to sink in the Mediterranean or to die on the trip up through Central America or in the deserts of the borderlands. Look at the way African immigrants in Europe are beaten by police. And yet, folks are forced to go northwards to escape the ravages of (neo)colonialism, neoliberalism, and environmental catastrophe caused in large part by these very same phenomena. They are forced to flee towards the metropole to work and to live and to send back something to those that remain. There is some hope of a future, of life, whether in Madrid or Chicago or Atlanta or Berlin or Paris. But also a thousand deaths to be found, a thousand iniquities and humiliations and obstacles and betrayals. So I don't see that moment a hundred or so years ago as that different. Nor do I see the violence of Jim Crow as being that different from the carceral police state that Black folks inhabit today. In fact, it is all eerily similar.

Your play Dead Are My People, *focuses on Arab immigrants in the early twentieth century. As Arab Americans who are, technically, settler colonialists ourselves living on Native American land, how can we simultaneously justify the fight for the end of settler colonialism in the Middle East while we simultaneously colonize Native lands here?*

IK: Yes, I think it is integral for those of us who came here as refugees and immigrants especially and those of us fleeing settler colonialism or the effects of imperialism to acknowledge and to act with that very much present in our daily lives. I think the challenge is to make it real, to actually create alliances with Indigenous folks and to follow their lead. And to investigate and interrogate what it means to participate in or be complicit in a settler colonial system, even if from the margins. I often think, for instance, about friends of mine who are indigenous to North America and how it must feel to walk around their lands and to see them occupied and transformed by entitled settlers. I know how that makes me feel when I go to Palestine and I see how the land is defiled and deformed and transformed, just in the space of decades, and it is profoundly disturbing to me, it is sad and enraging. It helps me understand, even if only in part, what it must feel like here in the Americas for native folks. I also have those conversations and it is something that we still all have to figure out. We can all talk a good game in progressive circles about decolonizing but what does it mean? What does "land back" mean and what do those things mean to Indigenous folks? And again, there is no monolith here. But I think the answers are not always simple. I think October 7th was a reminder of the real world difficulty of the terrain. But for me, the question of the violence is like the question of the "political." The status quo is inherently political and violent, even if it is "peaceful." Peace for whom? For the colonized and the oppressed everything is political and everything about the status quo is violent. So why is it only our reactions to this ever-present political violence that are qualified as "political" or "violent"? I know this is not an answer to what you asked, but it is a way of saying that I hate living in settler colonial societies, and I have also lived for ten years in Chile, another product of settler colonial violence.

In your play Final Status, *Mazen and Edriss are left in a ruined Gaza as "two washouts who failed their country but sacrificed their blood in return." With the destruction of Gaza, the desecration of the Freedom Theatre by IDF troops, and the arrests and jailing of Palestinian theater producer Mustafa Sheta, what do you see the role of Palestinian/Palestinian American theater being for the Palestinian people/cause?*

IK: Well I think that line has more to do with the failed leadership of the Palestinian national movement, and the most mediocre, reactionary, and sclerotic elements of older generations effectively blocking the circulation of the Palestinian body politic for years and years and doing great damage to the cause. Edriss represents the more enlightened and prescient of that older generation, of course, and Mazen the opposite, which is the faction that has unfortunately and by design dominated Palestinian politics for several decades. But that is a whole discussion in and of itself.

In terms of theater, I think it goes to the previous answer, about cultural resistance, memory, and imagining the future. And also making the present more bearable. There is a reason why so many of our artists have been assassinated or jailed or exiled over the years. The list is long. And recently the Freedom Theatre and its artists have been the target. It speaks to the power and the potential in art. Every colonial and authoritarian power has known this. In the case of the Freedom Theatre they are also located in Jenin, which has always been an epicenter of Palestinian resistance, armed and unarmed, and therefore a target of the colonial powers, whether the Brits or the Zionists. Listen, if your art is making enemies for you among the powerful then you are doing something right. I think theater and cinema and music and literature have a huge role to play in our collective liberation.

In your essay about Naomi Wallace's work you wrote, "I have tried in my own writing to tackle the question of Palestine for American audiences in the face of varying degrees of misunderstanding, censorship, and at times, downright bigotry." Since you began your career, have you seen any improvement in the conditions you've faced as a Palestinian American playwright working in the American theater? What, if anything, has changed?

IK: The short answer is no. There is a shift at the grassroots level, a sea change in fact. But institutionally the changes are not yet as profound, I think. There is still fear and dependence on reactionary donors and board members. There are of course more artists now, younger generations, who are super-talented and will, I think, break through as the cracks in the walls get bigger and the mythologies of Zionism are exposed and as the older generations that have been instrumental in propping up those mythologies begin to fade away. But at the end of the day, as long as we are dependent upon or seeking the recognition of the mainstream and therefore of capital, we are kind of missing the point. Once they let you in, in other words, it is most likely because you are no longer dangerous to them and their interests. There are exceptions and ways around it perhaps, and ways to subvert. But for the most part, the gatekeepers are incredibly adept at appropriating, at defanging, and ultimately monetizing. Representative liberal identity politics is the perfect example. So I am weary of that always, even if I regularly have to catch myself, like anyone, yearning to be let in, or at least to make a decent living from my work, or to feel like one has "broken through." So I guess what I am saying is that it is, again, something we need to be alert to as artists. It requires vigilance and principles and unfortunately it is sometimes hard to pay the bills with principles. But there is often a cost to be paid either way.

How do you see the role of Palestinian American theater moving forward? Can these plays, in your opinion, serve as a testament to Palestine and the Palestinian diaspora?

IK: I think the important thing is we evolve. We strive for artistic excellence and growth and courage while also engaging in liberatory struggle. And once we achieve liberation, and we will, then what? Are we to be content with a state? So I think the struggle goes on and it is not about statehood. For me it is about liberation from the system which has been bred by settler colonialism and racial capitalism and patriarchy. And to learn the lessons of why Palestine has become a rallying cry for so many. It is not because folks care about us as Palestinians more than others. It is not because our olive oil is better or our embroidery or our bravery or our dancing. That is when we get caught up in our own mythologies and run up against the limitations of nationalism in my opinion. The reason Palestine matters, I think, is because it is about everything. It is a litmus test because what is done to us has been done before and is being done again in order to pave the way to do it elsewhere to others. Palestine is an anti-colonial struggle but is also a feminist struggle and an environmental struggle. It is an abolitionist struggle and a queer struggle and it is a struggle against white supremacy and anti-semitism and Islamophobia, all in one. So yes, I hope they serve as a testament to the diaspora and to Palestinian literary output but not in a strictly nationalistic sense. I hope they are a testament and a record of something that speaks to the Palestinian experience, of course, and our identity, but I am truly more interested in how our experience relates to the universal and vice versa. I am interested in Palestinian memory and Palestinian liberation as a part of a project of collective memory and imagination and liberation.

In Truth Serum Blues, *Abu Ali says, "The American in me started hating the Arab in me. So I smuggled that part of me back home. For safekeeping." This speaks to a feeling or psychic state that many Arab Americans may share, especially—or perhaps increasingly—in the context of the twenty-first-century US political climate and the latest siege on Gaza. How have the potential contradictions and dissonance of your Arab American identity shaped your work?*

IK: You know, it sounds cliché and I am also aware that I say this from a place of relative privilege, but I feel quite out of place in the US even though it is probably the place I am most culturally fluent or adapted having grown up there. I speak English with an American accent, it is also my strongest language. I grew up playing baseball, listening to hip hop, and all that. I studied in the US and, of course, it should be mentioned that I also benefit from white-skin privilege being light skinned and light eyed. So I am not easily profiled appearance-wise as my other Arab friends are, for example. Not to speak of being far removed from the daily experience of being Black. That said, I have always felt myself to be the other, politically and even culturally, in the US. I have always felt myself to be the enemy and for good reason. In my lifetime the US has been in constant war with the Arab and Muslim world. And there is, as discussed above, an additional layer of disdain and discrimination and demonization reserved for Palestinians in American popular mainstream culture and politics. The things one can say about Palestinians in the US today are quite difficult to say out loud about any other group. I think in the coming years we will see the ratcheting up of this kind of racism towards Chinese folks by the way.

So yes, for me I write to and for Americans as a kind of internal outcast. There are things I love about the US, and most of them are things that come from its margins and its underclasses, its rebels and radicals.

Your work so poetically treats the subject of Palestine not only as a political, national, or cultural cause, but profoundly as a cause of human dignity and justice. How would you describe your journey to this voice that you have honed so beautifully through your craft? What were some of the growing pains and lessons learned along the way?

IK: I think the growing pains are constant. I think, again, constantly questioning the role of class and race and trying to constantly learn and evolve and become more self-critical and less self-important. I mean, again, I think that one of the central parts of my journey has been to really clock the nefarious and ultimately reactionary role played by the virtue signaling of liberal pageantry and representative identity politics. Like, I really don't give a fuck if you are Palestinian or a person of color if you work in the Pentagon. I have more in common with a radical anti-capitalist, anti-Zionist anarchist Jew, for example, than a capitalist Palestinian who wants to end the occupation in order to create a Palestinian state built on principles of capitalism and patriarchy. So yeah, I mean Lloyd Austin coordinating with the Israeli army to enact genocide or Linda Thomas-Greenfield raising her hand to veto resolutions at the UN. Or Barack Obama, for that matter, are for me, not symbols of progress or Black liberation. They are just faces of the empire and no better or worse than Bush or Rumsfeld or Biden. So anti-imperialism is both a constant for me but also an evolving thing. Just as the empire evolves and adapts so must we who oppose it.

Perhaps it's an understatement to say that the United States has had a tumultuous and schizophrenic relationship to political correctness. Yet, as a wordsmith, you don't shy away from painful or triggering statements in your work, perhaps to the detriment of its reception at times. How have you navigated these cultural shifts and pitfalls? How have producers and audiences responded to your work in relation to this issue?

IK: Well, we are all on the same roller-coaster ride of political correctness, and as one gets older it is harder to keep it all straight. I think it is a game of parsing out what is actually radical and progressive in political correctness and what is a product of identity politics bullshit meant to distract and divide. I have had hard discussions, for example, about the use of the N word in *Dead Are My People*. That is the term that white folks employed in the deep south and far north too, it should be remembered, at that time, and long after Jim Crow. So there is historical accuracy there. And I talked to a lot of Black colleagues about it throughout. Anyway, I don't know, I think trigger warnings are fine, and I think if one is employing these terms responsibly and in conversation with anti-racist principles, which I try to do in my work, then that is one thing. I do think one has to be aware and sensitive of course, and informed. And there is no doubt that some people abuse it, like [Quentin] Tarantino, who is a good example of crossing the line. On the other side of the coin, I have heard non-Black folks speaking for Black folks about what triggers Black folks. That is wild to me, and silly and a different kind of racism. It is kind of like the Germans being the gatekeepers of what is and what is not anti-Semitic. And I also think progressive allies, including POC, can be guilty of both being too flippant or insensitive as well as being too sensitive and woke.

I have also been censored for telling Palestinian stories or for not "including the other side" whatever that means. I have been censored, in the case of my adaptation with Naomi Wallace of Ghassan Kanafani's *Returning to Haifa*. I mean Kanafani, a Palestinian Marxist Leninist refugee, is definitely not politically correct in mainstream US theatre. So yeah, sometimes you have to push back, sometimes you have to laugh, and sometimes you have to learn and adapt and recalibrate accordingly.

The American theater purports to be a beacon of progressive values, especially in the aftermath of recent social justice movements like #MeToo and Black Lives Matter that have compelled the industry to self-reflect and change (to varying degrees of success, of course). However, when it comes to Palestine and Arab Americans, the institution remains overtly and covertly complicit in erasure and/or silencing. How would you compare these conditions internationally, in your work outside the US? What lessons can American theater learn from abroad?

IK: Well, everything is different post-October 7 and in the wake of the genocide in Gaza and we have yet to see how things will play out, but there is a battle going on between these two forces unleashed this year, on the one hand this ultra-Zionist anti-Palestinianism and on the other this awakening to the plight of Palestinians at the hands of Zionism. So I cannot really say how things will change for the better or the worse. I think for the time being it will be a mix of the two competing forces overlapping and there being on the one hand less space and on the other more if that makes sense. But again, as I said before, what does it mean when things gain traction in the mainstream. What is the line between change and being appropriated? #MeToo and the movement for Black lives are examples of movements and moments that produced both real change and were also appropriated and monetized by capital. How do we make radical art without being totally sidelined and invisibilized and how do we become visible without selling out? How do you reimagine what is the center, as it were. How do we decolonize our expectations and our definitions of success? When and where and how can we actually infiltrate the mainstream and be subversive? What voices are being heard at my expense and at whose expense is my voice being heard? I think for me, we need the presence of a combination of these questions (and others) and asking and answering them honestly and constantly along the way to stay principled. That seems part of the work we need to be doing.

In the previously mentioned preface to Tennis in Nablus *you write, "[A]t the heart of the question of Palestine are a plethora of issues that go far beyond Palestine. They include settler colonialism, white supremacy, imperialism, ethnic cleansing, human rights, international law, refugee rights, anti-Semitism, and Islamophobia among others." One important issue that I would argue threads through many of the ones you list is trauma, because it weaves across -isms and generations inextricably. How would you describe your work in relation to trauma? What about trauma do you want to communicate to audiences through your work?*

IK: I think the traumas unleashed by the ongoing genocide in Gaza are going to be far-reaching and long-lasting. Most directly and horrifically for the millions of Gazans subjected to the apocalyptic violence, but also for those of us in the diaspora. It is another layer of trauma. And just like the Nakba, just like dictatorships, just like all wars and occupations and just like the Holocaust and slavery, this unspeakable savagery will imprint itself on generations to come. The hope is the way in which it can mobilize and move people to act. Let us hope that the positive outcomes can help to mitigate some of the suffering or at least not let it be in vain. I don't know how my writing will change because of what we are witnessing, but I am sure it will. One cannot live through or witness such carnage and not be changed.

Bibliography

Works about Ismail Khalidi

Abbitt, E. S. (2019), "*Returning to Haifa*. By Ghassan Kanafani. Adapted by Ismail Khalidi and Naomi Wallace. Directed by Caitlin McLeod. Finborough Theatre, London. March 3, 2018," *Theatre Journal* 71 (1) March: 106–8.

Brock, W. (2010), "Brits' Cluelessness Brings Levity to Palestinian Tragedy," *The Atlanta Journal-Constitution*, February 5. Available online: https://www.ajc.com/entertainment/celebrity-news/brits-cluelessness-brings-levity-palestinian-tragedy/gj4wnKKhI5q45Xcy3qNBGP/ (accessed January 10, 2024).

"Dead Are My People" (2018), *New York Theatre Workshop*, November 4–11. Available online: https://www.nytw.org/show/dead-are-my-people/ (accessed January 16, 2024).

Dorman, A. (2017), "*Sabra Falling*: Pangea World Theater: Review," *Talkin' Broadway*. Available online: https://www.talkinbroadway.com/page/regional/minn/minn638.html (accessed January 10, 2024).

English, G. (2016), "American Theatre and Palestine," *Howlround Theatre Commons*, December 21. Available online: https://howlround.com/american-theatre-and-palestine (accessed January 10, 2024).

"Foot: Exitosa Obra Del Teatro Palestino En Valdiva, Chile" (2016), *Liga Latinoamerica Por El Retorno a Palestina*, September 24. Available online: https://ligapalestina.org/foot-exitosa-obra-del-teatro-palestino-en-valdivia-chile/ (accessed January 15, 2024).

Froomkin, D. (2012), "Reading Takes Intimate Look at Middle East," *Columbia Spectator*, October 9. Available online: https://www.columbiaspectator.com/2012/10/08/reading-takes-intimate-look-middle-east/ (accessed January 16, 2024).

"Gaza Vigil" (2009), [TV program] Chicago Independent Television, March 1. Available online: https://archive.org/details/CITV_Episode45_podcast_file (accessed January 15, 2024).

Harris, M. (2010), "Theatre Review: Tennis in Nablus," *RoughDraft Atlanta*, February 9. Available online: https://roughdraftatlanta.com/2010/02/09/theatre-review-tennis-in-nablus/ (accessed January 10, 2024).

Hetrick, A. (2010), "Benator, El-Attar and Chrysan to Play *Tennis in Nablus* at the Alliance," *Playbill*, January 7. Available online: https://playbill.com/article/benator-el-attar-and-chrysan-to-play-tennis-in-nablus-at-the-alliance-com-164738 (accessed January 15, 2024).

Holman, C. (2010), "Theater Review: Tennis in Nablus Finds Faults in Palestinian History," *Creative Loafing*, February 13. Available online: https://creativeloafing.com/content-181146-theater-review---tennis-in-nablus-finds-faults-in-palestinian (accessed January 10, 2024).

Howell, L. (2005), "New Playwright Ismail Khalidi Represents the Undistorted," *Pulse of the Twin Cities*, September 29.

Mashini, F. (2017), "'Foot': La crudeza de la esperanza," *Embajada Del Estado de Palestina Buenos Aires*, November 13. Available online: https://palestina.int.ar/foot-la-crudeza-la-esperanza/ (accessed January 15, 2024).

McAteer, E. (2015), "Heartbreak and History Collide in Palestinian Drama," *Electronic Intifada,* September 28: 1.

Moawad Muftah, S. (2016), "Ismail Khalidi's 'Dead Are My People' Examines White Supremacy & Immigration in America, Then and Now," *Arab America*, October 8. Available online: https://www.arabamerica.com/ismail-khalidis-dead-people-examines-white-supremacy-immigration-america-now/ (accessed January 12, 2024).

Moosavi, M. (2017), "Inside/Outside: Six Plays from Palestine and the Diaspora: Reviewed by Marjan Moosavi," *Critical Stages/Scènes critiques*, June/Juin, 15. Available online:

https://www.critical-stages.org/15/insideoutside-six-plays-from-palestine-and-the-diaspora/ (accessed January 10, 2014).

Mullenneaux, L. (2011), "Tennis in Nablus Revives the Arab Revolt," *Washington Report on Middle East Affairs,* December: 57–8. Available online: https://www.wrmea.org/2011-december/music-arts-tennis-in-nablus-revives-the-arab-revolt.html (accessed January 10, 2024).

Najjar, M. (2015), *Arab American Drama, Film and Performance: A Critical Study, 1908 to the Present.* Jefferson, NC: McFarland, 131–5, 170–5.

Najjar, M. (2015), "*Inside/Outside: Six Plays from Palestine and the Diaspora*: Book Review," *Arab Stages,* 2 (1) Fall. Available online: https://arabstages.org/2015/10/insideoutside-six-plays-from-palestine-and-the-diaspora/ (accessed January 10, 2024).

Najjar, M. (2021), *Middle Eastern American Theatre: Community, Cultures and Artists,* London: Bloomsbury, 54, 78–80, 149–50

Nassar, H. (2015), "*Inside/Outside: Six Plays from Palestine and the Diaspora*: Book Review," *Arab Stages,* 2 (1) Fall. Available online: https://arabstages.org/2015/10/insideoutside-six-plays-from-palestine-and-the-diaspora/ (accessed January 10, 2024).

"Review: Original Play Challenges with Blend of Tragedy, Comedy" (2011), *The Daily Gazette,* September 12. Available online: https://www.dailygazette.com/ticket/review-original-play-challenges-with-blend-of-tragedy-comedy/article_a43eee01-6c3f-59e5-8d95-1992c9c70641.html (accessed January 10, 2024).

Samel, D. (2011), "Tennis in Nablus—Well Worth the Trip to Hudson," *Mondoweiss,* September 18. Available online: https://mondoweiss.net/2011/09/tennis-in-nablus-%E2%80%93-well-worth-the-trip-to-hudson/ (accessed January 10, 2024).

Sears, J. (2012), "Tennis in Nablus: Between Stereotypes and Illumination," *Arablit & Arablit Quarterly,* October 13. Available online: https://arablit.org/2012/10/13/tennis-in-nablus-between-stereotypes-and-illumination/ (accessed January 10, 2024).

Singh, K. (2023), "Dipankar Mukherjee's 'Returning to Haifa' is a Powerful Play About Displacement, History and Human Complexities," *American Kahani*, April 25. Available online: https://americankahani.com/perspectives/dipankar-mukherjees-returning-to-haifa-is-a-powerful-play-about-displacement-history-and-human-complexities/ (accessed January 15, 2024).

Sutama, H. and D. Anwar (2019), "State Domination Enforcement in *Tennis in Nablus* (2015) by Ismail Khalidi," *E-Journal of English Language and Literature*, 8 (3): 58–68. Available online: https://ejournal.unp.ac.id/index.php/ell/article/view/105696/102246 (accessed January 10, 2024).

Rickwald, B. (2016), "Noor Theatre Announces 7th Season of Highlight Reading Series," *TheaterMania*, September 19. Available online: https://www.theatermania.com/news/noor-theatre-announces-7th-season-of-highlight-reading-series_78501/ (accessed January 10, 2014).

Yankee, L. (ed.) (2022), "The Interviews: Conversations with Acclaimed Playwrights, Critics, Librettists, and Lyricists," in *The Art of Writing for the Theatre: An Introduction to Script Analysis, Criticism, and Playwriting.* New York: Methuen Drama: 116–17, 142, 127, 184.

Ziter, E. (2017), "Naomi Wallace and Ismail Khalidi, Eds., *Inside/Outside: Six Plays from Palestine and the Diaspora*: Reviewed by Edward Ziter," *International Journal of Middle East Studies*, 49 (2), May: 357–9.

Works by Ismail Khalidi

Khalidi, I. (2003), "Review: 'Real DJs Do Real Things' by DJ K-Salaam," *The Electronic Intifada*, January 27. Available online: https://electronicintifada.net/content/review-real-djs-do-real-things-dj-k-salaam/3442 (accessed January 12, 2024).

Khalidi, I. (2004), "The Intellectual, the Maestro, and the 'Piece Process'," *The Electronic Intifada*, August 17. Available online: https://electronicintifada.net/content/intellectual-maestro-and-piece-process/5198 (accessed January 12, 2024).

Khalidi, I. (2004), "Three Poems," *Mizna*, 6 (2): 15–20.

Khalidi, I. (2006), "Letters to Our Parents," in D. Berger, C. Boudin, and K. Farrow (eds.), *Letters from Young Activists: Today's Rebels Speak Out*, 8–12. New York: Nation.

Khalidi, I. (2006), "Two Poems," *Mizna*, 8 (1): 23–6.

Khalidi, I. (2007), "DJ Revolutions: Spinning Beats for Freedom," *The Electronic Intifada*, February 22. Available online: https://electronicintifada.net/content/dj-revolutions-spinning-beats-freedom/6769 (accessed January 12, 2024).

Khalidi, I. (2007), "Excerpt from *Foot*," *Mizna*, 9 (1): 46–52.

Khalidi, I. (2010), "Debunking the Palestinian Stereotype," *The Atlanta Journal-Constitution*, February 10. Available online: Gale OneFile: News, link.gale.com/apps/doc/A218607079/STND?u=euge94201&sid=bookmark-STND&xid=bb117577 (accessed February 15, 2024).

Khalidi, I. and J. Marlowe (2011), "Remembering Juliano Mer-Khamis," *The Nation*, April 11. Available online: https://www.thenation.com/article/archive/remembering-juliano-mer-khamis/ (accessed January 12, 2024).

Khalidi, I., E. B. Mee, and N. Wallace (2012), "Creation Under Occupation," *American Theatre*, 29 (2): 28–31, 84.

Khalidi, I. (2013), "Being the 'Other': Naomi Wallace and The Middle East," in S. T. Cummings and E. S. Abbitt (eds.), *The Theatre of Naomi Wallace: Embodied Dialogues*, 211–13. New York: Palgrave Macmillan.

Khalidi, I. (2013), "Bill Ayers: Radical Acts," *Guernica Magazine,* November 15. Available online: https://www.guernicamag.com/radical-acts/ (accessed January 10, 2024).

Khalidi, I. (2013), "The Courage to Be Dangerous," *Pressenza*, 6 November. Available online: https://www.pressenza.com/2013/06/the-courage-to-be-dangerous/ (accessed January 14, 2024)

Khalidi, I. (2013), "Excerpt from *Sabra Falling*," *Mizna*, 14 (1): 38–45.

Khalidi, I. (2014), "Max Blumenthal: To Zion and Back," *Guernica Magazine*, July 15. Available online: https://www.guernicamag.com/to-zion-and-back/ (accessed January 10, 2024).

Khalidi, I. (2015), "A Brief Historical Note," in *Inside/Outside: Six Plays from Palestine and the Diaspora*. New York: Theatre Communications Group.

Khalidi, I. (2015), "Putting Palestine on the Map … and the Fútbol Jersey," *ReMezcla*, March 17. Available online: https://remezcla.com/features/sports/club-palestino-soccer-chile/ (accessed January 12, 2024).

Khalidi, I. (2016), "Reflections on *Sabra Falling*: Inspiration, Challenges, and Experiences in Writing and Producing the Play," in S. Orlov and S. Sabawi (eds.), *Double Exposure: Plays of the Jewish and Palestinian Diasporas*, 265–6. Toronto: Playwrights Canada Press.

Khalidi, I. (2017), "'Prisoners in Parallel': Film Review", *Daily Beast*, April 24. Available online: https://www.thedailybeast.com/prisoners-in-parallel (accessed January 12, 2024).

Wallace, N. and I. Khalidi (2017), "Shattering the Spectacle of Trump: Toward a Theatre of Holistic Dissent," *American Theatre*, 34 (9): 38–42.

Wallace, N. and I. Khalidi (2017), "Trump-ocalypse Now?" *American Theatre*, October 24. Available online: https://www.americantheatre.org/2017/10/24/trump-ocalypse-now/ (accessed January 8, 2024).

Khalidi, I. (2018), "Writing Palestine's Invisible History," in J. Khoury, M. Najjar, and C. Pond (eds.), *Six Plays of the Israeli–Palestinian Conflict*, 97–132. Jefferson, NC: McFarland, 95–6.

Khalidi, I., ed. (2018), "Foreword," *Mizna: The Palestine Issue*, 19 (2): 5–8. Available online: https://mosaicrooms.org/product/the-palestine-issue/ (accessed January 10, 2014).

Wallace, N. and I. Khalidi (2018), "The Last Taboo? The 'Palestine Exception' in American Theatre," *The Dramatist*, January 1. Available online: https://www.dramatistsguild.com/thedramatist/last-taboo-palestine-exception-american-theatre (accessed June 21, 2024).

Khalidi, I. (2019), "The Slumlords' Peace," *Al Jazeera*, June 25. Available online: https://www.aljazeera.com/opinions/2019/6/25/the-slumlords-peace (accessed January 12, 2024).

Khalidi, R. and I. Khalidi (2020), "Narrating Palestine: A Conversation with Rashid Khalidi and Ismail Khalidi," *NYUAD Institute*, June 8. Available online: https://youtu.be/BwQHgZC4B00?si=mAyd8LbvwZpqD2tk (accessed January 16, 2024).

Khalidi, I. (2021), "A Redacted Requiem for the Wretched of the Earth," *Pangea World Theater*. Available online: https://www.pangeaworldtheater.org/projects/a-redacted-requiem-for-the-wretched-of-the-earth (accessed January 12, 2024).

Khalidi, I. (2023), "The Bringers of Violence," *Mizna*, October 28. Available online: https://mizna.org/literary/the-bringers-of-violence/ (accessed January 12, 2024).

Plays by Ismail Khalidi

Khalidi, I. (2015), "Tennis in Nablus," in N. Wallace and I. Khalidi (eds.), *Inside/Outside: Six Plays from Palestine and the Diaspora*, 7–65. New York: Theatre Communications Group.

Khalidi, I. (2016), "Sabra Falling," in S. Orlov and S. Sabawi (eds.), *Double Exposure: Plays of the Jewish and Palestinian Diasporas*, 191–264. Toronto: Playwrights Canada Press.

Khalidi, I. (2018), *Push/Pull*, The Kenyon Review, October 3. Available online: https://kenyonreview.org/kr-online-issue/2018-septoct/selections/ismail-khalidi-373633/ (accessed January 12, 2024).

Khalidi, I. (2018), "Tennis in Nablus," in J. Khoury, M. Najjar, and C. Pond (eds.), *Six Plays of the Israeli-Palestinian Conflict*, 97–132. Jefferson, NC: McFarland.

Khalidi, I., N. Wallace, and S. Antoon (2018), "The Corpse Washer," in W. Wegener (ed.), *Humana Festival 2019: The Complete Plays*. New York: Limelight Editions.

Khalidi, I., N. Wallace, and G. Kanafani (2018), *Returning to Haifa*. London: Faber & Faber.

Related Readings

Abu-Manneh, B. (2018), "Returning to Kanafani," in N. Wallace and I. Khalidi (eds.), *Returning to Haifa*. London: Faber & Faber.

Al-Hout, B. N. (2004), *Sabra and Shatila: September 1982*. London: Pluto Press.

Clifton, T. and C. Leroy (1983), *God Cried*. London: Quartet Books.

Darwish, M. (1995), *Memory for Forgetfulness: August, Beirut, 1982*. Berkeley, CA: University of California Press.

Gualtieri, S. M. A. (2009), *Between Arab and White: Race and Ethnicity in the Early Syrian American Diaspora*. Berkeley, CA: University of California.

Hooglund, E. J. (1987), *Crossing the Waters: Arabic-Speaking Immigrants to the United States Before 1940*. Washington, DC: Smithsonian Institution.

Jacobs, L. K. (2015), *Strangers in the West: The Syrian Colony of New York City, 1880–1900*. New York: Kalimah.

Khalidi, R. (1986), *Under Siege: PLO Decisionmaking During the 1982 War*. New York: Columbia University Press.

Naff, A. (1985), *Becoming American: The Early Arab Immigrant Experience*. Carbondale, IL: Southern Illinois University Press.

Petran, T. (1987), *The Struggle Over Lebanon*. New York: Monthly Review Press.

Roediger, D. R. (2005), *Working Toward Whiteness: How America's Immigrants Became White: The Strange Journey From Ellis Island to the Suburbs*. New York: Basic.

Sayigh, R. (1994), *Too Many Enemies: The Palestinian Experience in Lebanon*. London: Zed Books.

Shakir, E. (1997), *Bint Arab: Arab and Arab American Women in the United States*. Westport, CT: Praeger.

Schiff, Z. and E. Ya'ari (1984), *Israeli's Lebanon War*. New York: Simon & Schuster.

Contributor Biographies

Hala Baki is a lecturer in the Theatre and Dance Department at California Polytechnic State University, San Luis Obispo. She earned her PhD in Theater, Dance, and Performance Studies with an Interdisciplinary Emphasis in Global Studies from the University of California, Santa Barbara. Her research interests include Arab American theater, conditions of theatrical production, and diaspora theories. She has presented her work at IFTR, ASTR, and ATHE, and has published in *Modern Drama*, *Theatre Journal*, *Theatre Topics*, *Asian Theatre Journal*, and the *Oxford Research Encyclopedia of American History*. She co-edited *The Vagrant Trilogy: Three Plays by Mona Mansour* (Methuen Drama 2022) and authored a chapter in the volume *Arabs, Politics, and Performance* (2024). She is also a theater director and dramaturg whose recent credits include Yussef El Guindi's *Wife of Headless Man Investigates Her Own Disappearance* (LaunchPad 2023), Mona Mansour's *unseen* (OSF 2022), the devised ensemble play *Writer's Block* (2021), and Kareem Fahmy's *American Fast* (LaunchPad 2021).

Ismail Khalidi is a playwright and director who has written, directed, performed, curated and taught internationally. Khalidi's plays include *Tennis in Nablus* (Alliance Theatre, 2010), *Truth Serum Blues* (Pangea World Theater, 2005), *Foot* (Teatro Amal, 2016–17), *Sabra Falling* (Pangea World Theater, 2017), *Returning to Haifa* (Finborough Theatre, 2018), and *Dead Are My People* (Noor Theatre, 2019). Khalidi's plays have been published in numerous anthologies. His writing on politics and culture has appeared in *The Nation*, *Guernica*, *American Theatre Magazine*, and *Remezcla*. His poetry and plays have been published by *Mizna*, and he co-edited *Inside/Outside: Six Plays from Palestine and the Diaspora* (2015). Khalidi has received commissions from the Actors Theatre of Louisville, Noor Theatre, Pangea World Theater, and The Public Theater, and Visiting Artist at Teatro Amal in Chile. He holds an MFA in Dramatic Writing from NYU's Tisch School of the Arts.

Michael Malek Najjar is Professor of Theatre Arts with the University of Oregon. He is the author of *Middle Eastern American Theatre: Communities, Cultures and Creators* and *Arab American Drama, Film and Performance: A Critical Study, 1908 to the Present*. He edited *Heather Raffo's Iraq Plays: The Things That Can't Be Said*, *The Selected Works of Yussef El Guindi*, and *Four Arab American Plays: Works by Leila Buck, Jamil Khoury, Yussef El Guindi, and Lameece Issaq & Jacob Kader*. He is co-editor of *Mona Mansour: The Vagrant Trilogy* (with Hala Baki) and *Six Plays of the Israeli–Palestinian Conflict* (with Jamil Khoury and Corey Pond). He has directed mainstage productions with Silk Road Rising, Golden Thread Productions, and New Arab American Theatre Works.

Naomi Wallace's plays have been produced in the United States, the UK, Europe, and the Middle East. Awards include the MacArthur Award, Obie Award, Susan Smith Blackburn Prize, Fellowship of Southern Writers Drama Award, Horton Foote Award, Arts and Letters Award in Literature, and the inaugural Windham Campbell prize for drama. Wallace is currently writing the book for the Loretta Lynn musical and the John

Mellencamp musical *Small Town*. She is presently co-writing a new play with Ismail Khalidi for Ashtar Theatre in Ramallah.

Edward Ziter is a theater historian with a particular interest in the intersections between European and Arab performance traditions. His most recent book, *Political Performance in Syria: From the Six-Day War to the Syrian Uprising* (2014), was co-winner of the Joe A. Calloway Prize for the Best Book on Drama or Theater. Other publications include *The Orient on the Victorian Stage* (2003) as well as articles on Shakespearean actors and comic actors of the Romantic and Victorian periods and on contemporary theater and film in the Arab world. He served as Middle Eastern area editor for the *Cambridge Encyclopedia of Stage Actors and Acting* (2015). He is Affiliate Faculty in the Kevorkian Center for Near Eastern Studies, the Department of English, the Department of Performance Studies, and the Theater Program at NYU Abu Dhabi. His current research focuses on nationalist performance during the Arab Renaissance (the late nineteenth to early twentieth centuries), focusing on Arabizations of Romantic dramas and Shakespeare.